The Da

Ho
& Sell Cars
2000

The Daily Telegraph

How to Buy
& Sell Cars
2000

Honest John

ROBINSON
London

Robinson Publishing Ltd
7 Kensington Church Court
London W8 4SP

First published by Robinson Publishing Ltd 2000

A copy of the British Library Cataloguing in Publication Data
is available from the British Library

ISBN 1–84119–122–1

Designed and typeset by Word_Space, Lewes, East Sussex

Printed and bound in the EC

10 9 8 7 6 5 4 3 2 1

CONTENTS

Part 1: Ways and Means

Part 2: Makes and Models

PART 1

WAYS AND MEANS

CONDITION OF SALE

What you need to know about this book before buying it

This book is intended to help you understand the motor trade before you commit yourself to the second-most expensive purchase you will probably ever make.

However, the advice is not infallible because all anyone ever knows for certain is that things are going to change. For this reason I can't guarantee that everything I write will still apply when you try to apply it. The economy may be in boom or recession. Taxation may have changed. Law very probably will have. Even dealers and agents who seemed honest enough when I included their telephone numbers could be preparing to cut and run.

So, just like buying a car at auction, use your common sense before you make a move. Neither I, nor *The Daily Telegraph*, nor Robinson Publishing, nor anyone else mentioned or involved, will accept any liability whatsoever for any inaccuracies or the dating of any information in this book. Of course, unlike cars at auction, you can sneak a look between the covers and give it a 'read-test' at the bookshop, so you know exactly what you're getting before you make your bid to the cashier.

I don't need to tell you much more about the book, because the chapter headings take you through every aspect of buying and selling cars I could think of, while the Car by Car Guide starting on p. 89 tells you what's good and what's bad about most popular models, together with what to look out for and known recalls up to the point at which I had to stop writing in order to get the book to the printers.

BUYING NEW

Understanding the system

If you want to beat the system, first you have to understand it.

For the past three years and at other times in the past, UK pre-tax car prices have been out of kilter with those in the rest of Europe (not to say the rest of the world). There are six reasons for this.

First, the UK is a right-hand-drive country in a part of the world where every other country drives on the left. It is inconvenient and expensive for mainland European manufacturers to turn out right-hand-drive cars for a mere 10% of the European market. It also creates an exploitable difference between Europe and the UK (25% of the world, including the UK, South Africa, Japan, India, Australia, New Zealand, Indonesia, Thailand and Malaysia, is RHD; the other 75%, including the USA, Europe, Russia and most of Africa, is LHD).

Factor two is that the UK has proportionally the biggest fleet market in the world. Around 60% of all new cars registered in the UK are destined for fleets of 25 cars or more. Add the numerous smaller fleets, and the total business market is estimated to be between 70% and 80% of all new cars sold in the UK. Fleets don't pay UK 'list prices' for cars, and the bigger their order, the bigger the discount, rebate or volume bonus they get. UK 'list prices' are inflated, partly so that the private buyers who pay them help to fund the fleet discounts, and partly to create a 'two-level playing field' upon which fleets are able to 'buy cheap and sell expensive'. Since the public provides the market for virtually all ex-fleet cars, the fleets want us to buy their cast-offs at prices which reflect list prices rather than the discounted prices the fleets paid.

Fleet discounts are not all huge, and may be as little as 5% for a car where demand considerably outstrips supply. But where cars are in a serious 'oversupply' situation, and the order is for 500 cars or more, fleet discounts have been as much as 55%. You can safely reckon that fleets buy mass-produced, mass-market cars at an average discount/rebate/volume bonus of 20%–30%. Where the fleet owners actually own the franchises through which the cars are obtained, they can get them at even bigger discounts.

The third reason is good old-fashioned British snobbery. This makes some of us suckers enough to pay as much as £10,000 over list price for an exciting new car which is 'hard to get'. Naturally, the manufacturers of such cars make them as hard to get as possible. So while British status-seekers are paying huge 'overs' on top of a high list price for RHD German roadsters and coupes, Belgians are getting discounts on considerably lower list prices.

The fourth reason why cars are sold at different pre-tax prices is the widely differing car purchase tax and VAT regimes in different European countries. Countries like Holland and Ireland still have a registration tax of around 30% added to the price of the car as well, as VAT at 17.5%. VAT on cars in Europe varies between 16% (in Germany, Luxembourg and Spain) to 25% (in Denmark, which also has a high registration tax). Other high-VAT countries are France (23%), Finland (22%), Ireland (21%), Belgium (21%), Austria (20%), Italy (19%) and Greece (18%). One school of thought within the Treasury is that if UK car prices were cut by 30%, VAT on cars would have to rise to a rate of 25% to make up the VAT revenue shortfall. However, this ignores the fact that at least 60% of new cars in the UK are sold to fleets at discounts of 20%–30% anyway. And the fact that many private new car buyers would spend the same amount of money they had planned to spend, but get more car for their money.

Factor five is currency variation. When Sterling is strong, this can shift even the 'on the road' difference in the price of cars to 30% or more, even after all taxes are paid. A new VW Golf V5 Highline, priced at £13,500 on the road in Germany, can be £18,700 in the UK. A mid-range Mondeo, priced at £10,000 in Spain, can be £14,000 in the UK.

The sixth and final reason is specification. 'Base' specification cars don't sell well in the UK. Though there are notable exceptions, such as the Perodua Nippa, Suzuki Alto and Daewoo Matiz, most new cars in the UK have power steering, airbags and at least a 1,200cc engine as standard equipment. Add to this the safety and emissions equipment necessary to pass EU-legislated standards and the manufacturing cost of a car can be 50% higher than that of, for example, the Indonesian Toyota Kijang. At Rp13,000 to the pound, this air-conditioned 1,800cc 7–9 seater estate car sells for £4,230 in Indonesia. But it lacks a catalytic converter, cold-start equipment, rear seatbelts, side impact protection and a multiplicity of other legislated equipment that would be deemed essential within the EU.

Block exemption

The method by which manufacturers have controlled local markets since 1985 is known as 'Block Exemption'. From 1985 to 1995, the EC allowed the motor industry to opt out of article 85(1) of The Treaty of Rome. This has enabled manufacturers to preserve an area franchise system, preventing competing dealers from selling their new cars at lower prices within each franchise area. The ten-year block exemption from European competition law was extended in 1995, but came under review by the EC again in July 1999.

At the same time, after a damning House of Commons Trade & Industry Select Committee report by MP Martin O'Neill, and a similar condemnation by John Bridgeman of The Office of Fair Trading, the Monopolies & Mergers Commission were investigating whether or not at least 25% of the UK market was unfairly rigged against the UK consumer.

By the time you read this, the MMC will have reported, and the UK Government should have taken whatever action was deemed necessary. In the meantime, the large manufacturers were planning to anticipate Government action either by cutting UK list prices or discounting them at the optimum point just before they were forced to.

The irony is that this will not necessarily reduce the average price paid for cars in the UK, for the simple reason that most of them were sold to the fleets at significant discounts on UK prices anyway.

But what it will do is give us a fairer system. Company car drivers who drive around 75% of the new cars on UK roads will no longer be taxed as though their car had been priced up to 55% higher than was actually paid by the fleet owners. And private buyers will no longer be faced with piddling discounts of a mere 5%–10% off a price which is on average 30% higher than that paid in other European countries.

This may mean the end of three years 'free' servicing, two years 'free' insurance, 0% finance, over-valued part-exchanges and other deals subsidised by high new car prices to private buyers. But at least we will be getting what we can plainly see is a fair deal.

If this *hasn't* happened, it is essential for you to read on. If it has happened, you will still be able to make savings on the new lower UK list prices, just as you can in Europe on Europe's lower prices.

Beating the system

How can you beat the system? There are numerous ways. The three most obvious are: buy a right-hand-drive EU type-Approved car in another European country such as Germany, a process which can save you up to 30% of the UK list price, all taxes paid; buy an independently imported new car from a car supermarket at a 15%–20% saving on UK list price; or buy 'nearly-new', either at auction or from a car supermarket. This last way you can obtain a 6–9-month-old car with 5,000–15,000 miles on the clock, at a saving of between 20% and 50% of the list price of a new car.

Another way is to buy pre-registered stock from franchised agents. These are cars registered by the agent to meet a monthly or quarterly volume bonus. Depending on how old they are at the time of sale, the savings on these cars can be as much as 20%. However, your choice will be strictly limited to oversupplied cars. There would be no chance of obtaining a much desired new model, such as the new BMW 3-Series, in this way.

Other methods save you less money, but involve less risk, less hassle and usually a greater degree of choice.

Buying via a broker

New car brokers act as middlemen between private car buyers and dealers. Since the contract is between the car buyer and the dealer, and since good brokers demand no deposit, this is a safe way to buy a car which is reasonably available. The broker takes a small commission from the supplying dealer for his part in the transaction.

The most you can save this way is the dealer discount of 5%–15%, plus any volume rebate being offered by the manufacturer, minus the small profit made by the dealer and the broker. It works best where the broker puts customers directly in touch with a family-owned dealership and, in effect, acts as their salesperson.

Two well-established brokers who can be recommended are: Steve Tokatlian at Quote to Quote on 0171 603 9999 (6 lines) and Pat Lawless at Carfile on 01335 360763/360022 (9.15–5.45), 0410 081984 (evenings and weekends). Neither asks for a deposit.

By bulk buying of Renaults in particular, Nationwide Vehicle Contracts is reported to be offering fleet discounts of as much as 25% to private buyers (tel: 01483 306906). Other brokers include Vehicle Sourcing (tel: 01865 358921); Motafile (tel: 01992 500595); and Grosvenor (tel: 0181 845 1538).

Buying from a franchised dealer

If you are a good negotiator, you should be able to buy a new unregistered car from a dealer for even less than you would pay via a broker. But in practice you will find yourself up against some very hard-nosed people, such as salespeople on commissions which depend on what they sell the car for and which can work out at more than the broker's commission.

But during comparatively slack months such as December, play your cards right and you can get 10%–12% off 'list price'. The best way to achieve this is to know precisely what the 'on the road' price of the car should be, take off the cost of Vehicle Excise Duty and the £25 First Registration tax, then subtract 15% from the remainder. On the premise that 3%–5% profit is better than no profit at all, many dealers will play ball, particularly towards the end of the month.

On the other hand, where they have more customers than cars, they won't play this game. You are unlikely to get more

7

than 4% or 5% off a car you have to order then wait several months for.

The part-exchange trick

If you have a car you want to part-exchange for a new one, it's no good getting a decent discount then giving it all back by accepting too little for your trade-in.

Be very well aware of what your existing car is worth. Compare it with similar models of similar age and mileage which the dealer has for sale, and don't accept less than £1,000 or 10% (whichever is the greater) less than the sticker price on these cars. This £1,000 or 10% may sound a lot, but remember that the dealer will usually negotiate downwards from these sticker prices when selling his used stock.

Also remember, what you get for your part-exchange is not the most important factor. The 'cost to switch' is. Always compare the total financial outlay involved in one deal compared to another.

For example, dealer 'A' has a Mondeo which lists at £15,000. He offers you £4,000 for your part-exchange, but no discount on the Mondeo, so the cost to switch is £11,000.

Dealer 'B' has a Vectra which lists at £15,000. He offers you £3,500 for your part-exchange, plus £750 off the price of the Vectra. The cost to switch is therefore £10,750, so the Vectra is £250 cheaper than the Mondeo even though you get less for your part-exchange.

Is the Mondeo worth £250 more than the Vectra? Or can you use the Vectra deal to chip £250 or more off the price of the Mondeo?

This is the way you should be thinking. It's not hard, is it?

Importing a car yourself

It is against European Community Law for any manufacturer to place any impediment in the way of any EU citizen buying any car at the pre-tax price in any other European country.

EC Regulation No. 1475/95 states, 'The consumer's freedom to buy anywhere in the Common Market is one of the fundamental achievements of the European Community and the Regulation reinforces this right.'"

But it goes on to state, 'The consumer's right is not accompanied by an obligation imposed on dealers to sell since it is normally in a dealer's interest to maximise its profits.'

Where a model of car is in short supply, a continental dealer may perfectly reasonably take the view that he will generate more profit by selling the car to a local who will probably insure, finance and service the car through him and even part-exchange it in a few years to come.

But where the model is freely available and the dealer simply wants to maximise turnover, he will usually be happy to play ball. At the time of writing, such dealers included: (Alfa Romeo) Koen Quintens, Alfa Romeo Ghent, tel: 0032 893 04930; (BMW) Zwartepoorte BMW, Rotterdam, tel 0031 165 576376; (Ford) Zunn Motors, Brussels, tel: 0032 2 3773500; (Peugeot) Leon Van Bruniesse of Netherlands Car Trading, Utrecht, tel: 0031 3024 75100; (Renault) Diffusion Automobile Calasienne, 58/60 avenue de Saint-Exupery, BP 154–62103 Calais, tel: 00 33 321 19 15 58, fax: 00 33 321 19 15 59 (also at Calais Carrefour Hypermarket); (VW) Autovroon, Amsterdam, tel: 0033 20 6869611; (Volvo) Bluekins Volvo, Roosendaal, Holland, tel: 0031 165 553040.

A typical Belgian pre-tax price breakdown is as follows:-

- Full UK spec Alfa 156TS   Bfr717,404
- Metallic Paint   Bfr14,876
- Sub total: Bfr729,280
- After 6% discount   Bfr688,000
- Transit Plates   Bfr10,000
- Total to pay   Bfr698,000
- @ 60 Bfr to £1   £11,633.33
- Ferry Costs   £150
- UK VAT @ 17.5%   £2,062
- Total Cost   £13,845
- UK List Price   £17,537
- Saving   £3,692

However, this involved a long wait for an RHD car, and a substantial up-front deposit. To protect yourself from currency fluctuations, the best thing to do is to open a foreign currency account at your bank. Transfers from Sterling into the account are made at the commercial rate for the currency (several points more favourable than the tourist rate). You get the rate at the time you order the transfer. And your deposits earn interest at a rate based on the base rate for the currency. But movements in and out of the account take several days and transfers to another account in another country (the dealer's) are likely to take a week. If Sterling were to plummet, VAT on import of the car would be due on the Sterling equivalent of the price paid, rather than the Sterling equivalent when you transferred your funds to your foreign currency account.

A reader-recommended Dutch broker who will do most of the work for you and still sell you a car at a sensible saving is Intercar at Brunssum in Limburg in the South of Holland (tel: 0031 45 525

3494; http://www.intercar.nl; e-mail: sales@intercar.nl).

Another company offering an import website is Import Marques: http://www.importmarques.com. This provides import quotations for virtually all makes and models linked to 15 specialist importers and apparently offers savings of as much as £3,500 on a Ford Puma or a Ford Focus. However, deposits of 10%–20% are asked for, and delivery can be three months or more. Since you might not know exactly where your deposit is going, it should only be made by a credit card offering credit card protection.

Broadspeed and Stena Lines are now organising car purchase cruises to Europe at an all-in price of £299 for two cruises for two people (to order, and then to collect the car) with overnight accommodation and expert help available. Call Broadspeed's 24-hour information line on 0171 413 9940/ 9950/9960/9970/9980 or point your internet browser at http://www.car-prices.com. Book tickets by calling Stena Lines on 01233 646881.

Step-by-step guide to importing a car from Europe

1 Get the relevant Government booklets and forms. First phone the DVLA on 01792 772134 and ask for the pack on personal imports. This includes a booklet, 'How to Import a Vehicle Permanently into Great Britain'; Form V100, which explains registering and licensing procedures and gives a list of Vehicle Registration Offices; and Form V55/5, which is an application form to license a vehicle in the UK for the first time. (Alternatively, phone the DETR on 0207 676 2094, write to DETR VSE1, Zone 2/01, Great Minster House, 76 Marsham Street, London SW1 4DR, or visit the DETR website at www.roads.detr.gov.uk/vehicle/vse1/index.htm).

Then phone your local VAT enquiry line listed under 'Customs & Excise' in the telephone directory and ask for the 'VAT Notice 728 Pack' which includes form Appendix D 'New Means of Transport – Notification of Acquisition'. (Don't call C&E on either 0171 864 3000 or 01304 224372, as these lines have become overwhelmed with enquiries.)

2 Decide which makes and models you are interested in and obtain the UK brochures for these cars. Then phone the manufacturer's UK customer helpline, say you have one of their cars and ask for a current list of continental service dealers.

3 Choose the car and specification you want, then start phoning. When you find a cooperative dealer, fax the exact specification of car you want and ask for a quote, to include temporary registration and export plates. The best countries to buy in are likely to be Holland, Belgium, Germany or France. Remember, if you buy in Europe, you will be buying a Europe-spec car with RHD as an extra. Other things, such as a radio, tinted glass, alarm/immobiliser and seven seats in an MPV may be extras too.

4 Order your car from the dealer offering the best combination of price and delivery date. Delivery could easily be 6–8 months for a car such as a VW, Mercedes Benz or Alfa Romeo. You will be asked to pay a deposit of between 10% and 30% when you place your order, either by credit card, Switch or international bank credit transfer. Make sure the dealer faxes, e-mails or posts you a receipt for this and a confirmation of your order.

5 Decide on whether you are going to gamble on Sterling rising or falling against the currency in which you will be buying the car. If you gamble on Sterling rising, leave your funds in a high interest Sterling account. If you gamble on Sterling falling, open a foreign Currency Call Account at

your bank. This is a deposit account in a foreign currency offering interest based on the much lower base rates for the foreign currency.

6 Keep in touch with the dealer by phone, fax or e-mail to make sure your order is being processed. Within two months of the delivery date, start asking for a scheduled build date for your car.

7 Once the dealer gives you a delivery date, ask for the Vehicle Identification Number (VIN number) of the car and insure it on the VIN from the date you propose to collect it. Then organise your flight out and ferry back and a bank draft to pay for the car.

8 When you go to collect the car, inspect it carefully to make sure it complies with the specification you have ordered. Make sure the dealer gives you a Certificate of Conformity to European Type Approval ('C of C'); Registration Certificate naming you as the keeper; insurance document to prove the car was insured in the country of origin (often combined with temporary registration); and, of course, the dealer's invoice. Make sure you buy some petrol in the country of origin and keep the receipt. Keep any hotel and restaurant receipts. And keep the ferry ticket.

9 As soon as possible (this must be within seven days of arriving back in the UK with your new car), fill in the form 'New Means of Transport – Notification of Acquisition' (Appendix 'D') which came with VAT 728 and take it, together with completed form C55/5, the dealer's invoice, the foreign registration document, the Certificate of Type Approval Conformity, your petrol receipts and any other foreign receipts to prove you have driven the car abroad, your ferry ticket, and your UK insurance certificate based on the VIN number, to your nearest Vehicle Registration Office. On payment of a £25 first registration fee and either six or

twelve month's VED, they will issue you with a registration number and a VED disc. The date of first registration will now be the date the car was first registered in the UK, provided this is within fourteen days of the purchase date, or within thirty days if the purchase date is immediately preceding a registration letter change.

10 The VRO will send form NMT Notification of Acquisition on to Customs & Excise, who will then send you an invoice VAT 413 for UK VAT at 17.5% of the cost of the car, which you have thirty days to settle. Once this is paid, you will receive a receipted VAT 413.

11 Order a set of plates. Phone the manufacturer's customer helpline number to put the car on their UK database for warranty purposes and in case of any recalls. Though HMC&E only insist you keep the purchase invoice and the receipted VAT for six years as proof that VAT has been paid, it's advisable to keep all the documentation, including petrol receipts and ferry tickets, in a safe place with them, to pass on to the new owner when you sell the car.

Single vehicle approval (SVA)

The above 'step by step' guide explains how to get the relevant official guides, documents and forms when importing a car from Europe which carries a Certificate of Conformity to EC Type Approval.

Up to March 2000, the following list of vehicles can also be registered in the UK without obtaining a 'Minister's Approval Certificate' (MAC):

- Personally imported vehicles over three years old
- Any vehicle which is over ten years old
- Motor Caravans

- Motor ambulances
- A vehicle which has been issued with a Minister's Approval Certificate on the basis that it has been suitably approved and registered in another EEA member state.
- A vehicle which is used by a member of a 'visiting force'.

In any other case, obtaining a MAC involves the vehicle passing a Single Vehicle Approval Test. This costs £165 for cars and £60 for the more limited test for commercial vehicles, and is carried out by Government Vehicle Inspectors at HGV testing stations. The relevant booklet is SVA1, 'The Single Vehicle Approval Scheme', from the Vehicle Certification Agency, tel: 0117 951 5151. You can buy a copy of the 'Single Vehicle Approval Inspection Manual', priced £25, order code 'SVA 01', from the Vehicle Inspectorate, PO Box 12, Swansea SA1 1BP.

Unfortunately MACs are subject to rationing under a quota system which restricts the number of independent trade imports to 50 of any one make and model of car in each year. Some ttade inmporters get around this by having the cars SCA-tested to UK staqndards inother EU countries, which the Vehicle Inspectorate now allows.

The system is set to change from March 2000. The annual trade quota of 50 of any one make and model will be replaced by a total of 1,000 cars in March, rising to 10,000 cars a month by December 2000 and being lifted altogether by January 2001. But at the same time, the loophole by which individual private imports between three and ten years old were not subject to the SVA test will be closed, and all non-European imports up to ten years old will become subject to the SVA test. Proving overseas ownership to escape the SVA test might mean living overseas for twelve months and having the vehicle registered to you there for six months. The SVA test itself will also be 'enhanced' in terms of 'key environmental, safety and anti-theft items to apply to commercially traded vehicles.'

As far as can be ascertained, all vehicles over ten years old, whether imported privately or by the trade, will continue to be free of the SVA test, but will need to pass a UK MOT test before they can be registered in the UK.

Where to shop and how to find the car

Order the relevant car magazines from an international newsagent, or pick them up at the airport when you land: *DAZ*, *Motor Markt*, *Auto Motorrad Freizeit* and *Auto Motor und Sport* for Germany, *Auto Week* for Holland, *Coche Actual*, *Autopista* or *Top Auto* for Spain, *Irish Auto Trader* for Eire; and start phoning dealers with the intention of buying a car already in stock, either pre-tax or with the forms to reclaim the local taxes. (One very good reason for choosing Dutch or Irish dealers, of course, is that they all speak English.) Once you have located a car, send your deposit by telegraphic transfer (which takes three working days). When the car arrives at the dealer, obtain the VIN number and arrange for the car to be insured in the UK on the VIN. (If your insurer won't do this, brokers ABM will; tel: 0181 681 8986). Send the rest of the money by telegraphic transfer (three working days again), take a flight to the relevant country, get the dealer to fix you up with 'export plates' and insurance, and make sure that the car comes with an EU Type Approval 'Certificate of Conformity' or you won't be able to register it in the UK. Then simply drive to the nearest ferry and follow the rest of the 'step by step' guide's instructions.

If you have bought an LHD it's a relatively simple matter to change over the lights and the foglamp, have the speedo altered to mph by Reap Automotive Design (0181 863 2305), have the car inspected and get it registered via your local VRO. With Europe-wide Type Approval for European cars from January 1998, there is no need for an SVA for a new European car, but you must make sure you get a 'Certificate of Conformity' with it, otherwise it will be subject to SVA.

If you order a car from a mainland European dealer, the biggest worry you are likely to face is that he may demand a substantial deposit, possibly up to 30%. If his franchise is pulled or he goes bust before you take delivery of your car, the situation is the same as in the UK: your deposit becomes one of the assets of the company and you will be way down the list of creditors and thus unlikely to get it back.

If a continental dealer tells you he would like to sell you an RHD car but is being pressurised by the manufacturer not to, report the matter to The European Competition Commissioner, DG IV, European Commission, 200 Rue de la Loi, 1049 Brussels, Belgium.

Warranty claims with Euro-imports

As long as you have registered your car with the UK manufacturer or an official UK importer, the car will be subject to the same pan-European warranty that applies in the country of origin and which must cover at least 12 months.

It will not be subject to a UK 3-year warranty unless a 3-year warranty applies in the country of origin. (A Nissan from Eire is covered by a 3-year warranty as long as Nissan GB can be furnished with a copy of the invoice.)

But if the car proves to be seriously faulty, it is not covered by the UK's 'Sale and Supply of Goods Act 1994' which, subject to case law, would otherwise allow you to reject it. The car will only be covered by consumer protection law in the country of origin. If this allows for rejection, then the car must be returned to the supplying dealer in that country.

However, if you buy your car directly from an independent import supplier in the UK, and the car is first registered in the UK rather than collected by you from mainland Europe, then you can invoke the UK's 'Sale and Supply of Goods Act 1994' and reject the car by returning it to the UK importer.

Over the next year the EC might introduce new pan-European consumer protection laws, but there was no Directive to this effect at the time of writing.

Buying foreign in the UK

Rather then go to another country to place an order for an RHD car which may be delayed and which might not come in the UK specification, you can actually buy a UK-spec car in the UK through the manufacturer's export sales division.

What you do is you say you are a UK ex-pat, working in another EU country for a year and living at a friend's address in that country. You then order the car in RHD UK spec to take with you to that other country at the equivalent of the pre-tax price prevailing in that country. You give your true UK address as an accommodation address in the UK for the car to be registered to, so it gets UK plates. You then decide to 're-import' the car to the UK, paying UK VAT, and the car is yours, here, with a full UK warranty, but at a price 15%–25% lower than the UK list price.

This may seem like a dishonest trick. But in fact all you have done is force the manufacturer to sell you a car at a price he should have been prepared to sell it at anyway.

Import agents

The alternative is to use an agent, such as Origin Euro (tel: 0181 381 3000). If you do, make sure the final price (or price parameters) are pre-agreed in Sterling, in writing on the contract.

Write down the exact specification you are contracting to buy on the contract (don't make the mistake one reader made of 'assuming' a VW Sharan would automatically come with seven seats and a driver's manual in English) and also make sure that any deposit you make is either paid by credit card or paid into an 'escrow' account from which you still have some chance of getting it back if the worst comes to the worst.

The advantages of dealing with Origin Euro are that it imports its cars by transporter to its own UK compound, so the first place they are registered is the UK rather than the country of origin. Origin Euro settles the VAT bill for you. And because Origin Euro has the financial resources to pay for the car, you don't have to pre-pay the final amount until collection day.

Other agents include Park Lane on 01420 544300, Carfax International on 0181 288 3536, PCA Car Brokers on 01892 516261, Eurocar on 0800 068 0303, Euro Continental Cars on 01703 470208 and Auto Liberté on 01491 412468. Though agents get you through the hoops, they do, of course, charge for their services, and your saving on the car will be greatly reduced.

A further source worth consideration is cancelled RHD export orders. When the economies of RHD Pacific Basin countries collapsed, UK companies started specialising in diverting RHD exports to the UK. Some of these cars came with EU Certificates of Conformity. If the car you are thinking of buying doesn't, until March 2000 it remains subject to a Single Vehicle Approval Test and the SVA import quota of just 50 of each model a year. Enquiry line on quotas: 01792 454255.

Japanese imports

In 1997 and 1998 the strong pound made new RHD imports from Japan very attractive – especially some of the 'Evolution' four-wheel-drive saloons. But in 1999 the rising Yen has been making Japanese imports progressively more expensive. Specialist importers include Park Lane on 01420 544300, Warrender of Bolton on 01257 427700, Orbis International (part of Sidney Newton PLC) on 0208 965 9666; MMC International Holdings Ltd. on 0208 656 1555 (website http://www.mmc-intl.com), Intercar on 0208 203 3399, and Direct Vehicle Rental on 01902 353393.

American imports

As in Japan, like for like, new cars sell in the USA for half to two-thirds of their price in the UK. A new Ford Cougar 2.0 litre, for example, costs less than the dollar equivalent of £11,000. There are also something like 200 million vehicles on US roads compared to the 28 million registered in the UK. So it's a huge market and it doesn't take any nonsense such as the ridiculous list prices forced on private buyers in the UK.

But even if they can be imported within the quota, lhd right-dipping American vehicles often cannot pass the SVA. One brand-new pickup (a commercial vehicle and thus subject to a less stringent test than for cars) failed on the design of its braking system – something that could not be changed – forcing the owner to reclaim his VAT and then try to get it passed in another EU country to be sold there, or otherwise to reclaim both the VAT and EU import duty and send the vehicle back to the USA where it would be sold at a considerable financial loss.

UK companies importing new cars from the USA include American Car Imports on 0208 889 4545, the American Carriage Company on 0208 549 3151, Brooks Kensington on 01869 325551 and Bauer Millet on 0161 831 7447.

Japanese cars and the SVA

Japanese-spec cars are not necessarily suitable for use in the UK. When their ECUs are electronically interrogated, the information may be in Japanese. The engine may be programmed to expect a higher quality of petrol than is available in the UK. Tyres may be speed rated to 112mph. Low mileage in a Japanese car may also mean countless hours idling in Japan's notorious traffic jams, which wrecks engines. A useful appraisal of the situation is provided in Automobile Buyers Services' Technical Information Sheet 27, from ABS, Adelphi Mill, Grimshaw Lane, Bollington, Macclesfield, Cheshire SK10 5JB, tel: 01625 576441 (ABS Vehicle Inspections: 0345 419926). You should also speak to Intech (01264 773888) or Protech (01179 861611), because they know what is needed to get individual models through the SVA test. Though the SVA test did not become compulsory until 1st May 1998, an official SVA certificate is the only sure way to know that any grey import you buy is likely to pass a future MOT.

As mentioned earlier, to get round the fifty-car-a-year quota, large numbers of Japanese cars were illegally brought into the UK by traders as 'personal imports' subject to no more than a UK MOT before resale to unsuspecting members of the public. Many of these cars have untraceable histories. A three-year-old Japanese grey import with a dodgy MOT could be as illegal to drive in the UK as one with no MOT at all. Buy one and you may not find out until its next MOT that the car is illegal, by which time the trader who sold it to you could have hitched up his caravan and scarpered. You have been warned.

Import agents' deposits

Agents usually ask for a deposit of at least 10% and sometimes as much as 30%. You can protect this deposit against the agent going bust or doing a runner by paying it by credit card (credit card, *not* charge card) or by insisting it is paid into a UK 'escrow' account where the agent cannot touch it until the deal is done and it does not form part of his assets if he goes bust.

I should add that, though a number of dealers and agents have been mentioned here, their financial and company status has not been checked out, so please do not take any of these names as recommendations. I take no responsibility whatsoever for anything going wrong with any deal you may make with any of them.

Buying on finance
Personal contract purchase (PCP)

This is a form of lease purchase which has sprung up during the 1990s and now seems to be offered by most manufacturers over periods of two or three years. It is also offered independently of the manufacturers by Swan National Car Choice, which is able to obtain fleet discounts on the cars it buys and pass on some of the savings to its private customers.

You pay a deposit (either cash or your trade-in). You then make monthly repayments which pay off roughly half the amount of money borrowed and the interest on all of it . At the end of the two or three years, you have three options: pay off the remaining lump sum and keep the car; use any equity you have in the car (the difference between the lump sum to clear the debt and the trade value of the car) as the deposit on another PCP on another new car; or simply walk away with no debts but no car.

Most new private cars in the USA are leased this way. But, of course, in the USA the payments form a much lower percentage of the average person's income than they do in the UK (they're richer in the USA and their cars are much cheaper).

PCPs are best for people who are in steady, secure jobs, who are happy leasing rather than owning, and who don't mind both the dealers and the finance companies profiting from this. If you're worried about your job, you can take out redundancy insurance on the debt, but this is expensive and makes the car even more expensive than it already is.

Compare any offer from a franchised dealer with what's on the table from Swan National Car Choice (0500 28 29 30) before making a final decision. And always remember, if the market slumps against the price you paid for your car on a PCP, as happened in thousands of cases during 1999, you may be left with no equity in it to finance the deposit of your next PCP.

50/50 finance

This is another form of lease purchase. You cough up 50% of the car's price straight away, and the remaining 50% in two year's time.

It looks like a free loan for two years but, of course, it isn't. In this world, nothing is for nothing. The car that is on the 50/50 deal is usually the sort of car which sells for 60%–70% of its new price at 8 months old with 8,000 miles. At two years old it will probably be worth 40% of its new price. So it isn't really worth 100% of its new price in the first place, and the difference between what it's really worth and its new price partly finances the finance and partly goes towards the dealer's and the manufacturer's profits and the salesman's commission.

I'm well aware that many people feel that a 50/50 deal suits them; I just want to be sure you know what you're getting into.

Straight finance

APRs vary and dealers earn commission on finance. Even with base rate at 8%, the true APR could be 25%.

All you have to do is follow the golden rule of comparing your total outlay on the deal with your total outlay on any other deal.

Let's return to the Mondeo/Vectra example we looked at earlier. The same straight deals are still on the table, but, after the cost of finance, the £11,000 outlay for the Mondeo rises to £13,000 over two years while the £10,750 outlay on the Vectra rises to £13,500. The Ford dealer clearly has the advantage, but, if you have your heart set on the Vectra, keep dealing and ask if there is some way the Vauxhall dealer can do the deal for £13,000 or less.

He may increase the p/x allowance, increase the discount, or sacrifice some commission on the finance. He may even offer to throw in a set of floormats to complete the deal and make you feel good about it. If he says no, he clearly doesn't need your business.

One final point: if you buy a car on finance, the law says that the supplier (i.e. the dealer) and the finance house are jointly liable for any defects. If the car proves to be faulty, you reject it under the Sale and Supply of Goods Act 1994 and the supplier accepts the rejection, don't then take any heavy-handed treatment from the finance house.

However, until the rejection is accepted by the supplier, you must keep up the payments or you could find yourself in serious financial trouble.

Bank or building society loans

This is usually the cheapest way to borrow, but if you borrow using the equity in your house as security, you don't get the same level of protection that you get through buying on the dealer's finance.

BUYING USED

Buying used privately
Buying from someone you know

Ask yourself how well do you know this person, and how well do you know the car?

You wouldn't be the first to buy a disaster zone just because someone in the family was selling it. Nor would you be the first to overlook faults because you didn't want to upset Uncle Albert and Auntie Gwen and the entire mother's side of your family.

So think about this very carefully. Obviously, if the car is literally being given away, take it. It's being offered to you at a knockdown price, make sure the price is knockdown by looking it up in 'Parker's Guide' or the *What Car* Price Guide. If the price is merely a fair price, weigh up what you know about the car against what you're being asked to pay. How long has the owner owned it? Is the mileage genuine? How often was the car serviced? Is there anything wrong with it? How much will the faults cost to put right?

I accept you may have private reasons for giving too much for a car to an impecunious, elderly or sick member of the family. It's a diplomatic way of helping them out. But otherwise you should not let your relationship with the seller colour your judgement. The car is a purchase you are going to have to live with, and if it proves to be a money pit you'll have to live with that too.

Buying used from a friend of a friend

The same cautions apply here as above – but to a much greater extent. How well do you know your friend? If you fall out with *his* friend, where do you stand? Where does *he* stand?

Buying used from an advertisement

First, you need to establish the status of who you are buying from. If he is a trader, he is required by law to put a 'T' or the word 'trade' in his ad. Don't be put off if he has. It gives you rights you do not have against a private seller; in fact the very same rights you have when buying from a swanky, carpeted car showroom.

To try and get out of this, some scurvy 'home traders' try to hide the fact that this is what they are. So when you call a number in the advertisement which does not contain a 'T' or the word 'trade', say you are calling about 'the car'. A private seller is unlikely to have half a dozen parked up and down the street, so will immediately know which car you mean. A trader who has more than one car will have to ask you 'which car?' But even if there is only one car for sale, the seller could still be a smalltime trader.

So your next question should be, 'How long have you owned it?' (You may well feel the vendor squirming at the other end of the line.) Any less than six months should then prompt the follow-up question, 'Are you a private seller or a trader?'

If the answer to this is something evasive or a final admission of trader status, ask yourself if you really want to deal with someone who has already lied in his advertisement.

Assuming from now on we are dealing with a genuine private seller rather than a trader, you need to establish some more facts about the car. First concentrate on content of the advertisement.

By '"M" reg', does he mean 1995M or 1994M, or even 1973M for that matter? Which 'model year' is the car? For example, a 1994-model 'M' reg Astra 1.4iLS did not have power steering, but all 1995 model 'V-grille' Astras did, even though the '95 model may have been registered in late 1994.

Ask how many previous keepers are listed on the V5 registration document, and add one for the vendor to that number for the true figure. Ask if the advertised mileage is genuine, and if the answer is 'Yes', ask how they know it is.

By now, you'll be starting to feel the measure of the person you are dealing with and your instincts will be getting to work. Trust these instincts. They are what you were born with and have subsequently developed to protect yourself against danger.

If you're happy about the car and the person selling it, make an appointment to view. Unless the car is something rare and really special, don't be rushed into a hasty twilight or nocturnal encounter. You want broad daylight and you don't want rain. Rain is the most effective disguise for a chameleon colour scheme and a host of other defects.

Checking the car's history

There are several organisations that will check the car's history for you to make sure it is not on any registers as having been an insurance damage write-off, a finance bad debt, or stolen.

These checks are provided over the phone for a fee, payable by credit card, of around £32.50. The organisations are HPI on 01722 422422, AA/Experian Car Check on 0800 234999, ABS on 0800 3895169, and *What Car?* History Check on 0845 601 0804.

AA/Experian and *What Car?* have extended their services to a limited mileage check (where past mileages have been recorded), and HPI intends to follow suit as soon as its database contain what it considers to be enough accurate mileage information. But gathering this has been a nightmare, largely due to the reluctance of some fleets (the prime source of relatively young but high-mileage cars) to divulge mileages on disposal. These fleets know that if they have a reputation in the trade for not divulging mileages, they stand a better change of getting high 'clockers money' for their cars at auction. The worry HPI has is whether it is getting the correct information in the first place. If a vendor and a trader conspire to register a lower mileage than a vehicle has actually covered, then that's what goes on the DVLA records and is passed on to HPI and AA/Experian. Still, some record of mileage has to be better than none at all.

The best advice is to treat all odometer readings as suspicious and to get in touch with the previous owners listed on the car's V5. If you are buying from the first owner of the car and he is a man of the cloth, then the mileage is probably correct. If you are buying from a small businessman who has used the car to travel extensively on business, then, if the mileage is low, it is probably not correct.

Checking out a car

When you first see the car, what do your instincts tell you? Do you get a funny feeling in the pit of your stomach, or do you feel happy and excited?

Trust these feelings because, once again, they are your natural defence mechanisms at work. All too often we ignore our instincts and intellectualise ourselves into making a bad decision.

That's what salesmanship is: getting you to think nice thoughts about what you're going to do with the car or how easy it will be to pay for it, and to put out of your head the obvious fact that the car is a heap of junk.

Beware the car dealer who pre-qualifies your financial status over the phone so that, when you arrive at the car lot, the finance is set up and all you have to do is choose a car. By that time you are pre-sold on buying a car from that dealer, come what may, and, when you leave home, you leave your brain and your instincts behind.

Assuming, and only assuming, you have a good feeling about the car, you can check it out yourself or have it independently inspected. The downside of an independent inspection, of course, is that it may take some time to get an appointment, the dealer may sell the car in the meantime, and you'll still have to fork out the inspection fee.

So, even if you're not mechanically minded, it makes sense to carry out some preliminary checks before you go to the expense of an independent inspection.

Inspecting a car yourself

First and foremost, does the paint match? If every panel is a different shade of red, for example, the car has been in several accidents. If the paint is fresh and new and all the same colour, the car has been in a big accident and been rebuilt. If just part of the car has fresh paint, for example the bonnet, it may merely have had a minor scrape or been repainted because it was badly stone-chipped. Other tips for looking for signs of repaired accident are to peel back bits of rubber trim and look for 'tide marks' underneath, to open and close all the doors and check the shut lines, to look under the boot carpet for fresh paint and a lack of the usual manufacturer's stickers, to look under the bonnet at the inner wings and on the engine, gearbox and suspension for flecks of spray dust, to crouch down in front of the car and look for ripples in its sides. It's not that hard, is it? One final tip: when a front wing is replaced it is resprayed *in situ*, and they don't usually make much of a job of the section hidden behind the shut door. Feel the paint there, and if it's rough the car has had a new front wing. Rust is less of a problem than it used to be and paint is now so expensive it's simply not worth filling a car with pudding and giving it a 'blow over'. But if the car is getting on in years, check all the usual places – round the wheel arches, under the valences (if they're steel), round the edges of the boot floor, under the carpets if they will lift, in the bottoms of the doors, round the headlights and along the outer tops of the doors.

Next job, check the tyres. Uneven tyre wear may be due to incorrect alignment settings, or it may be due to bent suspension components from kerbing. So be particularly wary of uneven front tyre wear. Check the nearside front wheel for rim damage. Has it got a new wheeltrim? Does the wheeltrim match the others? Are all the wheeltrims wrong? (A cheap set of four costs less than one correct wheetrim from the manufacturer's agent.)

You've done paint and tyres. Now on to the interior. Dirt cleans off, but tears in the seats and broken bits of trim are notoriously difficult and expensive to put right. One fag burn can be invisibly repaired using new techniques, but a lot of fag burns will cost you £50 each and the repairs won't be invisible. If the entire interior stinks of tobacco smoke you'll be up against it to get rid of the lingering odour. Has there been a dog in the car? Has it scratched the paint? Has it left a smell? Don't feel you have to be polite about this to the car's owners, however nice they may be. It's your money they're after, not your friendship.

Open the bonnet and check all the fluids. Makers like Ford very helpfully label all the things to check yellow. But what you want to look at is the oil on the end of the dipstick. Is it up to the mark? What colour is it? Castor oil yellow is excellent; light brown is good; dark brown is okay; a tar-like black in a petrol engine spells disaster, though lubricating oil in a diesel engine will always be black.

Unscrew the oil filler cap. If there is a deposit of whitish or creamy grey 'mayonnaise' underneath, it means one of two things. The car has led a life of very short runs from cold starts, has never warmed up properly and the condensation this has created has mixed with the oil. Engines run like this have less than a quarter of the life of engines run properly, so a little old lady's car with 10,000 miles on the clock has really done the equivalent of at least 50,000 miles and should be valued accordingly.

The second problem that 'mayonnaise' can warn you of is a blown cylinder head gasket. It may be straightforward to replace this, or the head may need to be skimmed because it has warped. This gives the car a higher compression ratio and may mean that it simply won't run on 95Ron unleaded petrol. Have a look under the radiator cap or in the radiator expansion tank for similar emulsion to confirm this, and also look for white smoke (i.e. steam) coming from the exhaust.

Have a look at the condition of the power steering fluid. It should be red, not black. Same goes for the automatic transmission fluid (most autoboxes have a dipstick). It is a good idea for automatic transmission fluid to be changed every year (and is essential with CVT automatics). It is also vital (especially with CVTs) that the ATF level is kept up to the mark.

Look under the car for leaks. Is there oil on the vendor's driveway? A leak from a cam-cover gasket is common and no big deal, but a bad oil leak from a cylinder head gasket means the head has to come off and, if it does, manifold studs may break. A leak from the timing belt cover is bad news because it means that the camshaft end seal or a jackshaft seal has gone, contaminating the timing belt – so you won't just need a new seal, you'll need a new belt too. If the gearbox/final drive is leaking from an output shaft seal, the lack of oil in the transmission may have led to premature wear.

Now ask to see the service history. Not a book full of stamps – the *actual bills* for all the work on the car which the owner has paid for, or, if it's a fleet car, a computer print-out of its service history. If, from this, you find that the car has been 'over-serviced' (had its oil and filter changed every 4–6 months), then be willing to pay more for it than the guides suggest. If, on the other hand, it has been 'underserviced' (with gaps of more than a year), then pay substantially less than guide price. If the car has a timing belt rather than a chain, in general this needs to be replaced every 35,000–40,000 miles or every 3–4 years. On some cars, such as Ford Zetecs, the replacement cycle can be pushed to up to 5 years or 80,000 miles, whichever comes first, but no longer. If the service bills don't show a timing belt change, then budget between £60 and £200 to have it done. (The job is more expensive on Peugeots and Citroens because there is an engine mounting in the way.) Automatic transmission fluid should have been changed every year, or every two years at a push; brake and power steering fluid every two years, or every three years at a push – but every year if the car is fitted with ABS. If the car has a manual gearbox and the oil in that has been changed within its 18 months on the road it's a valuable plus point worth paying more for.

You have now made a number of checks which will have provided you with a lot of information without having to pay anyone. Now we'll get on to the road test of the car.

The road test

First, are you insured? If you own and insure a car yourself, your policy will usually cover you to drive another insured car third-party only. But this means you will be personally liable for any damage you do to the car.

Switch on the ignition and look at the lighting display. If there is an ABS light, make sure it goes off within seconds of starting the engine. The engine should start instantly. When it does start, are there any rattles? With hydraulic tappets you may hear a brief rattle before the tappets pump up, but this is nothing to worry about unless it persists.

If the car is manual, at which point in the pedal travel does the clutch take up? If near the top, there is likely to be less than 10,000 miles of life left in the clutch. If you can get it to slip, reckon on less than 2,000 miles.

If the car is front-wheel-drive, do a full-lock reverse turn in both directions. This will tell you more about the condition of the clutch, but if you also hear clonking, there is wear in the driveshaft universal joints and these are expensive to replace.

Does the car accelerate smoothly? If it's an automatic, do the gears change smoothly? But don't expect all automatics to change into 4th or even 3rd at town speeds. If it's a manual, do the gears change easily with no graunching, and can you change down smoothly, particularly from 3rd to 2nd, without having to double de-clutch? Is there any gearbox whine or whirring noise? A lot of gearboxes do whine slightly and, though it's an irritant, it may be nothing to worry about. Similarly, a bit of diff lash may be terminal, or the diff may soldier on for years. But the likelihood of a transmission repair should be budgeted for and the price you pay chipped down unless it already accounts for this.

Do the brakes stop the car straight and true? If you feel juddering, the discs may be warped. If retardation is slow, the discs, pads, drums and linings may be worn or grooved. Do the brakes lock up front or back during an emergency stop? If so, the rear brake compensator may be u/s.

Finally, check all the electrics: wipers, sunroof, windows, everything. If the car has a computer, get the owner to run through its functions. (But, obviously, if the car is cheap, you don't worry about a non-functioning computer.)

Having the car inspected

The four main used-car inspection organisations are: AA (0345 500610); ABS (0345 419926); Green Flag/National Breakdown (01254 355606); and RAC (0800 333660). Others are AAA Motor Vehicle Inspections (London area only: 0705 0158123); Autocheck GB Ltd (0181 678 7060); and D S Crawford (Central Scotland only: 0131 453 4393). ABS also offers a Helpline on 01625 576441. (ABS are by far the best for 'grey imported' Japanese cars because they know what to look for.)

Inspections tend to cost from £50 to £150 for the average car, the inspectors 'come to the car', and you are provided with a written report afterwards. Some, such as D S Crawford in Scotland, include an HPI status check in their very reasonable price of £55. The RAC has been known to charge up to £250 for inspecting personally imported cars.

Sports and high performance cars need specialist inspections by experts in the particular make and model. An AA or RAC inspection of a Porsche, for example, simply isn't enough. Best to get a written report from a Porsche agent or specialist and to pay the extra for a compression test on all six cylinders.

The problem is, no vendor with any sense will give you right of first refusal on a car subject to inspection at a later date, unless you pay them a non-refundable deposit. If you can't cut a deal like this with the vendor, they will simply sell the car to the first buyer who comes up with the right money and you could end up forking out an inspection fee for a 'sold' car.

Condition of older cars

Where cars are more than ten years old, whatever the make, there is likely to be some rust somewhere.

In general, German cars with metallic paint finishes seem to rust the least. But this is an over-simplification, because German build quality slipped quite a bit between 1988 and 1992. Since 1986, all Audis have incorporated hot-dip or electro-galvanized panels, but, since 1988, so have most Fiats, starting with the Tipo and carrying on even with Unos and Pandas from around 1990.

Whereabouts the car has spent its life also affects its propensity to rust. Nothing rusts a car worse than a salt solution, which acts as an electrolyte between the different metals in a car's body and suspension. In northern counties such as Northumberland, roads are heavily salted from November to March, and if you go into any Northumberland market town you can see the effect this has on the cars. Cars in coastal areas are affected by airborne salt and sea spray.

In general, cars that have spent their lives in the south east and more than 20 miles from the coast are least likely to have been affected by premature rusting.

Keeping a car in a garage does not necessarily prevent rusting. If a car is put away wet and salty in a poorly ventilated garage, the atmosphere in there will accelerate the rusting process. On the other hand, a warm, dry car driven into a dry, well-ventilated and possibly even heated garage is least likely to rust while stored. Remember, though, the floors of most garages, even integral garages, are usually below the damp course of the house, and condensation is likely inside such garages during the winter.

Combined inspections and used car warranties

Cover Plan Direct, in association with ABS, now offers a used vehicle inspection combined with a warranty on the vehicle after purchase. For information, tel: 01625 576441.

Motor Warranty Direct (0800 097 8001) also offers private used car warranties. White Knight (0870 601 6055) offers a combined warranty and purchase contract (details below in 'Making a Purchase Contract'.)

Agreeing a price

How good are you at negotiating? Most used car sellers will have checked the value of their car as a 'private sale' in one of the consumer car price guides available from newsagents. ('Parkers', the *What Car?* Price Guide, etc.) They are likely to have followed the guide advice to build an amount into the price for negotiation.

The simplest way to check out their bottom line is to say, 'OK, I know the advertised price, but what's the lowest you're prepared to take for the car?' They may smile sheepishly and tell you straight away, or getting to their bottom line might be like pulling teeth.

Remember, though, that even when you get to what they have told themselves is their 'bottom line', it might not be as low as they are prepared to go. Much will depend on circumstances, such as the urgency of the sale, how long the car has been on the market, and/or how few people have come to see it so far. So think like a detective. If the bloke's bags are already packed, his furniture gone and his curtains down, he's probably leaving for Australia that afternoon. If he's already bought a replacement car, he may need to sell the older one urgently. Just chatting to the fellow may elicit little hints that tell you the true circumstances. It's hardly a Christian approach, but it's up to you to take advantage of whatever information you can get.

Making a purchase contract

An insurance company trading under the brand name 'White Knight' has come up with a great idea for private purchase contracts and a subsequent 'warranty'.

First, understand that all a second-hand car warranty can ever be is a form of insurance policy. ('Mechanical Breakdown Insurance' is the correct term.) For an insurance underwriter to meet any claims on such a 'warranty', there must have been nothing wrong with the car when it was sold. They will not meet 'warranty' claims for faults which were already present.

White Knight recognises this by creating a contract between vendor and buyer in which the vendor lists all of the car's major parts in good working order and White Knight covers them with its MBI. If any of these parts fail within 21 days, White Knight then either pays for the repair or has the AA inspect the vehicle in order to decide if the fault was present when the car was sold. If it was, the vendor is held liable for the repair. After these 21 days the buyer has cover for the remainder of the 6 or 12 months warranty period purchased.

The plan can be used to cover any car up to 10 years old and up to 110,000 miles. The cost is fixed at £99 for six months or £149 for twelve months, and the policy can be taken out either by the vendor or by the purchaser. To obtain a contract form with full instructions, call 0870 601 6055.

Phone for the pack anyway because the private sale/-purchase contract is an excellent model for any private contract between buyer and seller. Because its terms are crystal clear, both of you will know where you stand.

Long gone are the days of a scruffy bit of paper with the registration of the car, the date, the words 'accepted as seen', and both signatures scrawled over a 20p stamp.

Unless, of course, that's what both of you want.

Buying from a company
Buying your 'company car'

Your company car may be owned by your company or it may be leased.

If it's the company's own car, the company may have a policy of offering it to an employee at a favourable price as a perk. But if whoever runs the fleet gets performance-related pay for saving the company money, forget about getting an excellent deal.

And if the car is leased, you can expect the first price the leasing company quotes you to be close to retail. They want to make money and you're a captive market, so you can't blame them.

Be very sure of your ground. You know your car better than they do. Is it so good that you want to lay out your own money on it? It may have reliable during your tenure over three years and maybe sixty thousand miles. But over the next forty thousand miles it could need tyres, exhaust, clutch, water pump and all the other things that fail just after fleets get rid of their cars.

'Cold buying' from a company

Traders constantly phone the fleet and 'human resources' managers of companies to try to buy company owned cars as they come off the company fleet. The bad news is there are a lot of closed 'sweetheart' deals involving bungs which keep outsiders out. Or the company's accounts may be so strictly audited that it is compelled either to sell its cars by tender or put them out to auction.

But you never know unless you try. So check the businesses in your locality and spend a morning phoning them.

Inevitably, you will get a lot of brush-offs, but if you 'score' just one car in a morning at £1,000 below trade book, you've done rather well. That £1,000 below book will probably finance running the car for the next six months. No wonder traders are thicker-skinned than the average rhinoceros.

Buying used from a dealer
'Franchised' dealers

Most franchised dealers now offer used car schemes support-ed by manufacturers, such as Ford's 'Ford Direct' and Vauxhall's 'Network Q'. Where the warranty is backed by the manufacturer (e.g. Ford Direct) rather than simply an insured warranty, these give peace of mind but can come at a fairly high price.

Nevertheless, once you've shopped around a bit and got the feel of prices at the car supersites, it's worth paying the franchised dealers a visit. They have been known to beat supersite prices, and if their prices, inclusive of a cast iron war-ranty, are only a few hundred more than those of the supersites, you may be better off with the franchised dealers.

Where you want to part-exchange your old car, franchised dealers almost always give better part-exchange allowances than the supersites. But here you need to compare the total 'cost to switch', not merely the part-exchange allowance offered.

Specialist dealers

These are dealers who specialise in a particular type of car, usually sports cars, prestige cars or 4x4s, but you also find '7-seater Centres', 'Mini Centres', 'Cavalier Centres' and so on.

To maintain attractive stock levels, they usually have to pay more for their cars, especially at auction, and this is likely to be reflected in the prices they ask.

You have to weigh up the convenience and time-saving they offer you against these slightly higher prices. And if they have any sports or prestige cars on offer which are less than three years old, you should question the wisdom of buying from them rather than from a franchised dealer.

The best specialists are keen enthusiasts of a marque, such as Porsche, BMW or Volkswagen, with workshops on the premises.

Independent dealers

These are your old-school car dealers as seen by the hundred on the Romford Road and stretches of the A24 through Tooting, Balham and Clapham.

Some of them are really nice people. Some of them are right old rogues.

'Home' traders

These people are much maligned, usually by magazines with a vested interest in maligning them. (Obviously if a magazine's main source of income is from dealer advertisements, it isn't going to recommend the little guys who undercut those dealers.)

A proper trader who openly trades from a home of his own is bound by all the same consumer protection laws as a dealer with large, expensive premises. He'll be watched fairly carefully by the local trading standards office. The only way he can make an honest living is by offering deals that beat those on offer from the big boys.

That 'home of his own' bit is important. If he's operating from rented accommodation you may have no more come-back against him than from a 'traveller' working from a big shiny caravan.

Make sure he invites you into the house (it may not be his house). And if he's the least bit aggressive, shifty, bad tempered or has a vicious looking dog on a chain, make a polite excuse and get the hell out of there.

Never buy a car in a car park or a lay-by or from a dealer working from a mobile phone number who brings the car round to your house. Always check (HPI or AA/Experian) cars offered by home traders and look for verification that the mileage is genuine.

For this purpose, a fleet car's computerised service history print-out is a far better bet than a lot of stamps in a service book. For example, unless the car is a manual Volvo T5, if the tyres seem to have been changed every 5,000 miles you'll instinctively know something isn't quite right.

Buying at auction
Advantages and disadvantages

Auctions can be the best places to source a car. After all, unless its a 'classic car auction' aimed at the public, the cars there should sell for the trade prices the market puts on them on the day.

Auctions, especially 'classic car auctions', are also a lion's den for the naïve and unwary. Remember, from a seller's point of view, auctions provide quick sales with no comebacks.

In the old days it was common for traders to buy a car either in the trade or at auction, strip all the good bits off it (tyres, battery, up-graded stereo, etc.), replace them with duff bits, then put the car back through the auction. This still happens, and the more luxurious the car the worse it can be. Often little things, like good electric mirrors, are swapped for u/s bits. Occasionally, big things like a good engine and transmission or a good diff are swapped for a bad one. Of course, if a car is coming up for a £2,000 service, it will be put through the auction before rather than after.

Different types of car auction

There are a lot of different types of car auctions, and some are a lot safer for the private buyer than others.

Manufacturer Sales of 'nearly-new' ex-rental and ex-demo fleet cars can be a good bet. The cars are clean, usually have some warranty left, and you know where they're coming from. However, such sales are increasingly aimed at the private buyer as well as the trade, and it can be difficult for obvious private buyers to buy at true trade money. Either rival trade bidders or the auctioneer may 'run up' your bids, and if the auctioneer runs you past your limit, the car will simply be re-entered in a subsequent auction.

True trade money for a car changes through the course of the sale, and self-tracks to a variation of no more than £100 for a given make, model and mileage in a similarly desirable colour. If you write down all the prices paid, you will be able to see this for yourself.

With manufacturer sales, do listen carefully to the auctioneer (what he says is taped) because some of the cars may be faulty and have been returned to the manufacturer for a refund, either under a special scheme or simply under the Sale and Supply of Goods Act 1994.

Dedicated Fleet Sales can be good, too. These are where a section of the sale is given over to cars from a single named fleet source. MFL (Motability Finance Ltd) has the largest fleet in Europe, and its cars tend to be low-mileage, less than three years old, with a good sprinkling of power-steered automatics.

You need to be a bit more wary where the named fleet also has its own retail outlets (I'd better not name any names here) because you have to ask yourself why it has not retailed the cars itself rather than consigned them to auction. Some fleets retail their ex-fleet cars from their own sites, then enter the cars they take in part-exchange in their dedicated sections, so not all the cars in their dedicated section are genuinely ex-fleet.

West Oxfordshire Motor Auctions (01993 774413) holds ex-police vehicle evening sales twice a month. Blue lights, sirens, radios, 'jam sandwich' fillings, will all have been removed, so there's no chance of impersonating a police officer on the drive home. And the specification of all but 'undercover' cars tends to be a bit basic (no sun roofs, for example). But it's a great way to pick up a high mileage, well maintained ex-Panda Escort or Astra, or even a full blown 3-litre Omega, BMW 325TDS or Volvo T5. Well worth a visit. (They also do Britain's best auction house bacon rolls, with optional chili sauce.)

Fleet/Finance Sales may offer a mix of cars from named and un-named fleets and repossessed cars from finance houses. A dedicated Finance House Sale can be an excellent source, particularly where it includes pre-registered zero-mileage dealer stock which had not been sold before the dealer's creditors pulled the plug and did a midnight swoop on his premises.

Theme sales such as 'Diesel Cars', 'MPV & 4x4', 'Japanese', and 'Late-year low-mileage' are designed to help the trade shift metal and can catch private buyers out. Most of these vehicles will be trader's cars, bulled up for the occasion, on which the trader hopes to make his living. He may even be there on the floor bidding against you. It need not be a catastrophe for a private bidder to buy such a car from a trader, especially at one of the bigger auction houses which don't tolerate 'low lifes'. But be extra attentive to the auctioneer's description, make sure the mileage is 'warranted' and that the car comes with its V5 listing the previous owners so you can check the mileage yourself within the auction house warranty time limits.

For General Sales, the same applies. But these sales often also include 'wrong make' part-exchanges such as Mazdas from Renault dealers and vice-versa. If you happen to make the top provisional bid for a car that's already been through the halls 'over reserved' several times, the chances are the vendor will instruct the auction house to 'get it gone' and you'll lay your hands on a bargain.

Dedicated part-exchange sales designed to shift generally older excess stock taken in by larger groups such as Inchcape and Hartwell can be good sources. Inchcape rarely warrants any mileages, but 'gut-feel' and some broad hints from the auctioneer should tell you which cars are right and which are wrong. If, for instance, the auctioneer reads out the car's entire service history, you don't usually have to worry that the mileage is not warranted.

Classic & Historic is another form of general sale aimed principally at the public. About half the cars will be entered by traders or restorers. But the others will be genuine private and executor entries. Pick of the bunch are often those on the supplementary list rather than in the catalogue. Classics are rarely sold with warranted mileages, due to the impossibility of checking back, and it really is up to the buyer to satisfy him or herself of the car's true condition prior to bidding. Remember also that the public is easily hoodwinked by shiny paintwork and glittering chrome. It can be well worth a trader's while to fill a rusty old classic with 'pudding', give it a respray and try to get bids of £3,000 to £5,000 more then he paid. So classic auctions are one type of sale to which it's still worth taking a magnet.

Time of year

While we still had the August plate change there was always a price crash at some point between September and November.

After the frenzied activity of August, with around 500,000 used cars released in just one month, the trade was faced with a residue of cars and a market which declined from September until Christmas.

It usually picked up in January, so the wise buys were made at the bottom of the market – at the point where retail sales had slowed down but just before the big players start buying for the new year.

But the March and September registration plate changes of 1999 changed everything.

The March 'T' plate ensured that the market was well supplied with part-exchanges in the peak Spring selling season. No less than 370,000 new cars were registered in March 1999, delivering an equal number of part-exchanges or retired fleet cars into the system.

But, though 'high status' cars in the £15,000–£50,000 bracket continued to sell well throughout the summer of 1999, there was plenty of fall-out among the mass-market motors. Even before September, values were dropping at least £500 a month. Consumer resistance had hardened against paying 'rip-off' UK prices for new cars and there was wide expectation of an imminent fall. So the only way the 400,000 registrations for September 1999 could be 'got gone' was at discounts which brought their prices much closer to those paid by our continental cousins.

The process created more delay, leading to a considerable surplus of part-exchanges and de-fleeted cars over October and November, by which time the market was thinking of Christmas presents and celebrating the Millennium.

But I think that sales will pick up in 2000 for several reasons: One is the status of having a 2000 'V', or a 2000 'W'. The other is a heavy fall-out of older cars 12–15 years old being scrapped because they won't run properly on unleaded petrol or because of a Government cashback offered to scrap an old car in order to buy a new one.

So, until the 'World Crash of Year 2K' (if it happens), I reckon the car market will be pretty healthy. And 4–7 year old used cars could be up by as much as 25% on 1999 levels.

Auction buying hints and tips

When visiting an auction, and particularly when bidding, it is vital for the private buyer to keep a low profile. Noisy family groups carrying 'Parkers Guide' or the *What Car?* 'Price Guide' are a dead giveaway. So don't wave your newsagent price guide around. Look up prices on the sly, and keep the guide hidden when bidding.

Give the cars you're interested in a good onceover in the auction marshalling yard. Look for obvious signs of a repaint (spray dust, over-bright paint, rubbing compound, tide marks under rubber trim strips). Check for matching shut-lines, especially between the bonnet and wings and the front wings and doors. Crouch down in front of the car and look along the sides for ripples. Check the condition of the tyres for uneven wear. (And if it's a Renault, Citroen or Peugeot, feel under the back to make sure it still has a spare wheel.)

When they come to start it up, look for excessive smoke from the exhaust, and ask the yard boy how much clutch it has left. As it moves into different light, you may spot faults you missed before. But don't be 'all over' the car as it drives into the auction hall.

Find a spot where the auctioneer can see you very clearly, but where most rival bidders can't see you. Let the bidding start and wait until it slows down or shifts from £100s to £50s or £25s before making your bid. Do this by waving your catalogue to catch the auctioneer's eye. Then, once he knows you are in the bidding, a simple nod will suffice for each increment. If you want to get out, shake your head as soon as he looks at you for a next bid. The more you appear like a trader from out of the area, the less chance you have of being 'run up' next time you get into the bidding.

Bidding at auction for the first time can be both nerve-wracking and addictively exciting. Remember, though, you're there to buy a car as cheaply as possible, not get high on the adrenaline rush.

Auction warranties

Auction houses usually charge a 'buyer's premium', which is higher for the public than the trade. If the car is described as 'with warranty', this will include limited cover warranting title to the car, described condition, and mileage if the vendor has warranted this. If the car is described as 'without warranty' or 'as seen', the only guarantees are your title to the car.

These 'buyers premiums' have risen over the past few years, and for a £20,000 car could be as much as £500, so check this carefully before starting to bid.

Employing an auction buyer

If you're nervous of buying at auction, at least two organisations offer to source the car for you.

Julian Trim & Co. (01747 838888) charges the auction hammer price plus 6%.

Douglas Coker Associates (0181 351 7976) will source the car either directly from a fleet or from auction, with full service histories if requested.

Yet another car sourcing specialist is Sam Davies of Autobarn Direct (0181 367 1647).

List of UK auction houses

Specific sale dates and times continually change, so you should *always* phone the auction centre before setting off. Many auctions will now take Switch or Delta card payments (not credit card payments). Again, check this before leaving for the auction and make sure you have sufficient funds in your account.

London area

CHARLTON: BELMONT CAR AUCTIONS Penhall Road, Charlton, London SE7, tel: 0181 858 5429. General Sales Tuesday & Thursday 6.30pm.

CROYDON: DINGWALL MOTOR AUCTIONS, Sidney House, Beddington Farm Road, Croydon, Surrey CR0 4XB, tel: 0181 684 0138. General Sales Wednesday 6.00pm; Friday 6.30pm.

EDMONTON: STONEHILL PARK MOTOR AUCTIONS, Stonehill Business Park, Harbet Road, Edmonton, London N18, tel: 0181 807 2300. Car Sales Monday, Wednesday, Friday 7.00pm; Van Sales Wednesday 6.30pm. 'Bargain Basement' 15–30 cars with no reserve Friday sale. Fax-U-Back catalogues 0336 415637 after 1.00pm on sale day.

ENFIELD: BRITISH CAR AUCTIONS, 620 Gt Cambridge Road (A10), Enfield, Middx EN1 3RL, tel: 0181 366 1144; fax: 0181 367 1009. (M25, J25). Website: www.bca-group.com General Car Sales Tuesday 11.00am, Thursday 11.00am, Saturday 10.00am. Distributor part-exchanges Thursday & Saturday 12.00 midday. Fleet Sales: Tuesday 2.00pm. Fleet, Finance and Lease Sales: Thursday 11.00am. 'Premium Select' Sales: every 3rd Thursday 11.00am. Light Commercials: Tuesday 10.00am. Catalogue DIAL-A-FAX National Directory: 0336 411411, updated daily. Website: www.bca-group.com

SOUTH FULHAM: THAMES-SIDE MOTOR AUCTIONS,

Wandsworth Bridge Road North, Fulham, London SW6, tel: 0171 736 0086; 0171 736 0087. Sales: Tuesday and Friday 7.30pm; Saturday 1.00pm.

WANDSWORTH: GENERAL MOTOR AUCTIONS, 63/65 Garratt Lane, Wandsworth, London SW18, tel: 0181 870 3909. Sales Monday 2.00pm.

WEMBLEY: 'AUCTIONS AT WEMBLEY', First Way, Wembley Stadium Industrial Estate, tel: 0181 900 2344. Sales Tuesdays and Fridays 7.00pm; Thursdays and Saturdays 12.00 midday.

WIMBLEDON: MANHEIM AUCTIONS. Waterside Way, off Plough Lane (opposite greyhound stadium, beside Wickes); Wimbledon, London SW17 7AB, tel: 0870 444 0415. Catalogue Fax-U-Back 09003 416079 for Fleet and low mileage; 09003 416008 for budget cars. Sales Monday, Wednesday, Friday at 10.30am.

South of the Thames

ASHFORD: ASHFORD CAR AUCTIONS, Romney House, Ashford Market, Elwick Road, Ashford, Kent, tel: 01233 622222. Sales: Mondays 12.00 midday; Wednesdays 6.30pm.

BLACKBUSHE: BRITISH CAR AUCTIONS, Auction Centre (West of Airport on A30), Blackwater, Camberley, Surrey/Hants border (M3 J4a), tel: 01252 878555, fax: 01252 879599. General Car Sales: Wednesday 11.00am; Friday 10.00am; Fleet & Finance Sales: Monday, Wednesday and Friday 10.00am; Dealer Part Exchange Sales Monday and Friday 11.00am; Fleet and Distributor Part Exchange Sales Wednesday 10.00. Late Year, Low Mileage: Wednesday 11.00am. Top Car: Alternate Mondays 11.00am. Union Jack: First Wednesday of the Month 1.00pm; Premium Select: Third and 5th Wednesday 1.00pm. Hall 3 Select: Wednesday 1.00pm. Light Commercials Friday 10.00am. Classic & Historic 4–6 times a year, tel: 01252 877317.

Catalogue DIAL-A-FAX National Directory: 0336 411411, up-dated daily. Website: www.bca-group.com.

EASTBOURNE: EASTBOURNE CAR AUCTIONS, Arkwright Road, Lottbridge Drive, Drove Trading Estate, Eastbourne, tel: 01323 520295, fax: 01323 520330. Sales: Wednesday 1.00pm; Friday 6.00pm. Auction catalogue Fax-U-Back: 0336 406088.

ERITH: NORTH KENT MOTOR AUCTIONS, 188 Manor Road, Erith, Kent, tel: 01322 350500. Sales: Wednesday and Friday 7.00pm.

GUILDFORD: GUILDFORD CAR AUCTIONS LTD., Slyfield Green, Slyfield Industrial Estate, Guildford, Surrey, tel: 01483 537879. Sales: Monday 6.30pm, Thursday 7.00pm, Saturday 12.00 midday, Sunday 11.30am.

PADDOCK WOOD: BRITISH CAR AUCTIONS, Eldon Way, Paddock Wood, Kent (M20 J2), tel: 01892 836611. General Sales: Tuesday and Friday 10.00am. Distributor/Part Exchange Sales: Tuesday and Friday from 10.00am. Fleet Sales: First and Third Tuesday 10.00am; Fleet Special Sales: Tuesday from 11.45am; Late year Low Mileage: Tuesday from 11.00am; Premium Select: Alternate Tuesdays 11.30am; Light Commercials: Thursday 11.00am. Catalogue DIAL-A-FAX National Directory: 0336 411411, updated daily. Website: www.bca-group.com.

POOLE: SOUTH WESTERN VEHICLE AUCTIONS, 61 Ringwood Road, Parkstone, Poole, Dorset, tel: 01202 740066 and 01202 745468, fax: 01202 732036. Sales: Tuesday 5.00pm; Friday 12.30pm. Catalogue Fax-Back: 0336 416239.

PORTSMOUTH: SOUTH HANTS CAR AUCTIONS, 1-3 Dragonair Estate, Fitzherbert Road, Farlington, tel: 01705 384122. Sales: Tuesday and Thursday 7.30pm; Saturday 11.30am.

SHOREHAM: SHOREHAM CAR AUCTIONS, Chartwell Road, Churchill Industrial Estate, Lancing, W. Sussex BN15 8UB, tel:

01903 851200, fax: 01903 851100. General Sales: Monday 7.00pm, Thursday 12.00 midday (includes fleet and distributor direct); Prestige Cars: alternate Thursdays 12.00 midday; Commercials: alternate Wednesdays 11.00am.

SOUTHAMPTON: SOUTHAMPTON CAR AUCTIONS, Southern Road, (next to Dock Gate 10), Hants SO15 1DH, tel: 01703 631631, fax: 01703 631662. Sales: Wednesday and Saturday 12.00 midday; Thursday 7.00pm. Commercials: alternate Thursdays 7.00pm.

North of the Thames

AYLESBURY: AYLESBURY MOTOR AUCTIONS, Pembroke Road, Stocklake, Aylesbury, Bucks HP20 1DB, tel: 01296 339150, fax: 01296 339140. General Sales: Tuesday and Thursday 6.30pm; Prestige and 4x4 Sale last Wednesday of month at 2.00pm.

BEDFORD: BRITISH CAR AUCTIONS, Mile Road, Bedford (M1 J13), tel: 01234 218161. General Sales: Monday 12.30pm, Wednesday 11.00am; General and Distributor Thursday 6.00pm; Distributor Part Exchanges: Wednesday 6.00pm; Fleet Advantage: Every fourth Monday 1.30pm; Fleet Direct: Every second Monday; Fleet, finance and lease: Monday 12.30pm; Foreign: Every first Monday 1.30pm; Premium Select: Every second Wednesday 1.30pm; Light Commercials: Monday 11.00am; Light Commercials Fleet Direct: Every second Monday 11.00am. Catalogue DIAL-A-FAX National Directory: 0336 411411, updated daily. Website: www.bca-group.com.

HIGH WYCOMBE: WYCOMBE CAR AUCTIONS, Cressex Business Park, High Wycombe, tel: 01494 444200. Sales Tuesday and Thursday 6.30pm, Saturday 11.30am.

LEIGHTON BUZZARD: LEIGHTON BUZZARD CAR AUCTIONS, Corner Chartmoor Road and Grovebury Road, Leighton Buzzard LU7 8SQ, tel: 01525 853912, fax: 01525 370505.

MILTON KEYNES: MILTON KEYNES STADIUM MOTOR AUC-
TIONS, Ashland, Milton Keynes South, tel: 01908 666835. Sales
Wednesday and Friday 6.30pm.
OXFORD: OXFORD STADIUM MOTOR AUCTIONS, Oxford
Stadium, Sandy Lane, Cowley, Oxford, tel: 01865 395977, Sales
Monday 6.30pm.
WITNEY: WEST OXFORDSHIRE MOTOR AUCTIONS, Bromag
Industrial Estate, Old A40, Witney, Oxon (leave new A40 for
West Witney, right under dual carriageway, take first left, skirt
housing estate to your right all the way to T junction onto old
A40) tel: 01993 774413. Sales Tuesday and Thursday 6.30pm.
Most sales include a Fleet Direct section. Police Car Sales twice
a month. E-MAIL: buy@woma.demon.uk.

Essex and East Anglia

BOURNE: COUNTY CAR AUCTIONS, Eastgate, Bourne, Lincs,
tel: 01778 424201. Sales Tuesday and Thursday 6.30pm.
CHELMSFORD: CHELMSFORD CAR AUCTION, Drovers Way,
Chelmsford, tel: 01245 450700, fax: 01245 460695. Fleet Sales:
Wednesday 11.00am; Fleet and Private Cars: Saturday
11.00am; Older Cars Monday 6.30pm. Commercials: Monday
11.00am.
COLCHESTER: MANHEIM AUCTIONS, Frating, Colchester, Essex
tel: 0870 444 0403. General Sales: Thursday 6.00pm; Fleet Sales:
Tuesday and Thursday 11.00am; Late Year Low Mileage: Tuesday
and Thursday 11.00am; Light Commercials: Wednesday
11.00am. Budget: Thursday 6.00pm. Monthly Manufacturer
Sales. Monthly Prestige and Performance car Sales. Auction catalogue Fax-U-Back 09003 416006 (Tue sale); 09003 416013 (Wed
sale); 09003 416009 (Thur sale); 09003 416005 (Mgf sales).
IPSWICH: IPSWICH CAR AUCTIONS, Wherstead Road, Ipswich,
tel: 01473 685868. General Sales including dealer direct, fleet

direct, private cars: Monday and Wednesday 6.30pm.

KINGS LYNN: ANGLIA CAR AUCTION, The Cattle Market, Beveridge Way, Kings Lynn, tel: 01553 771881. General Sales Wednesday 6.00pm; Friday 6.30pm.

NORWICH: EAST ANGLIAN MOTOR AUCTIONS, 261 Aylsham Road, Norwich, tel: 01603 409824. Fleet and Late Date Cars: Thursday 12.00 midday. Budget Sales: Tuesday 6.30pm.

NORWICH: EASTERN CAR AUCTIONS, Norwich Livestock Market, Hall Road, Norwich, tel: 01603 503037. Main Agent Direct and Private Cars: Thursday 6.30pm, Saturday 11.00am.

PETERBOROUGH: BRITISH CAR AUCTIONS, Boongate, Peterborough, tel: 01733 568881, fax: 01733 588297. General Sales: Wednesday and Friday 12.00 midday; Evening Sales: Monday 5.00pm; Fleet Advantage: last Friday of the month 1.00pm; Fleet, Finance and Lease: Friday 12.00 midday; 'Posh Parade': second Wednesday of the month 1.30pm; Union Jack: second Wednesday 12.30pm; Premium Select: third Wednesday 2.00pm; Light Commercials: first and third Friday 11.00am. Catalogue DIAL-A-FAX National Directory: 0336 411411, updated daily. Website: www.bca-group.com.

South-West England

BRIDGWATER: BRITISH CAR AUCTIONS, Bristol Road (A38), Bridgwater, Somerset TA6 4TN (M5 J23), tel: 01278 685511, fax: 01278 685353. General Sales: Wednesday and Friday 10.00am; Distributor and Part-Exchange: Wednesday and Friday 12.00 midday; 'Fleet Advantage': second and fourth Friday of the month 2.00pm; Fleet and Lease Rental: Wednesday and Friday from 10.00am; 'Premium Select': second Wednesday 12.30pm; Light Commercials: Wednesday 10.00am. Catalogue DIAL-A-FAX National Directory: 0336 411411, updated daily. Website: www.bca-group.com.

BRISTOL: MANHEIM AUCTIONS, Ashton Vale Road, Ashton Vale, Bristol BS3 2AX, tel: 0870 444 0402. Fleet Sales Tuesday and Thursday 10.30am. Catalogue Fax-U-Back 09003 416084.

GLOUCESTER: MANHEIM AUCTIONS, Berkeley Road, Cam, Dursley, Gloucestershire GL11 5JB, tel: 09003 416052. Fleet Sales: Wednesday 11.00am; Main Dealer p/x & overage: Saturday 11.00am. Catalogue Fax-U-Back 09003 416052 (cars); 09003 415666 (LCV's).

EXETER: EXETER CAR AUCTIONS, Matford Park Road, Marsh Barton, tel 01392 425481. General Sales: Monday 1.00pm, Wednesday 5.00pm; Fleet Sales Late Year: Monday 1.00pm.

FALMOUTH: CORNWALL MOTOR AUCTIONS LTD., Station Road, Penryn, Falmouth, Cornwall, tel: 01326 372955. Sales: Tuesday and Friday 6.00pm.

SALTASH: SALTASH CAR AUCTIONS, Gilstone Road Industrial Estate, tel: 01752 841444. Sales: Tuesday 12.00 midday, Thursday 6.00pm.

SOUTH MOLTON: NORTH DEVON MOTOR AUCTIONS, Dart Park, New Road, Devon, tel: 01769 572167 and 01769 572549. Sales: Saturday 1.30pm.

TAUNTON: TAUNTON MOTOR AUCTION, Taunton Market, Canal Road, Taunton, tel: 01823 334136. Sales: Tuesday and Thursday 6.00pm.

TEWKESBURY: BRITISH CAR AUCTIONS, Newtown Industrial Estate, Northway Lane, Tewkesbury, Gloucestershire GL20 8JG (M5 J9), tel: 01684 292307, fax: 01684 294246. General Sales: Wednesday 10.30am, Friday 1.00pm; Fleet Sales: Friday 2.30pm; 'Premium Select': fourth Wednesday of month 12.30pm; Light Commercials: Friday 11.00am. Catalogue DIAL-A-FAX National Directory: 0336 411411, updated daily. Website: www.bca-group.com

WESTBURY: WESTBURY MOTOR AUCTIONS, Brook Lane, Westbury, Wilts, BA13 4EN, tel: 01373 827777, fax: 01373

864286. Sales: Tuesday and Thursday 11.00am, Friday 5.30pm. Commercials Sales: first and third Wednesday of month 11.00am.

Wales

ANGLESEY: GWYNEDD MOTOR AUCTIONS, Gearwen, tel: 01248 723303. Sales: first Thursday of the month at 5.30pm.

BRIDGEND: BRIDGEND AUCTIONS, Newport Auctions Ltd., Brackla Industrial Estate, tel: 01656 767767. Sales: Tuesday and Thursday 7.00pm.

DEESIDE: CLWYD CAR AUCTIONS, Hollywell Road, Ewloe, tel: 01244 532821. Sales: Wednesday and Saturday 2.00pm.

MERTHYR TYDFIL: MERTHYR MOTOR AUCTIONS, Pant Road, Dowlais, tel: 01685 377818. Sales: Monday 5.00pm, Wednesday 6.00pm, Saturday 2.00pm.

NEWPORT: BRITISH CAR AUCTIONS, Meadows Road, Queensway, Meadows Industrial Estate, Newport, Gwent NP9 0YR, tel: 01633 270222, fax: 01633 270444. General Sales: Monday and Thursday 10.30pm; Distributor and Lease Rental: Thursday 11.30am; Evening Sale: Thursday 6.30pm; 'Fleet Advantage': third Monday of month 12.00 midday; Fleet, Finance and Lease: Monday 1.00pm; 'One Owner' section: Monday 12.00 midday; Light Commercials: Monday 11.00am. Catalogue DIAL-A-FAX National Directory: 0336 411411, updated daily. Website: www.bca-group.com.

NEWPORT: NEWPORT AUCTIONS LTD., Dockland Distributor Road, Newport, tel: 01633 262626. General Sales: Wednesday and Friday 7.00pm; Budget Cars: Monday 7.00pm.

QUEENSFERRY: TMA MOTOR AUCTIONS, Station Road, Deeside, tel: 01244 812811. Sales: Tuesday 5.30pm, Friday 1.00pm.

RHYL: NORTH WALES MOTOR AUCTIONS LTD., Marsh Road, Rhuddlan, tel 01745 590176. Sales: Thursday 1.00pm.

South-West Midlands

LEOMINSTER: LEOMINSTER CAR AUCTIONS, Kingsland, Leominster, tel: 01568 708561. Sales: Thursday 6.00pm.

LEOMINSTER: RUSSELL BALDWIN & BRIGHT COUNTY VEHICLE AUCTIONS (UK's largest 4x4 sales), Office: 38 South Street, Leominster, Herefordshire HR6 8JG, tel: 01568 611166, fax: 01568 611802. 4x4 Sales: first and third Tuesday of the month 11.00am; Public Authority Vehicle Sales followed by General Sales: fourth Tuesday 11.00am. AUCTIONS HELD AT LIVESTOCK MARKET; sale-day tel: 01568 611325.

WARWICK: WARWICK MOTOR AUCTIONS, 67 Emscote Road, Warwick, tel: 01926 495221 and 01926 491821. Sales: Monday and Wednesday 7.00pm.

West Midlands

BIRMINGHAM: BIRMINGHAM CAR AUCTIONS, 302-312 Moseley Road, Birmingham B12, tel: 0121 446 4000. Sales: Tuesday and Thursday 6.30pm, Saturday 12.00 midday.

BIRMINGHAM: BRITISH CAR AUCTIONS, Hayward Industrial Estate, Langley Drive, Birmingham B35 7AD (M6 J5 or 6), tel: 0121 749 1331; fax: 0121 747 2481. General Sales: Monday and Thursday 10.30am; 'Birmingham Combination' Sales: alternate Thursdays 11.00am; Distributor and Part Exchange: Monday and Thursday from 1.00pm; Fleet, Finance and Contract Hire: Monday and Thursday 10.30am; Premium Select: second Monday of the month 2.30pm; Light Commercials: Wednesday 10.30am. Catalogue DIAL-A-FAX National Directory: 0336 411411, updated daily. Website: www.bca-group.com.

BIRMINGHAM: MANHEIM AUCTIONS, Whitworth Close, Heath Road, Darlaston, West Midlands, tel: 0870 444 0401.

General Fleet/Finance Sales: Wednesday 11.00am, Friday 10.30am. Catalogue Fax-U-Back 09003 416081 (cars); 09003 416086 (LCVs).

BIRMINGHAM: PORTWAY MOTOR CENTRE CAR AUCTIONS, Alcester Road, Portway, Birmingham B48 7HX (500 yards from M42 J3 on A435 Redditch Road), tel: 01564 822877. (Regular Saturday Classic Car Auctions.)

COVENTRY: MANHEIM AUCTIONS, Rowley Drive, Coventry CV3 4FG tel: 0870 444 0404. Fleet Sales every Monday 11.00am; Manufacturer Closed Sales on other days of the week. Catalogue Fax-U-Back: 09003 416026.

MEASHAM: BRITISH CAR AUCTIONS, Tamworth Road, Measham, Swadlincote, Derbyshire DE12 7DY (M42 J11), tel: 01530 270322, fax: 01530 273595. General Sales: Tuesday and Friday 10.30am; Distributor Sales: Tuesday and Friday 11.00am; Contract Hire, Fleet, Finance: Friday 10.00am; 'Foreign Cars': third Tuesday of the month 2.00pm; Top Car: first Tuesday 11.00am; Lease Rental: Tuesday 10.30am; Union Jack: second Thursday 2.00pm; 'Premium Select': fourth Tuesday 2.00pm; 'Measham Select': Tuesday 1.00pm; Light Commercials: Tuesday 10.00am; 'Top Van': Tuesday 1.00pm. Catalogue DIAL-A-FAX National Directory: 0336 411411, updated daily. Website: www.bca-group.com.

NEWCASTLE-UNDER-LYME: NEWCASTLE MOTOR AUC-TIONS, Silverdale Road, Newcastle-under-Lyme, tel: 01782 617930. Sales: Saturday 2.00pm.

PREES HEATH: PREES HEATH MOTOR AUCTION, Whitchurch, Shropshire SY13 2AR, tel: 01948 663166 and 01948 663177, fax: 01948 665318. Sales: Tuesday 1.00pm, Thursday 6.30pm.

REDDITCH: ARROW MOTOR AUCTIONS, Bartleet Road, Washford, Redditch, tel: 01527 510923. Sales: Monday and Wednesday 6.00pm.

STAFFORD: STAFFORD MOTOR AUCTIONS, Back Browning

Street, Stafford, tel: 01785 243470. Sales: Tuesday and Thursday 7.00pm.

STOKE-ON-TRENT: NORTH STAFFORDSHIRE MOTOR AUCTIONS, Sutherland Road, Longton, tel: 01782 332719. Sales: Thursday 6.30pm.

TELFORD: TELFORD AUCTIONS, Rookery Road, St. Georges, Telford, Shropshire, tel: 01952 610033. Sales: Thursday 6.30pm.

TELFORD: TELFORD MOTOR AUCTIONS, Trench Lock 2, Telford, Shropshire, tel: 01952 257751. Sales: Wednesday 12.00 midday, Friday 6.00pm.

WALLSALL: BRITISH CAR AUCTIONS, Green lane, Walsall, West Midlands, WS2 7BP, tel: 01922 721555, fax: 01922 613188. General Sales: Tuesday 10.30am, Thursday 3.30pm; Distributor and Lease Rental: Tuesday from 10.30am, Thursday from 3.30pm; Evening Sales: Thursday from 3.30pm; Fleet, Finance and Lease: Tuesday from 10.30am, Thursday from 3.30pm; British Car Contracts and Rover Finance: Thursdays from 3.30pm (phone to check). Catalogue DIAL-A-FAX National Directory: 0336 411411, updated daily. Website: www.bca-group.com

WOLVERHAMPTON: BOWMAC MOTOR AUCTIONS, Dale Street, Bilston, tel: 01902 490884. Sales Monday, Wednesday and Friday 7.00pm.

North and East Midlands

CHESTERFIELD: CHESTERFIELD CAR AUCTION, Lockford Lane, Chesterfield, tel: 01246 277999. General Sales: Monday and Friday 6.00pm, Wednesday 1.30pm.

DERBY: BRITISH CAR AUCTIONS, Raynesway, Derby, Derbyshire DE21 7WA, tel: 01332 666111, fax: 01332 660186. General Sales: Wednesday 11.30am; Distributor Part-Exchanges: Monday 4.00pm; Evening Sales: Monday 4.00pm;

Fleet, Finance and Lease: Wednesday 12.00 midday; Late Year Low Mileage and Lease Rental: Wednesday 11.30am; Special bank Holiday Monday Sales 11.00am; Light Commercials: first and third Thursday of month 11.00am; Police and Public Authority: third Thursday 11.30am. Catalogue DIAL-A-FAX National Directory: 0336 411411, updated daily. Website: www.bca-group.com

LEICESTER: LEICESTER CAR AUCTIONS, 8 Commercial Square, Freemans Common, Leicester, tel: 0116 255 6606. General Sales: Monday and Thursday 6.15pm.

LEICESTER NORTH: MANHEIM AUCTIONS, Charnwood Road, Shepshed, Leics LE12 9NN (M1 J23), tel: 0870 444 0408. Local fleet sales Mondays 3.00pm: Fleet Sales Thursdays 11.00am; Closed Sales Wednesdays 11.00am. Auction catalogue Fax-U-Back 09003 416080.

MANSFIELD: MANHEIM AUCTIONS, Fulwood Industrial Estate, Common Road, Huthwaite, Sutton-in-Ashfield , NG17 6AD. tel: 0870 444 9460. Fleet Sales: Tuesdays 12.00 midday, Thursday 6.30pm; Part Exchanges: Thursday 5.00pm; Light Commercials: Tuesday 3.30pm; Motorcycles: last Wednesday of the month 6.00pm. Auction Catalogue Fax-U-Back: 09003 416076 (cars); 09003 416078 (commercials).

NORTHAMPTON: MANHEIM AUCTIONS, The Auction Hall, Salthouse Road, Brackmills Industrial Estate, Northampton, tel: 0870 444 0412. Under 5 years old Thursdays 1.00pm; General Sales Tuesdays 5.30pm; P/ex sales Thursdays 6.00pm. Catalogue Fax-U-Back 09003 415667.

NOTTINGHAM: BRITISH CAR AUCTIONS, Victoria Business Park, Netherfield, Nottingham NG4 2PE (M1 J24 or 26), tel: 0115 987 3311, fax: 0115 961 7296. General and Distributor Sale: Wednesday 11.00am; General Sale: Friday 11.00am; Diesel, 4x4, MPV: first Friday of the month 12.00 midday; Distributor and Lease Rental: Friday 11.00am; Fleet and

Contract Hire: Friday 12.00 midday; KLM: second Wednesday of the month 12.00 midday; Late Year Low Mileage: Wednesday 1.00pm; Premium Select: fourth Wednesday 12.00 midday; Top Car: third Thursday 11.00am; VQ Sale: first Wednesday 1.00pm; Light Commercials: second and fourth Friday 11.00am. Catalogue DIAL-A-FAX National Directory: 0336 411411, updated daily. Website: www.bca-group.com

Yorkshire and Lincolnshire

ADWICK-LE-STREET: ADWICK MOTOR AUCTIONS, Church Lane, Doncaster, S. Yorks, tel: 01302 722251. General Sales: Tuesday and Thursday 7.00pm; Weekend Car Bazaar: Saturday and Sunday 10.00am–5.00pm.

BAWTRY: BAWTRY MOTOR AUCTION, Corner Garage, Bawtry, tel: 01302 710333. Sales Monday, Wednesday, Friday 7.00pm.

BEVERLEY: BEVERLEY MOTOR AUCTIONS, Tokenspire Business Park, Woodmansey, tel: 01482 887555 and 01482 888111. Sales: Wednesday and Friday 7.00pm.

BRADFORD: BRADFORD MOTOR AUCTIONS, Midland Road, Bradford, tel: 01274 774444. Sales: Tuesday and Thursday 6.30pm; Sunday 2.00pm.

BRIDLINGTON: BRIDLINGTON MOTOR AUCTIONS, Pinfold Lane, Bridlington, tel: 01262 674044. Sales: Tuesday and Thursday 7.00pm.

BRIGHOUSE: BRITISH CAR AUCTIONS, Armytage Road, Brighouse, West Yorks HD6 1XE (M62 J25), tel: 01484 401555, fax: 01484 406686. General Sales: Thursday 10.00am; Diesel Sales: last Thursday of the month 12.00 midday; 'Brighouse Direct': Monday 10.00am; Fiat: first Thursday 1.30pm; Top Car: second Thursday 12.00 midday; 'Union Jack': third Thursday 2.30pm; Light Commercials: Friday 10.30am; Top Van: Friday 12.30pm. Catalogue DIAL-A-FAX National Directory: 0336

411411, updated daily. Website: www.bca-group.com

GRANTHAM: GRANTHAM MOTOR AUCTION LTD., Tollemache Road North, Spittlegate Level, Grantham, tel: 01476 594022. General Sales: Monday and Wednesday 6.30pm; 4x4 Sales: last Wednesday of month 6.30pm; Sports and Performance Sale: second Wednesday 6.30pm.

KNOTTINGLEY: MANHEIM AUCTIONS (formerly A1 Motor Auctions), Tadcaster Road, Brotherton, Knottingly, Yorks, tel: 0870 444 0416. Dealer p/ex sales Tuesdays 1.00pm and Fridays 11.00am; Budget Sales (under £2,000 reserve) Tuesdays 6.00pm. Other Budget Sales Thursdays 6.00pm

LEEDS: MANHEIM, Pontefract Road, Rothwell, Leeds LS26 0JE, tel: 0870 444 0407. Fleet Sales: Mondays and Wednesdays 11.00am; Police Sales: second and fourth Wednesday of month 12.00 midday; P/ex Sales: Wednesdays and Saturdays 11.00am; mgf open sales Tuesdays 11.00am; mgf closed sales Thursdays 11.00am. Catalogue Fax-U-Back: 09003 416054.

LEEDS: LEEDS LTD. MOTOR AUCTIONS, Hillidge Road, Leeds (M1 J46), tel: 0800 4581000 or 0113 272 6800. Part exchange and trade retail vehicles up to £5,000: Monday and Wednesday 6.00pm; Direct main dealer, fleet and ready to retail: Tuesday 1.30pm; Main fleet sale, main dealer direct and ready to retail: Friday 12.30pm.

LEEDS: PREMIER MOTOR AUCTIONS, Cross Green Industrial Park, Pontefract Lane, Leeds, tel: 0113 294 1111. Sales: Monday, Wednesday, Thursday 6.30pm; Tuesday and Friday 12.30pm.

LEEDS: WEST RIDING MOTOR AUCTIONS, Bruntcliffe Lane, Morley, tel: 0113 252 1046. Sales: Monday and Tuesday 1.00pm; Wednesday and Friday 6.00pm.

NEWARK: EAST OF ENGLAND MOTOR AUCTIONS, The Showground, Winthorpe, tel: 01636 671167. General Sales: Tuesday and Thursday 6.30pm.

ROTHERHAM: MANHEIM AUCTIONS, Canklow Meadows Industrial Estate, West Bawtry Road, Rotherham S60 2XL, tel: 0870 444 0413. Budget dealer direct and overage (under £3,500): Mondays 6.00pm; Fleet Sales: Wednesdays 11.00am; Fridays 10.30am. Catalogue Fax-U-Back 09003 424593.

TATTERSALL: CASTLE MOTOR AUCTIONS, 57 Sleaford Road, tel: 01526 342921 and 01526 342924, fax: 01526 342945. Sales: Monday and Wednesday 7.00pm.

North-West England

ALTRINCHAM: ALTRINCHAM MOTOR AUCTION, Old Market Place, Altrincham, tel: 0161 928 3725. Sales: Monday 7.00pm.

BLACKBURN: EAST LANCS MOTOR AUCTIONS, Highfield Road (off Bolton Road), tel 01254 670190. Sales: Tuesday and Thursday 7.00pm.

BLACKPOOL: WEST COAST MOTOR AUCTIONS, Poulton Industrial Estate, Garstang Road East, Poulton-le-Fylde, tel: 01253 892488. Sales: Mondays and Wednesdays 7.00pm.

BURNLEY: BURNLEY AUCTIONS, Liverpool Road, Rosegrove, tel: 01282 427231. Sales: Monday and Thursday 7.25pm.

CARLISLE: HARRISON & HETHERINGTON VEHICLE AUCTIONS, Borderway Mart, Rosehill, Carlisle, tel: 01228 640908. Sales: Tuesday 11.00am.

CHESTER: DIRECT MOTOR AUCTIONS, 9 Hartford Way, Sealand Trading Estate, Chester, tel: 01244 383789. Sales: Monday and Wednesday 6.30pm; Saturday 2.30pm.

CHORLEY: CHORLEY MOTOR AUCTION, Cottam Street, Chorley, tel: 01257 262091. Sales: Tuesday and Friday 8.00pm.

ELLESMERE PORT: ELLESMERE PORT MOTOR AUCTION, Rossfield Road, Rossmore Industrial Estate, Ellesmere Port, Wirral, tel: 0151 357 2040. Sales: Monday and Friday 7.00pm; Wednesday 2.30pm.

HAYDOCK: NATIONAL CAR AUCTIONS, Yewtree Trading Estate, Kilbuck Lane, Haydock, Lancs, tel: 0870 444 0406. Dealer direct sales Tuesdays 6.00; Light Commercials: second Tuesday of the month 11.00am; Budget Sales Thursdays 6.00pm; Fleet Sales Fridays 11.00am. Catalogue Fax-U-Back 0336 416074.

LIVERPOOL: LIVERPOOL MOTOR AUCTIONS, Dorset House, west Derby Road, Liverpool, tel: 0151 263 7351. Sales: Monday 6.00pm, Wednesday 3.00pm, Friday 4.00pm.

MANCHESTER – BELLE VUE: BRITISH CAR AUCTIONS, Belle Vue Auction Centre, Belle Vue, Manchester M12 4RX, tel: 0161 230 6000, fax: 0161 220 8065. General Sales: Tuesday and Friday 10.30am; Diesel, 4x4, MPV: second Tuesday of the month 12.00 midday; Distributor Sales: Tuesday and Friday 10.30am; Contract Hire, Fleet and Finance Sales: Friday 11.30am; 'Executive Cars': fourth Tuesday of the month 12.00 midday; 'Union Jack': third Tuesday 12.00 midday; 'Premium Select': first Tuesday 2.00pm; Light Commercials: Wednesday 11.00am; 'Top Van': Wednesday 1.00pm. Catalogue DIAL-A-FAX National Directory: 0336 411411, updated daily. Website: www.bca-group.com

MANCHESTER – BELLE VUE: STOODLEY VEHICLE AUCTIONS, Hyde Road, Belle Vue, Manchester, tel: 0161 223 3882. Sales: Monday and Wednesday 6.00pm; Saturday 12.00 midday.

MANCHESTER: MANHEIM AUCTIONS, Richmond Road, Trafford Park, Manchester M17 1RE, tel: 0870 444 0409. Finance Sales Tuesday 6.00pm; Fleet Sales Thursday 11.00am. Catalogue Fax-U-Back 09003 416053.

MANCHESTER: RADCLIFFE & DISTRICT MOTOR AUCTIONS, Unit 7, Globe Industrial Estate, Spring Lane, Manchester, tel: 0161 724 0805. General Sales Monday, Wednesday and Friday 7.00pm.

PRESTON: BRITISH CAR AUCTIONS, Reedfield Place, Walton Summit, Preston PR5A 8AA (M6 J29 or M61 J9), tel: 01772

324666, fax: 01772 334838. General Sales: Monday and Wednesday 11.00am; 'Fleet Advantage': fourth Monday of the month 2.00pm; Fleet/Distributor: Monday 11.00am; "Premium Select": fourth Wednesday of the month 1.30pm; Light Commercials: Thursday 11.00am; Van Leasing Section: Thursday 12.30am. Catalogue DIAL-A-FAX National Directory: 0336 411411, updated daily. WEBSITE: www.bca-group.com

PRESTON: PRESTON OLYMPIA MOTOR AUCTIONS, London Road, Preston. tel: 01772 252428 and 01772 253230. Sales: Monday and Thursday 7.00pm.

RADCLIFFE: RADCLIFFE AND DISTRICT MOTOR AUCTION, Unit 7, Globe Industrial Estate, Spring Lane, Radcliffe, tel: 0161 724 0805, Sales: Monday, Wednesday and Friday 7.00pm.

ST. HELENS: ST. HELENS MOTOR AUCTIONS, East Lancs Road, Carr Mill, St. Helens, Lancs, tel: 01744 22513. Sales: Monday and Wednesday 7.00pm.

TELFORD: IMPORT MOTOR AUCTIONS, Telford, Shropshire (specialises in second hand Japanese imports. No more known.)

WARRINGTON: WARRINGTON MOTOR AUCTIONS, Lyncastle Way, Barley Castle Trading Estate, Appleton, Thorn, tel: 01925 265252. Sales: Tuesday and Friday 7.00pm.

WIRRAL: NEW FERRY AUCTION, 508 New Chester Road, Rock ferry, Wirral, tel: 0151 645 4006. Sales Tuesday and Thursday 6.30pm.

North-East England

BIRTLEY: SCOTTISH MOTOR AUCTION GROUP, Portobello Industrial Estate, Birtley, Co. Durham, tel: 0191 410 4243. Sales: Monday and Wednesday 7.00pm, Friday 1.00pm.

FERRYHILL: DURHAM COUNTY MOTOR AUCTIONS, Mainsforth Industrial Estate, tel: 01740 650065. Sales: Thursday 11.00am; Tuesday and Thursday 6.00pm.

MIDDLESBROUGH: MANHEIM AUCTIONS, Low Road, Maltby, Middlesbrough TS8 0BW, tel: 0870 444 0411. Fleet Sales: Tuesday 11.00am; Budget/Dealer Direct Sales: Monday and Wednesday 6.00pm; Dealer Direct, Finance and Main Agent Sales: Friday 11.00am. Catalogue Fax-U-Back 09003 424594.

NEWCASTLE-UPON TYNE: BRITISH CAR AUCTIONS, Whitley Road, Longbenton, Newcastle-upon-Tyne NE12 9SQ, tel: 0191 270 0077, fax: 0191 266 8786: General Sales: Tuesday 6.00pm, Thursday 12.00 midday; Contract Hire Sales: second Tuesday of the month 2.00pm; Diesel, 4x4 and MPV: third Tuesday 4.00pm; Distributor and Lease rental: Tuesday 4.00pm; Fleet, Finance and Lease: Thursday 1.30pm; Late Year Low Mileage: Tuesday 4.00pm; 'Tried and Tested': Tuesday 6.30pm; Light Commercials: second and fourth Tuesday 11.00am. Catalogue DIAL-A-FAX National Directory: 0336 411411, updated daily. Website: www.bca-group.com

NEWCASTLE-UPON TYNE: TYNE TEES MOTOR AUCTION, Coast Road Retail Park, A1058 Coast Road, North Shields, tel: 0191 296 2020. General Sales: Monday 2.00pm, Wednesday 5.30pm, Friday 4.30pm; Fleet Sales: Wednesday 1.00pm.

WASHINGTON: MANNHEIM AUCTIONS, District 15, Pattinson Road, Washington, Tyne & Wear, tel: 0870 444 0414. Fleet Direct: Weds 11.00am; Part-exchange and overage dealer stock: Tursdays 6.00pm; Fleet Direct, Main Dealer and Distributor; Fridays 1.00pm; Light Commercials: Wednesdays 11.00am; HGVs and Plant: Tuesdays once a month 11.00am. Catalogue Fax-U-Back: Cars Weds & Thus: 09003 416024; Cars Friday: 09003 416027; HGVs & Plant: 09003416059.

Scotland

ABERDEEN: SCOTTISH MOTOR AUCTION GROUP, Aberdeen Exhibition Centre, Bridge of Don, tel: 01224 822261. Sales

Monday and Thursday 7.00pm.

ABERDEEN: THAINSTONE VEHICLE AUCTIONS, Thainstone Agricultural Centre, Inverurie, tel: 01467 623700. Sale: Monday 6.30pm.

EDINBURGH: BRITISH CAR AUCTIONS, Edinburgh Exhibition and Trade Centre, Ingliston, Edinburgh EH28 8NB (A8 at M8/M9), tel: 0131 333 2151, fax: 0131 333 4608. General Sales: Monday and Thursday 12.00 midday; Diesel, 4x4, MPV: second Monday of the month 3.00pm; Evening Sales: Tuesday 6.00pm; Fleet, Finance and Lease: Monday 2.00pm; Top Car: third Thursday of the month 3.00pm; 'Union Jack': second Thursday 2.30pm; 'Premium Select': fourth Thursday of the month 2.30pm. Catalogue DIAL-A-FAX National Directory: 0336 411411, updated daily. WEBSITE: www.bca-group.com

EDINBURGH: SCOTTISH MOTOR AUCTION GROUP, 1 Murrayburn Road, Edinburgh, tel: 0131 443 7163. Sales: Monday and Thursday 6.30pm.

FORFAR: TAYSIDE MOTOR AUCTIONS, Carseview Road, Forfar, tel: 01307 462197. Sales: Tuesday 6.45pm, Friday 6.15pm.

GLASGOW: BRITISH CAR AUCTIONS, 999 Royston Road, Provanmill, Glasgow G21 2AA, tel: 0141 770 9661, fax: 0141 770 9592. General Sales: Wednesday and Friday 12.00 midday; Diesel & 4x4: third Wednesday of the month 1.00pm; Distributor: Friday 1.00pm; Evening Sales: Monday 6.00pm; Fleet, Finance & Lease: Friday 2.00pm; Late Year Low Mileage: Wednesday 2.30pm; 'Tried & Tested': first and third Wednesday of the month 1.30pm. Catalogue DIAL-A-FAX National Directory: 0336 411411, updated daily. Website: www.bca-group.com

GLASGOW: INTERCITY MOTOR AUCTIONS, 77 Melbourne Street, tel: 0141 556 3333. Sales: Wednesday 12.00 midday, Thursday 6.30pm, Sunday 1.00pm.

GLASGOW: SCOTTISH MOTOR AUCTION GROUP, 80 Burnfield

Road, Giffnock, tel: 0141 633 1134 and 0141 637 5014. General Sales: Tuesday and Thursday 6.30pm; Main Agent Direct: Thursday 7.00pm.

GLASGOW: STRATHCLYDE MOTOR AUCTION, 39 Bellgrove Street, Glasgow, tel: 0141 551 0123; fax: 0141 551 0777.

KINROSS: SCOTTISH MOTOR AUCTION GROUP, Bridgend, tel: 01577 862564. Sales Monday and Wednesday 6.30pm.

NEWMAINS: BRITISH CAR AUCTIONS, Main Street, Newmains, Wishaw, Strathclyde ML2 9PT, tel: 01698 383737, fax: 01698 383139. General Sales: Tuesday 11.00am; Evening Sale: Wednesday 6.00pm; Fleet, Finance and Lease: Tuesday 12.00 midday; Late Year Low Mileage: second Tuesday of the month 1.00pm; Light Commercials: Thursday 11.00am; 'Top Van': Thursday 1.00pm. Catalogue DIAL-A-FAX National Directory: 0336 411411, updated daily. Website: www.bca-group.com

PERTH: INTERCITY MOTOR AUCTIONS; Perth Agricultural Centre, East Huntingtower (on A85), tel: 01738 623333, fax: 01738 621000. Sales: Thursday 6.30pm, Sunday 2.00pm.

SHOTTS: SHOTTS MOTOR AUCTIONS, Stane Road (M8 J5), tel: 01501 823337, fax: 01501 823498. Sales: Tuesday 12.00 midday, Thursday 6.00pm.

Northern Ireland

BALLYCLARE: BALLYCLARE MOTOR AUCTION, 53 Park Street, Ballyclare, tel: 01960 323819 and 01960 352557. Sales: Wednesday 7.00pm.

BELFAST: CARRYDUFF AUCTIONS, 10 Comber Court, Carryduff, tel: 01232 813775. Sales: Monday and Wednesday 6.30pm.

MALLUSK: WILSONS AUCTIONS LTD., 22 Mallusk Road, Glengormley, Newtownabbey, tel: 01232 342646. General Sales: Tuesday and Thursday 7.00pm. Company Cars: alternate Wednesdays 2.15pm.

OMAGH: OMAGH AUCTION CENTRE, 24 Gortrush Industrial Estate, Derry Road, Omagh, tel: 01662 241514 and 01662 247940. Sales: Monday 7.30pm.

PORTADOWN: WILSONS AUCTIONS LTD., 65 Seagoe Industrial Estate, tel: 01762 336 433. General Sales: Monday and Wednesday 6.30pm; Saturday 10.30am.

Eire

DUBLIN: WINDSOR CAR AUCTIONS, Bewlgard Road, Dublin, tel: 00 351 1 4599 300. Fortnightly Sales of up to 500 RHD cars imported directly from Japan. ABS pre-checks available,

Buying to re-sell
Buying to re-sell at a profit

Doing this this privately is getting more and more difficult. The main reason is that the big auctions have increasingly oriented themselves towards the private buyer – the very sort of buyer you would hope to sell your auction-bought car to.

The result is prices achieved at auction are often above the sort of price you could expect to get selling the car from your doorstep. The other factor is that the big fleets set up their own sites to sell their ex-fleet cars direct to the public who would otherwise be your customers.

The trick, of course, is to circumvent the auctions and direct selling by fleets by buying direct from smaller fleets, from private vendors, or even from overstocked garages. But it's hard work and no way to a fortune.

Buying to cut re-sale losses

The way to do this was to buy at a market low and sell at a

market high. Traditionally, July, October, November and December were the 'low' months and March to June were the 'high' months. It used to be comparatively easy to pick up a car in October/November, run it until May, and still sell it at a profit.

Not any more. The new twice-a-year March and September registration system has changed all that. You can no longer rely on buying a car at a market 'low', running it for six months, then selling it on at a profit. You can't even rely on any advantage you may have gained through buying at auction being sustained for more than a month or two.

So unless you're prepared to go through the hassle of changing your car every few months (which effectively amounts to 'dealing' in the eyes of the local Trading Standards Office and the Inland Revenue), the only way you can motor for free is to predict accurately which cars will be in high demand and short supply in six months time.

This could mean buying imports (either new or used) in their countries of origin (not from a UK dealer or import specialist). Or it could mean playing the waiting-list game by getting your deposit down against a new, highly desirable model due to hit the market at some future date.

That said, there is some light on the horizon. The widespread scrapping of cars more than ten years old – either because they're taxed off the road, don't suit unleaded petrol or LRP, or are subject to a government scrappage incentive – is bound to increase demand for cars in the next age group up. So if you pick up the right car at sensible money in January or February of Y2K, you could well get your money back later in the year. The only trouble then is buying back into the market to stay mobile.

Buying 'nearly-new'

Remember, most 'nearly-new' mass-market cars are ex-rental or from 'fast rotation' fleets. The availability and prices fluctuate wildly according to supply and demand, and big manufacturers such as Ford and Vauxhall have now cut back the number of cars they register through rental fleets and 'fast rotators'. You may save as much as £5,000 buying a 9-month-old 9,000-mile Mondeo or Vectra – but equally the saving may be as little as £3,000.

Beware of 'customer service returns', which can be faulty new cars rejected by customers, taken back by the manufacturers and auctioned off to the trade. And beware of Fiats lacking a 'red key' for the alarm immobiliser system.

Some specialists are also offering new cars which have been imported from Eire, Cyprus or mainland Europe. Specifications of these cars and warranties on them may not be the same as official UK imports, and some may be up to 18 months old.

Finally, note that because these specialists operate on much tighter profit margins than franchised agents, they rarely offer as much for cars taken in part-exchange – usually no more than they know they can get for the part-exchanges at auction. Nor do they offer the sort of 'after sales service' UK car buyers have come to expect from franchised agents.

Nearly-new car specialists

London: The Great Trade Centre, Hythe Road (off Scrubs Lane – the original 'Car Supermarket') White City, London NW10. Tel: 0181 964 8080 and 0181 965 5511. (Advertises in the *Sun*, *Exchange & Mart*, *Thames Valley Trader*. Website: www.gtccar.co.uk). Hertz Car Sales, Gillette Corner, Brentford. Tel: 0181 560 1202.

South: Trade Sales of Slough, 353–357 Bath Road, Slough, Berks SL1 6JA. Tel: 01753 773763 (website: www.trade-sales.co.uk. Advertises in 'Telegraph Motoring' – note that 'DEAL 2' prices are after £500 minimum part exchange, plus £99 and only for cars sold on finance.) Offers an excellent, if expensive, 'bumper to bumper' warranty which even includes some consumables. CONCEPT Lakeside, Weston Avenue, West Thurrock, Essex RM20 3FJ, tel: 0800 783 3366. (Formerly CARLAND, taken over by Concept in Spring 1999. Concept specialises in pre-qualified finance packages, which means it makes sure it can offer you the finance before it shows you its cars.) Also at Staines Road, Chertsey, Surrey, tel: 01932 567000. InterKar, Camberley, Surrey, tel: 01276 671999.

Midlands: Motorpoint, Chartwell Drive, West Meadows, Derby, tel: 01332 347357 (website: www.motorpoint.co.uk. Advertises in 'Telegraph Motoring'.). Rayns of Leicester, Thurcaston Road, Leicester, tel: 0116 261 2200. Ian Shipton Cars, 24 Main Street, Stretton, Burton-on-Trent, tel: 01283 542983. CONCEPT at The Motor House, A5 Watling Street, Cannock, Staffs. Tel: 01543 506060 or 0990 289227. (1 mile from M6 J11). Motor Nation, Mackadown Lane, Garrett's Green, Birmingham. Tel: 0121 786 1111. Bristol Street Motors, 156–182 Bristol Street, Birmingham B5 7AZ, tel: 0121 666 6003. Motorworld, Dudley, West Midlands, tel: 0121 520 5533.

Wales and West: Carcraft at Empress Cars, Langland Way, Spitty Road, Newport, Gwent. Tel: 01633 284800. Ron Skinner & Sons, Roundabout Garage, A469 Rhymney, Gwent. Tel: 01685 842624, 01685 844370, sales hotline: 01685 844446. C P Motor Company, Tonteg, tel: 01443 218600. Sanderson Motorhouse, Cheltenham, Gloucs, tel: 01242 253053.

North-West: Fords of Winsford, Wharton Retail Park, Weaver Valley Road (off A5018), Winsford, Cheshire. Tel: 0845 607 3208, or 01606 861234. Faxback: 0891 715970. Motor Nation,

Widnes, Cheshire, tel: 0151 423 3342. Reg Vardy Motor Zone, Albion Way, Salford, Lancs M5 4DG. Tel: 0161 737 7333. Carcraft, Molesworth Street, Rochdale OL16 1TS. Tel: 01706 752500. Reg Vardy Motor Zone, 608 Penistone Road, Sheffield S6 2SZ. Tel: 01142 834949. Reg Vardy Motor Zone, Chancellor Lane, Ardwick, Manchester M12 6JZ. Tel: 0161 273 2273.

North-East: Reg Vardy Motor Zone, Stoddart Street, Shield-field, Newcastle-upon-Tyne NE2 1AN. Tel: 0191 232 3838.

Scotland: Reg Vardy Motor Zone, 5 Seafield Way, Seafield Road (between Portobello and Leith), Edinburgh. Tel: 0131 669 3000.

Ex-fleet car specialists

London: The Great Trade Centre, 44-45 Hythe Road, (off Scrubs Lane), White City, London NW10. Tel: 0181 960 3366. (Turn North from Western Avenue up Wood Lane at the BBC centre.) The Great Trade Centre is very cheap and stocks 2,000 cars, but requires a deposit for car keys and imposes a £41 sales charge. Midlands: Arriva Used Vehicle Sales, London Street, Smethwick, Birmingham B66 2SH. Tel: 0121 558 5141; Motor **Nation**, Mackadown Lane, Garretts Green, Birmingham. Tel: 0121 786 1111; Concept, A5 Watling Street, Cannock, Staffs. Tel: 01543 506060 or 0990 289227 (1 mile from M6 J11).

Used vehicle imports

Different pre-tax pricing to compensate for heavier taxation in other countries does not help the second-hand buyer in the same way as it helps the new car buyer. Used cars are generally little cheaper in countries such as Holland than they are in the UK. So for the used buyer there are no tax killings to be made.

What will help is any comparative strength of Sterling and a differently structured market.

Used German imports

With Sterling at around Dm3.0 / £1, Germany has been a good source of extremely well cared for high-performance cars. But a quick glance through a magazine shuch as *Motor Markt* soon shows you that, without the heavy supply of ex-fleet cars on its used car market, most bread and butter used cars aren't particularly cheap.

For example, at the equivalent of £9,338 in September 1999, an 8,000-km August 1998 Vectra 1.6 was actually more expensive than the same car in the UK. At £14,847, a 24,000-km June '98 MB C180 automatic estate wasn't particularly cheap either. But at £37,250, a 68,000-km March '97 Porsche 993 Carrera S looked an altogether better deal.

One problem can be certification. Every car sold in most European countries since January 1998 comes with a 'Certificate of Conformity' to pan-European Type Approval. Before that date most European countries recognised most other European other countries National Type Approval, so get that certificate, send it away to the Ministry, and your German purchase could be ratified.

But if the car comes with no certificate, if it's a trade import up to 10 years old or a private import up to 3 years old, it's subject to SVA and the 50-car quotas may apply. And, as from March 2000, all uncertificated cars up to ten years old which are not genuine personal imports by returning ex-pats will be subject to the SVA.

A specialist in importing Porsches from Germany is Nick Faure on 01483 414800.

Used Japanese imports

New cars in Japan, for example, sell for between half and two-thirds of the UK list price. But Japan also has a tough government testing regime designed to encourage Japanese owners to buy new every three, five or seven years. As a result, the already low prices of Japanese cars drop sharply once they are three years old, and once they are seven years old they are of little more than scrap value on the home market.

Until the Yen recovered, this made second-hand imports from Japan spectacularly cheap. From a list of cars which sailed on the *Asian Beauty* out of Nagoya in March 1997 I worked out some examples of UK landed trade prices, shipping and all taxes paid: 1990 Eunos Roadster (Mazda MX5), £3,976; 1992 Mitsubishi Galant 2.0 V6, £5,636; 1991 Toyota Celica Turbo, £7,325; 1994 Toyota Celica Cabrio, £8,838.

Unfortunately the potential fortunes to be made from this were spotted many years ago. So as well as the rising Yen, the export factor has increased values of used Japanese cars and they are not the bargains they once were. The second factor is the condition of these cars. Most Japanese cars spend much of their driving lives stuck in traffic jams. After 20,000 miles of this sort of treatment, the diesel engine in a Shogun, for example, can be ruined. The third factor is that because they don't keep their cars for long, a significant proportion of Japanese owners simply don't bother to service them. The fourth factor is that Japanese cars are set up to run on different petrol at different speeds than in the UK; the maximum speed in Japan is 55 mph, so tyres may not be suitable for the UK, suspension may be too soft, steering too light and so on.

There is an auction of used Japanese imports every month in Dublin (Windsor Car Auctions, Bewlgard Road, Dublin, tel: 00 351 1 4599 300). Specialist importers include: Park Lane:

01420 544300; Warrender of Bolton: 01257 427700; Orbis International (part of Sidney Newton PLC): 0181 965 9666; Windsor Motor City: 00 353 1 4061 000; Keith Chapman at Far East Services: 01322 529647; AJR Trading, tel 0161 723 3748, MMC International Holdings Ltd.: 0181 656 1555 (web site: http://www.mmc-intl.com); Intercar: 0181 203 3399; and Direct Vehicle Rental: 01902 353393.

You can also try using specialists who buy cars for you at Japanese auctions. These include Spectrum on 0081-48-833-0665, website: http://www.trade.co.jp; e-mail: spectrum@trade.co.jp; and Japan Car Direct on: 0081-339 280-935; website: http://www.isibike.com/isicar/; e-mail: isik@crisscross.com.

Specialists know how to get most Japanese cars through the SVA test for imports, mandatory from 1 July 1998 (£165 for cars or £60 for vans). The more complex the car, the more complex the modifications. Specialists in this area are Intech, based at Thruxton Circuit in Hampshire, tel: 01264 773888, and Protech, tel: 01179 861611.

Used American imports

Up to March 2000, 'personal imports' more than three years old remain subject to no more than the paying of import tax and VAT and the passing of a UK MOT before they can be registered. Remember, though, that you may have a bit of trouble with the headlights and the colour of the indicators. From March 2000, only cars more than ten years old can be personally imported without having to pass an SVA.

Think of the USA as a happy hunting ground for 60s to 80s muscle cars and leviathans, and for rust-free British sports cars in the dry states such as California, Arizona, and New Mexico. But please note that Florida is not a 'dry state' due to the extremely high humidity and its proximity to the sea.

Currency fluctuations

From 1997 to 1999, the growing strength of Sterling and the comparative weakness of domestic used car markets in other European countries made Europe a happy hunting ground for Brits.

The reasons for this were threefold. First, Britain had the highest interest rates in Europe, so currencies transferred to Sterling deposits would bring in a better return for Europeans than depositing the money in their own currencies in their own banks.

Second, the rest of Europe had its brakes on in order to qualify for the Single European Currency. How well Sterling will fare against the Euro in the long term could be a completely different matter.

Third, because Britain does not join the Euro in the first wave, Sterling remains a European hedge against it. From January 1999, Sterling's strength or weakness will mainly depend on the strength or weakness of the Euro.

Finding the car

The same rules apply here as for importing a new car. Check websites. Buy magazines. Preferably learn the language. Make use of friends in the country. *Hemmings* is the equivalent of a national classic car *Auto Trader* for the USA.

Shipping

This is no problem from Europe, of course. But some tips may help if you wish to import from Japan or the USA. Be warned that when importing from Japan, car space on the huge Wallenius Lines 'roll-on roll-off' ships may be limited and may be booked up months in advance.

A good shipper is Mann Motor Ships (tel: 01703 237711) which ships from Jacksonville, Charleston, Baltimore, New York and Halifax to Southampton and Liverpool, using Wallenius Lines. Mann only uses roll-on roll-off ships, but you can have a car shipped as deck cargo or fully containerised. Expect to pay between $495–$625 to ship a 'one-off' average car between 351 and 500 cubic feet. You'll also have to pay US wharfage of $75–$85 and UK wharfage of about £30. Insurance has to be negotiated with a stateside broker.

Two other shippers are: Prestige Shipping Services Ltd., tel: 0181 462 0292; and N.S.E.W., tel: 01394 674455.

Import duties from the USA and Japan

There is 10% European import duty to pay on the invoice price of the vehicle plus the shipping costs, then a further 17.5% UK VAT to pay. The appropriate two leaflets are: 'How to Permanently Import your Vehicle into Great Britain' (Department of Transport leaflet P12, printed December 1996); and 'The Single Vehicle Approval Scheme' (leaflet SVA1, also printed December 1996). Both are available from Department of Transport VSE1, Zone 2/01, Great Minster House, 76 Marsham Street, London SW1 4DR. Public Enquiries can be directed to tel: 0171 271 4800. An agent dealing in Japanese imports is Home Straight on 01932 843777.

Import agents' deposits

Agents usually ask for a deposit of at least 10% and sometimes as much as 30%. You can protect this deposit against the agent going bust or doing a runner by paying it by credit card (credit card, *not* charge card) or by insisting it is paid into an 'escrow' account where the agent cannot touch it until the deal is done.

As I stressed in the first section, though a number of agents have been mentioned here, their financial and company status has not been checked out, so please do not take any of these names as recommendations. I take no responsibility whatsoever for anything going wrong with any deal you may make with any of them.

SELLING PRIVATELY

How to prepare the car for sale

The public are suckers for clean looking cars. So, however much a heap of junk the car might be, if it can be made to look good, someone will invariably buy it.

Making a car look good is a matter of thoroughly cleaning it inside and out, thoroughly polishing it – paying particular attention to the windows, treating the plastic with a restorative, touching up or 'blocking in' as many paint chips as you reasonably can and blacking the tyres to make the whole show look new. An upholstery spray such as 'Apple Fresh' also goes down well. Whatever you do, don't spray the plastic around the dashboard with shiny glop. This looks and feels hideous and will make the public suspicious.

If you are selling the car privately from your doorstep, consider servicing it and putting it through a fresh MOT. It doesn't need to be a big service, but it will give buyers confidence and make then feel much better disposed towards you.

A couple of years ago I came across a lady with a Rover 800 Vitesse full of kids stuck by the roadside. The car was dead, I couldn't help, and the lads from the garage round the corner were called in. A few days later I asked Matthew what had been wrong with the car. 'Plugs and throttle valve completely choked up with muck. Hell of a state,' he replied. 'I asked her when she last had it serviced and she told me 16,000 miles ago. I offered to service it for her but she said, no, we're selling it next week.'

This is the worst way to sell a car because all any buyer will look at is the profit they can gain from cleaning it up and re-offering it. She'll have got about £2,000 less for it than she would have clean, freshly serviced and with a new MOT.

How to prepare your advertisement

If you're using a photo ad in one of the many 'Trader' publications, don't let their bloke come round and take the photograph. Especially don't let him take his snap of the car parked next to the dustbins round the back of a block of flats.

These days you get 24 exposures and a replacement free film for a fiver. Obviously it's well worth a bit of time and a fiver if a good snap is going to sell your car faster and for a lot more money.

So shoot the whole roll. Photograph the car against a variety of backgrounds. Side on, three-quarters, against a contrasting skyline, then pick the photo that both shows it off the best and is most likely to reproduce well in fairly grotty newsprint.

Describe the car accurately and simply using no superlatives. 'Nissan Primera 2.0SLX 5-door hatchback, 92K, 55,632 miles, full service history, met blue, electric sunroof and windows, power steering, good condition, £4,500' will go down a lot better with the general public than 'Beautiful Nissan Primera, two litre, top spec SLX model, K reg, 55k, FSH, stunning metallic blue, electric roof and windows, PAS, drives superb, first to see will buy £4,499'.

Where to advertise

This depends on the car and the price range.

For cars under £3,000, it's always worth putting a postcard in the local newsagent's window. Local newspapers or freesheets usually have sections for this type of car. People who buy *Loot*, the London classified newspaper, expect cars advertised in it to be cheap. *Auto Trader* magazines also offer sections for cheap cars. And if the car is a bit specialist, *Exchange & Mart* is worth a stab.

The photo ad section in *Classic Car Weekly* has become the best for 'classics' at the cheaper end and charges £20 a week. For more expensive 'classics' it may be worth going for a series ad in *Classic Car Weekly*, *Practical Classics* and *Classic & Sportscar*.

Mid-range family cars seem to go best either from the bigger local newspapers (or groups of newspapers) or from a photo ad in an *Auto Trader* (or at http://www.autotrader.co.uk, which costs £4.95) (see tips about taking the photo, in the previous section).

For sports or specialist cars it might be worth trying *Top Marques*, which is an upmarket national version of *Auto Trader*. If you have something you think a dealer or an enthusiast might be interested in, *Autocar* is worth a try. If attempting to get a high price or an 'over' for a car the demand for which exceeds supply, then you'll do best with an ad in the *Sunday Times* or in 'Telegraph Motoring' which appears on Saturdays. 'Telegraph Motoring' also has a photo 'Forecourt' section which can be particularly good for reaching a high circulation with a classic car.

How to answer the phone

Though you are a private individual, it's better to sound fairly

professional. Blaring television, loud pop music or kids fight-
ing in the background are a definite turn-off to the buyer.

Answer with a polite, upbeat 'Hello', followed by your telephone number. This immediately confirms that the caller has
phoned the right number.

There is than a 95% chance that the caller will say, 'I'm calling about the car.' This is your cue to say words to the effect of,
'Yes, the Nissan Micra (or whatever), and confirm to the caller
that you are not a 'home trader' who has a lot of different cars
for sale. Quickly add, 'What can I tell you about it?'

You're honest, you've put the buyer at ease, and you are
welcoming his or her questions. What more could the buyer
want? You must then try to answer every question as quickly
and straightforwardly as you can, which is not always easy
when they make ill-thought demands on you such as 'Does it
have any marks?' (Every car has marks, so your answer to this
is 'Nothing significant'.) Similarly, if they ask 'What sort of condition is it in?' you say 'Good condition – at least I think so.'

What they should be asking are questions such as, 'Are you
the owner of the car?', 'How long have you owned it?', 'Why are
you selling it?', 'When did you last have it serviced?', 'Can you
be sure that the mileage is genuine?', 'Do you owe anything on
finance for the car?', 'Is the colour Balliol Blue, Rimini Blue,
Ontario Blue, Cayman Blue, Java Blue, State Blue or Petrol
Blue?' (that would indicate that the caller knew his or her
Mondeos).

Remember, depending on the scarcity of the car and how
competitively you have priced it, the buyer may either be
working through a list or you may be the only vendor he is
phoning that night. If it's obvious he is working through a list,
you have to hook him and you'll do that by charm and hon-
esty, not by a load of old flannel.

Even if the seller does not yet want to make an appointment to view the car, be sure to get his name and phone number before you give him your address. When subsequent callers query how much interest there has been in the car, you can then read out a list of names and that might make them want to come and view the car immediately. The British are a bit peculiar like that. They always seem to want something if they think everyone wants it.

Getting the name and number of all callers also helps protect you against theft from your driveway or from the street. If you are selling a highly desirable, much stolen sportscar, take all caller's phone numbers, then phone them back on that number before divulging any address details. Smart thieves can get your address from your phone number anyway, but they're not all as smart as that.

How to demonstrate the car

It is illegal for anyone to drive your car if he or she is not insured to do so. In effect, most purchasers' private car policies will cover them to drive a car they wish to purchase on third party terms if that car (your car) is insured by someone else (you). But third party means just that. If the potential purchaser wrecks your car, his insurer will pay for any damage to third parties, but not to you. Similarly, if he steals the car from you, you will get nothing back either. And if he turns out not to be insured at all, then crashes your car, both you and he could find yourselves facing criminal charges.

So be very careful indeed about allowing other people to drive your car and don't even contemplate it unless you see their insurance certificate, or have an 'any driver' policy for your car, or have a trade policy.

Assuming the insurance question is satisfactorily answered, there is not much point in you driving the car with the purchaser as passenger unless that is specifically what they want.

Why not let them drive? The procedure is for the buyer to get into the driver's seat and you to get into the passenger's seat. Both of you then get comfortable, the buyer becomes familiarised with the controls, and you both put your safety belts on.

Then, and only then, hand him the key.

If you drive first, there are two safe ways to carry out the swapover. You climb from the driver's seat to the passenger seat and let the buyer walk round to the driver's seat. Or you both walk round but you take the key so he doesn't get hold of it until you're both belted in.

Never, ever, take more than one person on a test-drive unless you also take a big bloke as your own back-up.

How to do the deal

The buyer will try to chip you down on price. If you have accidentally underpriced the car (it can happen, I've done it) and the phone has hardly stopped ringing, you can be firm on your price. Simply and politely say you're sorry, but you know you have priced the car fairly and you know you will get the asking price, if not from the buyer in front of you then from someone else.

But, of course, if the car has stuck (this has also happened to me) you will be prepared to take a bath just to get rid of the damn thing. Whatever you do, don't make this too glaringly obvious. Still try and do a deal. Consult your wife. Fight for the last £25. Do whatever you have to. But don't let the car go cheap easily, both for your own sake and for the fact that to do so might make the buyer have second thoughts.

You need to have some kind of document to record the sale. 'Received the sum of £150 in exchange for Austin A35 reg XYX 101 – Accepted as seen and tested' written on the inside of an old fag packet might still do the trick. On the other hand you may prefer to protect yourself with a more professional bill of sale.

You can now buy 'pro-forma' private sales contract documents, and even one which contracts the buyer into a warranty. (See the section on 'Making a purchase contract' for details.)

How to take payment

There are only three forms in which to take payment for a car.

The first is a Building Society cheque issued by the Building Society itself, in which case you need to see the buyer's pass book to check the amount has in fact been withdrawn so you can satisfy yourself that the cheque is genuine.

The second is a Bank Draft which you must only take during banking hours so you can phone the bank that issued it and check it is genuine.

The third is 'Nelsons' (Nelson Eddies: Readies). The best advice when taking cash is to swap the V5 and keys for the cash in a bank so you can bank it safely straight away. Take cash on your doorstep and you won't be the first to receive a little 'cash relieving' visit shortly afterwards by big, nasty men you wouldn't want to argue with or to threaten your children.

Part-exchanging for a used car

The same rules apply as when part-exchanging a used car for a new car. But be doubly vigilant when part-exchanging for a 'nearly-new' or used car on finance. One well-know dealer offers two deals on his used cars. 'Deal 1' is a straight price, it-self very competitive, and negotiable if you find a cheaper deal for precisely the same make, model, colour, age and mileage. 'Deal 2' involves a price usually well below what you would pay at auction for the car. But the deal is subject to a minimum £500 part exchange allowance, payment of £99 and finance on the dealer's terms. The 'Deal 2' package is designed to be irresistibly tempting and the truth is it isn't bad if you don't mind tucking yourself up with fairly expensive finance. Even when you compare the true total cost of the deal (the 'cost to switch') you will probably come out better off than with a deal from a franchised dealer. Just know exactly what you're getting into.

Selling to a dealer

Unless the car is highly sought after and selling for an 'over', this is a desperation tactic.

If the car is relatively ordinary and the dealer wants stock, he has to build in a margin on top of whatever he offers you and has to include in that margin his own insurance that the car doesn't have some secret history you and HPI don't tell him about.

If your car is over the age of the dealer's stock, then the dealership may not make you an offer, but one of its salesmen might. These sort of offers are often derisory. In 1996, a reader was offered just £1,000 for an immaculate 50,000-mile BMW 320i Bauer cabrio. I told the reader to do what the salesman was planning to do with it – advertise it in *Top Marques* for £4,000 and be prepared to accept up to £500 less. He did, and got £3,750.

Okay, you can't do this if you're about to leave the country. But if you are all set to emigrate, don't be too greedy. Advertise the car for a tempting price, and take an offer. Don't hold out for more money until the day before your plane flies out or you could end up forced virtually to give the car away.

Selling at auction
Advantages and disadvantages

It's clear cut, simple and ideal for executors, finance houses and bailiffs who may be audited and must not show any favours.

Ordinary cars sold this way usually fetch no more than trade price, less the auction house entry fee and less its commission.

'Top Cars' may or may not sell to a member of the public, but usually need a bit of 'encouraging' to fetch top money – either from Joe Public or from a franchised dealer attending the auction who has an order for precisely that car.

Specialist cars in high demand and short supply will achieve what the people in the auction house that day are prepared to pay. 'Top Car' sales are often used by specialists who deal in such cars to test market price levels so they know what to pay and what to sell for. The classified ads in the weekend newspapers are no true indication because they are often placed by speculators who have bought in too late for too much money and missed the 'overs' market. On the other hand, a car for which demand suddenly exceeds supply, may sell for considerably more than the speculators are asking.

Executors who have classic cars to dispose of as part of the deceased's estate will usually get a better price selling at auction than they will from any dealer.

PART 2

MAKES AND MODELS

CAR-BY-CAR BREAKDOWN OF POPULAR MODELS

This section includes most recalls 1994–99. To check further, call the SMMT Recall Hotline, 0171 235 7000; ask for Consumer Affairs Department. Or ring the Department of Transport Vehicle Safety Branch on 0117 954 3300.

AC

MK IV AND SUPERBLOWER

WHAT'S GOOD

With 355bhp supercharged Ford V8 putting out 385lbs ft torque, they might as well have called this the 'Mindblower'. But there's nothing to be afraid of. Take it easy, 'point and squirt' at first and the informative chassis soon tells you that much more is possible. Original AC Cobra looks. Probably the most fun car there is. Beautiful; hand beaten aluminium body, but new £38,000 polycarbonate version with non-supercharged 240bhp Mustang engine from Summer 1999 is a great alternative to a TVR.

WHAT'S BAD

Driver and passenger get blown about a bit at over 100mph (on the track), nice gearchange has a narrow gate and first time out you may get 5th instead of 3rd.

WHAT TO WATCH OUT FOR

If you've got £69,795 for a fun car and you live on St George's Hill, Weybridge (spitting distance from the

Brooklands factory) there's no better way to spend your fat wedge than on this. Just think what people pay for 'real' Cobras that are inferior to drive.

AIXAM

MICRO-CARS

WHAT'S GOOD

Tiny French two and four seater micro hatchbacks. Have 2-cylinder 469cc Kubota diesel engines giving 55 mph and 75–90 mpg. Simple, exposed belt Variomatic transmission. Under the weight limit, so can be driven on a B1 motorcycle licence. Euro Type Approved. Should qualify for very low CO_2-based VED. First UK RHD sale May 1999.

WHAT'S BAD

Slow acceleration will take a bit of getting used to. Quite expensive at around £6,500–£8,000..

WHAT TO WATCH OUT FOR

Too soon to say.

ALFA ROMEO

33

WHAT'S GOOD

Zingy flat-four engine.

WHAT'S BAD

Poor substitute for Alfasud. Same rust problems. Gearboxes break. Condensation on flat-four causes poor starting. Seat trim falls apart. Gearboxes stiffen up and break. Electrics fail.

WHAT TO WATCH OUT FOR

Unless it's virtually being given away, this is one best avoided.

145/146

WHAT'S GOOD

Fabulous two-litre Twin-Spark motor, superquick power steering on 2-litre versions, brilliant oddball styling of the 145, good but not great handling. 1.8 and 1.6 Twin-Sparks also good. 3-year warranty on all Twin-Sparks.

WHAT'S BAD

The flat-fours in early models are nothing like as good as the straight-four Twin-Sparks. Dashboard a bit iffy. Not much room in the back when sitting behind a long-legged driver.

WHAT TO WATCH OUT FOR

Accident damage, lack of service history. Check electrics carefully. Oil leaks from gearboxes of flat-fours.

Starting problems with flat-fours. Make sure has 'Red Key'.

RECALLS

(April 1997 build): Tyres may lose pressure.

155

WHAT'S GOOD

Brilliant later engines – both Twin-Spark and 2.6 V6. Late 'Sport' models had 'quick-rack' power steering. 3-year warranty on later cars.

WHAT'S BAD

Terrible fall-apart dashboards. 'Italian Ape' driving position. Look like yesterday's car compared to 156. Avoid early pre-'Twin Spark' models.

WHAT TO WATCH OUT FOR

Tattiness. Kerbed alloys. Accident damage. Duff cats. Front tyre wear. Check all electrics. Sport spec well worth having. Make sure the car does have 'Quick Rack' (2.1

turns lock to lock) steering. Make sure has 'Red Key'.

156

WHAT'S GOOD

Fabulous styling. Brilliant engines. 1.8 and 2 litre Twin-Sparks are great. 190bhp 24v 2.5 V6 is a real hooligan. All have 'quick rack' steering. Pure, unadulterated handling well up to the job with Sports packs; less good without. 3-year warranty. 2 litre 'Selaspeed' with thumb operated gearchange buttons of steering wheel works very well indeed on country roads, but is less satisfactory in town. 136bhp 2.4JTD arrived in Summer 1999, offering 224 lb. ft. torque. Sport 1 spec adds carbon fibre console, bodykit, 16" alloys with 205/55 tyres, sports suspension and 'Blitz' cloth trim. Sport 2 spec adds Recaro front seats. Sport 3 spec adds Momo leather.

WHAT'S BAD

'Police Alert' spoilers optional on Sport 2 and Sport 3 spec. Sub-20mpg fuel consumption of V6 if you hoof it. Trim quality still not quite up to BMW standards. 5-speed gearchange on 1.8 and 2.0 can feel a bit floppy. Turn-in not as sharp as Peugeot 306 GTi-6 or 406 2 litre Coupe.

WHAT TO WATCH OUT FOR

Worn front tyres on V6. Accident damage. Kerbed alloys. Make sure aircon works properly. Feel the discs through the wheels for scoring or shouldering. Make sure has 'Red Key'. RECALLS: June 1999: Safety recall No 4054: Modify rear hinge mounting on all four side doors to prevent hinges splitting from doors.

164

WHAT'S GOOD

Brilliant engines, none more so than full house 3 litre 24-

valve mega-powerful 230bhp Cloverleaf V6 good for 150mph.

WHAT'S BAD

Old fall-apart Alfa trim, Alfa build quality and uneven quality of Alfa agents (some brilliant and enthusiastic, others completely the opposite).

WHAT TO WATCH OUT FOR

Electrics. Accident damage. Driveshaft wear. Gear selector problems. Worn front suspension springs shocks and joints. Scored or lipped discs (try to feel them through the wheels). Rear suspension bush wear. Tattiness. Make sure aircon works. Go for post May 1993 makeover improvements. Make sure has had a cambelt change within last 35,000–40,000 miles. Make sure has 'Red Key' (later models only).

RECALLS

1995 (to VIN 6272929): Corrosion of front

suspension spring support. (Earlier TSB check of timing belt.)

166

WHAT'S GOOD

Svelte replacement for 164. 2 litre 155bhp Twin Spark, 2.5 24v 190bhp V6 or 3.0 24v 220bhp V6. Autoboxes optional with V6s.

WHAT'S BAD

Not as charismatic as 156.

WHAT TO WATCH OUT FOR

Make sure has 'Red Key', otherwise too soon to say.

OLD SPIDER

WHAT'S GOOD

Lovely 'up and down' classic Alfa gearchange. Evergreen Alfa twin-cam motors. Early 1,570cc and 1,779cc boat tail cars had the looks. 1990 facelift brought with it a decent hardtop.

WHAT'S BAD

Scuttle shake. Progressively ruined over the years by ugly 'facelifts', but 1990 facelift an improvement. Early cars rusted from new. Later cars can still rust. 'B' pillar can dig you in the back when you try to get in. Ruined by catalytic converter.

WHAT TO WATCH OUT FOR

Tears in hood and trim. Soggy carpets. Rusty 'cornflakes under the carpet'. Rust around the fuel tank in the boot. Duff catalytic converters on later cars. Broken window-winder cables. Dripping heater matrix. Electrics. Noisy timing chain. 3,000 mile oil changes essential (I used to change mine every three months).

GTV and SPIDER

WHAT'S GOOD

We're talking about the latest model here, not the mid-60s Duetto that lasted into the 1990s. The good bits are fabulous looks, brilliant engines, 'quick rack' steering, better rear suspension than the saloons. 3-year warranty. Latest 3.0 24v V6 is Ferrari bait; 1999 MY RHDs have 220bhp and 6-speed gearbox.

WHAT'S BAD

Spider suffers scuttle shake. Virtually no boot room at all in the coupe. 'Saw their legs off' back seats. No RHD V6 Spider. No auto options.

WHAT TO WATCH OUT FOR

Kerbed alloys. Electrics. Porous wheel rims (symptom: soft tyres). Undeclared personal imports lacking 3-year warranty. Disguised 'envy' damage. Hood mechanism and tears in hood (don't forget to check hood if hood is down). LHD imports from Germany won't have 3-year warranty. Make sure has 'Red Key'.

ASTON MARTIN

DB7

WHAT'S GOOD

Nice compromise between handling and ride quality. Excellent 335bhp supercharged 3,239cc 6-cylinder engine with healthy 361lbs ft torque. Supplemented from Spring 1999 by 6 litre V12 Vantage version offering 420bhp, much praised by English motoring writers.

WHAT'S BAD

Expensive compared to XK8. (But Vantage comparatively 'reasonable' at £92,500.)

Cabin spoiled by cheap and nasty 'parts bin' switchgear. Hood of convertible does not fold away. Most 6-cylinder cars filled with old-fashioned 4-speed automatic gearbox which is difficult to override manually and changes gear half way round corners.

WHAT TO WATCH OUT FOR

For rich English people, chosen over XK8 for exclusivity of Aston Martin name. Must have top notch service history. Don't expect this car to be 100% niggle-free.

AUDI

A2

WHAT'S GOOD

High-tech aluminium space-frame constructed 12' 4" hatchback, with low drag coefficient of 0.28 built to take on the MB A Class. 75bhp 1.4 petrol engine offering a Euromix of 46.31mpg or a 3-cylinder 1.4 litre 75bhp TDI pump-injector diesel offering a Euromix of 67 mpg. Both do 108mph and 0-60 in 12 seconds. Two-deck rear luggage compartment. Rear seats completely removable. To reach UK September/October 2000, priced from around £14,000.

WHAT'S BAD

Looks like a chopped-up A6. Bonnet doesn't open, as servicing only to be carried out by agents. (Flap opens to reveal oil dipstick and filler caps for engine oil and screenwash. High rear door sills and sunken footwells make entry difficult for the elderly. Emergency spare wheel is an optional extra.

WHAT TO WATCH OUT FOR

Too soon to say.

80 (1986–91)

WHAT'S GOOD

Electro-galvanized body shell, hot-dip galvanized underside, so very little

chance of tin-worm unless accident damaged. Switchable ABS. Powerful 2 litre 16-valve engine. Euro Car Parts (0541 506506) supplies cheap parts.

WHAT'S BAD

Strangely-shaped, short, deep boot. Franchised agent service costs. Hard to sell without a sunroof. Tornado red paint oxidises in sunlight. Audi replacement autoboxes cost the wrong side of £3,000. BBS Replica alloy wheels on Sport models chip easily then oxidise.

WHAT TO WATCH OUT FOR

Duff catalytic converters, but can be 'de-catted' for £350. Accident damage repaired with non-galvanized panels. Rattly hydraulic tappets due to insufficient oil changes (sump only holds 3 litres). Worn CV joints. Rumbling wheel bearings. Don't buy early cars without PAS unless you want your arms to ache. Look for PAS leaks in cars which have it. Rear discs rust first, leading to failed MOT. Valve stem seals may need replacing at 100,000–130,000 miles – earlier if mileage clocked up slowly.

80 (1991–95; 1991–98 for convertible)

WHAT'S GOOD

Electro-galvanized body shell, hot-dip galvanized underside, so very little chance of rust unless accident damaged. Has switchable ABS (A4s doesn't switch off). Powerful 2 litre 16-valve engine. Smooth and punchy 2.6 V6. Economical TDI. All had PAS, folding rear seat and better shaped boot than previous model.

WHAT'S BAD

Franchised agent service costs. Hard to sell without a sunroof. Tornado red paint oxidises in sunlight.

WHAT TO WATCH OUT FOR

Duff catalytic converters. Accident damage repaired with non-galvanized panels. Coolant must be changed every two years especially on TDI or head gasket problems will result. Valve stem seals may need replacing at 100,000–130,000 miles – earlier if mileage clocked up slowly. Make sure ABS and ABS switch working properly. Rear discs rust first, leading to failed MOT. TDI may be worn out and oil-burning at 150,000 miles.

RECALLS

1997: 50,523 cars recalled due to possibility of "inadvertent deployment of airbags".

A3

WHAT'S GOOD

Image, quality, galvanized body. 3-year warranty.

100bhp 1.6, 125bhp 1.8, 150bhp 1.8 Turbo, new 200bhp S3 turbo. First application of Golf Mk IV platform. Front-drive alternative to the BMW Compact. Joint top of the class for secondary safety in NCAP crash testing. Handles better than Golf Mk IV. 5-door complements 3-door from autumn 1999.

WHAT'S BAD

Not much room in back whether 3 or 5 door. First tests seemed to indicate that 5-door A3 had lost the handling edge of the 3-door over the Golf Mk IV.

WHAT TO WATCH OUT FOR

Demand a proper Audi agent service history and evidence that recall work has been carried out. Sometimes bought as 'shopping cars' so be vigilant when checking the flanks for dings. Check for accident damage repaired with non-galvanized panels or with bad welds which can rust.

RECALLS

1997 (built Feb–March 1997): Check front seatbelt top mounting height adjusters. 1998: 2,822 cars recalled due to possible cracks in rear seatbelt brackets.

A4

WHAT'S GOOD

Handles well. Good looking, galvanized body. Old 150bhp 2.6 V6 is a nice engine and easily delivers 30mpg. TDI 90 and TDI 110 deservedly popular, delivering up to 50mpg driven fairly carefully. TDI V6 promises fantastic performance and economy combination, though likely to be front-heavy. Other engines: 100bhp 1.6, 125bhp 1.8 20v, 150bhp 20v Turbo, new 165bhp 30v 2.4 V6; 193bhp 2.8 30v V6; 265bhp S4 Quattro. Comprehensively re-thought in Spring 1999.

WHAT'S BAD

Takes a few days to get used to the steering, seats and over-servoed brakes. Weight of TDI V6 may take edge off handling. Limited market for 1.6s without sunroofs or a/c. Average performance in NCAP crash tests. New A4 due in Y2K.

WHAT TO WATCH OUT FOR

Rear discs rust first. Non Audi agent accident repairs. Rattling catalytic converters (especially on 2.6, which has two costing £650 apiece). Cats also fail on 1.9 TDIs built before August 1998. Quite a few coming off the fleets now, so look out for signs of clocking. Look for accident damage repaired with non galvanized panels or with bad welds. Possible oil consumption problem with 30-valve V6s, so have emissions checked for excessive HCs before buying. Some A4s develop a fault with the immobiliser ignition switch transmission reader coil. Some develop faults with both the reader coil and the key transponder. If the car comes with two different keys, this is why.

RECALLS

1997 (built Feb–March 1997): Check front seatbelt top mounting height adjusters. (Built '95–'96): Airbag may inflate while stationary. 1998: 4,574 2.4litre V6 cars built Aug '97–Feb '98: possibility of throttle jamming. 1999: 'S' reg 2.5 V6 TDIs recalled for brake modification; 2.5 V6 TDIs recalled for major engine modifications.

100 AND 'OLD' A6

WHAT'S GOOD

Galvanized against rust. 2 litre models handle better than heavier V6 and TDI. TDI 2.5 5-cylinder powerful and economical, especially with 6-speed manual gearbox.

WHAT'S BAD

Expensive agent servicing and parts. TDI fuelling needs re-setting regularly. TDI timing belt drives water pump and if water pump fails, so does belt.

WHAT TO WATCH OUT FOR

Worn autoboxes. PAS leaks and wear. Serious front tyre wear. Suspension joints. Wheel bearing rumble. Rattling cats, especially on 2.6. Ex-fleet examples may be clocked. Accident damage repaired with non galvanized panels or with bad welds which can rust.

RECALLS

1997 (2.8 V6): rumoured recall issued in April concerning driveline. 1997 (built Feb–March 1997): Check front seatbelt top mounting height adjusters. (Built '95–'96): Airbag may inflate while stationary.

NEW A6

WHAT'S GOOD

Good looking Passat-based Audi, especially 'different' at the back. 2.4 30-valve V6 is a nice, powerful (165bhp) engine. Handling is 'soft' but not floaty and grip is quite good. Estate car available. 230bhp twin-turbo 2.7T and 340bhp 4.2 V8 S6 launched autumn 1999.

WHAT'S BAD

Tiptronic gearbox lever works wrong way round (forward for upshifts, backwards for downshifts). Three-Star NCAP crash test rating. Reports of heavy oil consumption of 2.4 litre V6. TDI V6 should be brilliant, but handling is front-heavy.

WHAT TO WATCH OUT FOR

Audi agent service history. Accident damage repaired with non galvanized panels or with bad welds which can rust.

A8

WHAT'S GOOD

Advanced all-alloy 'ASF' space frame body construction. Lots of room inside. 300bhp 4.2 V8 is a high quality, quick, safe, luxurious car. S8 has 340bhp. Lesser versions are front drive 2.8 V6 and 230bhp 3.7 V8. 2.8 went 30-valve and got power hike from 174bhp to 193bhp in 1996. 3-year warranty.

WHAT'S BAD

Body dents easily and is very expensive to repair – requiring a special jig (makes insurance expensive). Ride quality not as luxurious as expected. Hasn't sold all that well.

WHAT TO WATCH OUT FOR

Don't confuse a £36,000 2.8 with a £55,000 4.2 Quattro Sport or a £61,000 S8. Mark price down heavily for event the smallest dent or scratch. Quattros must have full Audi agent servicing history, 2.8s not quite so important.

AUSTIN (ROVER)

MINI

WHAT'S GOOD

'Classic' car still being made (until the 'new' Mini arrives, anyway). Driving position can be adapted to suit six footers. Outlived the Metro. Lots of specials about, some with Jack Knight 5-speed manual boxes which are good but very noisy. AP autobox works well if the oil is changed every six months without fail. If oil not changed, it can be a disaster.

WHAT'S BAD

Hard, bouncy ride (Alex Moulton has a new mod for

this). Standard cars have just four gears and in the engine sump. Expect a noisy drivetrain. Heavy steering on wide 12" wheels. Not everyone can get comfortable. They're so low, winter road salt gets everywhere and they rust badly underneath. Bumpers far too low to be of any use.

WHAT TO WATCH OUT FOR

Rust in seams was always a Mini problem. Rust also found in sills, in area in front of the doors, in rear battery box and in rear subframes which can collapse. Early 'K reg' carb plus cat didn't work (insist on a new MOT). Water leaking from core plugs. Oil leaks. Head gasket problems (mayonnaise under oil cap may be gasket, may be from short runs). Noisy timing chain. Gears jump out of second due to internal selector collar moving down rod. Clonking drive-shafts. Wear on rear trailing arm bushes. Front tie bars can bend. Never buy a Mini

without a good look underneath, preferably on a garage hoist.

RECALLS

14/5/99: 5,000 Minis built from August 1999 recalled for rectification of a fault in the braking system causing it to lose fluid.

METRO

WHAT'S GOOD

Quite tough. Will still drag themselves along when little more than a crumbling shell. MG Metro quite well done and fun to drive. Clever separate double-folding rear seats give good luggage space. Driving position can be adapted to suit six footers. (For Rover 100, See 'Rover'.)

WHAT'S BAD

Ugly (apart from MG). Parts-bin stop-gap model – more a tribute to expedient ingenuity than proper all-new design. Rust badly at the front. Many began their lives with driving schools or as Panda Cars. Fuel splashes out of low-set filler onto rear n/s tyre.

WHAT TO WATCH OUT FOR

Rust in front bib, down front wings, in sills, in floorpan, in doors and in all body seams. Look for engine oil leaks from cylinder head gasket, water leaking from core plugs. Gears jumping out of second due to selector collar moving down rod. Clonking drive-shafts. Rattling timing chains. Leaking radiators and water pumps. Don't believe that they can do 10,000 miles between oil changes. Some were 'exported' to Jersey then re-registered in UK as a year younger than they really are. The last 1.0 and 1.3 'A' Series Metros had fuel tank filler directly over the rear wheel instead of in front. For automatics, see Mini.

MAESTRO

WHAT'S GOOD

Practical size, practical shape, very economical Perkins Prima DI and TDI engines. 2 litre MG version by far the best. MG Maestro Turbo a bit of a hooligan. Amazingly, you can still buy new 1.3s, built from CKD kits originally sent to Bulgaria and assembled with RHD and catalytic converters by Ian Yarsley of Parkway Service Station of Ledbury for a reasonable £5,300, tel: 01531 632320. (Also in LHD from Lifestyle Garages of Ctra de Mijas, Fuengirola, Malaga, Spain, tel: 00 345 952 580 077)

WHAT'S BAD

Tin shed construction. 'Red Robbo' build quality. Antidiluvian 'A' Series 1.3 litre engine. 1.3s are surprisingly horrible to drive – worse than you would ever have imagined.

WHAT TO WATCH OUT FOR

Rust in body seams. Water leaks. Dodgy engine management systems. Oil leaks from all engines. Core plug problems with 1.3. Avoid the MG 1600 Maestro due to hopeless twin carb set-up. 1600s and 2000s need regular cambelt replacement.

MONTEGO

WHAT'S GOOD

Very sensible, practical estates (7-seat 'Countryman' quite sought-after). Not bad to drive. Economical Perkins Prima TDI engines. LX models had decent spec, but most lacked power steering. Diesel or catalysed 2 litre only from 1992K. Lots of owners loved the estates and mourn their passing.

WHAT'S BAD

Rust in body seams. Hit and miss build quality of all but the last few years production. Saloons difficult to re-sell for more than buttons.

WHAT TO WATCH OUT FOR

Cracked Plastic bumpers. Fall apart trim. Oil/water leaks from cylinder head gaskets. Cambelts need regular replacement. Valve gear wears on 'O' Series engines (if it's particularly quiet, it's about to give way). Same engine management foibles as Maestro. Petrol Turbo may spell trouble, but may have enjoyed doting enthusiast care. The last saloons went as special order to taxi fleets and the MOD.

BENTLEY

MULSANNE AND TURBO

WHAT'S GOOD

Image. Huge performance from Turbo versions. Stiffer

suspension than Rolls Royce. Best colours: metallic bottle green or ink black. Gradually improved over the years with injection and ABS in October 1986, automatic ride control in 1987, four rather then 3-speed autobox in September 1991. Cats came in during June 1990, but were initially a no cost option. Standard Brooklands has 226 bhp and 340 ft lb torque. Continental R had 385 bhp and 553 ft. lbs torque; Turbo RT from 1997 has all of 400bhp and 580 ft. lb torque; Continental T has a truly awesome 420 bhp no less than 619 ft lb torque and handles its power and bulk very well.

WHAT'S BAD

Thirst. Stink of cigar smoke clings to the headlining. Labour might ban them. Resentful drivers don't let you out of side roads, particularly during recessions. Apt to get vandalised with rusty nails or keys while parked. Trim choice may be in bad taste. White or cream is hideous and suitable only for wedding hire.

WHAT TO WATCH OUT FOR

Anything over £15,000 must have a proper Rolls Royce agent or Rolls Royce specialist history. The engine is an old fashioned pushrod V8, so you don't want to hear ticking tappets or see any blue smoke from the exhaust pipe. Make sure the suspension is not unduly wallowy. Check expensive tyres for tread depth and uneven wear. With so much weight to stop, turbos can be heavy on their brakes, so check for signs of warp on your test drive. Best to have the car inspected by a different Rolls Royce specialist from the one who's selling it.

RECALLS

1997 (Bentley Azure): 101 cars recalled due to danger of fire from a short circuit. 1997 (Rolls /Bentley general): 29 left hand drive cars found to have potentially defective braking system.

ARNAGE

WHAT'S GOOD

BMW's relatively small but powerful 350bhp/420 lb. ft. twin-turbo 4,398cc V8 engine and 5-speed auto in a very British body. Optional 6,750cc Cosworth V8 from Turbo RT offers same staggering 400bhp and 619 lb ft torque with tougher GM 4-speed autobox.

WHAT'S BAD

Doomed wedding between Rolls Royce and BMW before VW turned up like Dustin Hoffman in 'The Graduate' and whipped the bride away. Values drop like a spanner down a lift-shaft. Power characteristics of twin turbo BMW V8 disliked by traditionalist customers.

WHAT TO WATCH OUT FOR

Thinking you want one, when it probably isn't a very good idea at all.

RECALLS:

1999: Possible wiring fault in heated seat circuit.

BMW

E30 3-SERIES (1983–91)

WHAT'S GOOD

Nice looking. 318iS, 320i, 325i and M3 still nice to drive. Some galvanized panels from 1988. American spec 325i auto only car I've ever driven with more than 1,000,000 miles on the clock and it still ran to 6,000 rpm with no trouble. 136bhp chain cam 16v M42 powered 318iS is already achieving classic status.

WHAT'S BAD

316 and 318 relatively slow and over-rated. Many drivers not ready for oversteer, especially in the wet. No room in the back of two door versions with big front seats. All models apart from 318iS had timing belts which need to be replaced every three years or 36,000 miles without fail.

WHAT TO WATCH OUT FOR

Clocking. Rust in early cars. Make sure cambelts and tensioners were recently changed. Cylinder head studs of 6-cylinder engines can shear. Heads of 6-cylinder cars can also crack. Prime candidate for fully synthetic oil (engine won't last forever without it). Repaired accident damage. Most convertibles have been 'customised' in questionable taste. Some nice, obviously well cared for M3s are coming over from Germany and M3s are all LHD anyway. (It's very hard to find a genuine old 3-Series these days.)

RECALLS

1998: 170,000 E30s recalled because radiator cap pressure valve may seize up and over-pressurise cooling system, leading to coolant leak and steaming up inside car

E36 3-SERIES (1991–1998)

WHAT'S GOOD

170bhp 323i is a strong performer also capable of delivering excellent mid-30s mpg. 6-cylinder cars have brilliant brakes.140bhp 318iS coupe and run-out special 318iS saloon by far the best 4-cylinder cars. Impressive build quality. Long-lived 'chain cam' 6-cylinder engines. Older iron block chain cam 325 twin-cam longest-lived of all.

WHAT'S BAD

Average performance in NCAP crash tests. 4-cylinder

disc/drum set ups nothing like as good, as 6-cylinder's discs. 316i and 318i saloons over-rated, under powered and pretty ordinary to drive. Non M42 8-valve 4-cylinder engines had timing belts up to September 1993 – chains thereafter. Some 'M52' 6-cylinder 323is and 328is have suffered premature bore wear. Early E36s suffered poor quality trim.

WHAT TO WATCH OUT FOR

Clocked mega mile ex-fleet cars (not all fleets register their mileages on disposal). Lots of early E36 3-Series suffered premature dashboard failure, so mileage on the clock may not be the mileage on the car. Earlier 4-cylinder cars still had cambelts which need changing every three years or 36,000 miles. Service indicator can be reset with £30 tool. Kerbed alloys may indicate front suspension damage from uncaring company driver.

Lift carpets to check for result of rainwater leaks through screen seals (condensation inside windows a sure sign of this). 'M52' engine 320i, 323i and 328i from December 1994/April 1995 may suffer premature bore wear due to high amounts of sulphur in some UK petrol. Solved by replacement block with steel-lined bores. 328is from April 1998 fitted with 'EU3' steel lined bores; 323is from September 1998 fitted with 'EU3' steel lined bores. A full BMW agent service history should tell you all recall work carried out.

RECALLS

1997 (E36 from January 1996): Tighten stub axle bolts. 1997 (E36 built Feb '91–Dec '94: 77,000 cars): Possibility of corroded steering shafts. 1997 (M3): Faulty bearings in Variable Valve Timing mechanism can deposit shards of metal in engine. Official recall. 400 cars affected. 1998: E36s built before Nov '94 recalled to fit new radiator cap.

E36 3-SERIES COMPACT

WHAT'S GOOD

As E36, but lighter and therefore quicker. 1.9 litre twin cam 140bhp 318Ti quickest of all. No sixes or 'M' versions so drivers less likely to be branded as status seekers.

WHAT'S BAD

As E36. Has simpler rear suspension based on E30 3-Series.

WHAT TO WATCH OUT FOR

As E36.

RECALLS

1997 (E36 from January 1996): Tighten stub axle bolts. 1997 (E36 – 77,000 cars): Possibility of corroded steering shafts. 1998: Compacts built before Nov '94 recalled to fit new radiator cap (very few cars

involved as Compact not launched until Sept '94).

E46 NEW 3-SERIES

WHAT'S GOOD

Fairly close to perfection. More comfortable and refined than E36. Good body control. 'Cornering Brake Control' makes it very safe. Up to 193bhp in standard range. All have steel bore liners eliminating problems of previous Nickasil lined all alloy blocks. Same 136bhp 2 litre direct injected diesel as Rover 75. Excellent secondary safety features. 2-door version arrived in Spring 1999; Touring autumn 1999. New 2-door M3 boasts 340bhp. Convertible expected late Y2K.

WHAT'S BAD

Lacks character, and lacks the visual impact of the Alfa 156. Performance and driving pleasure blunted compared to the best E36s. 'Cornering brake control' can take over – but does, of course, make the car safer in unskilled hands when a corner tightens up unexpectedly. Heavier, so uses more fuel than E36.

WHAT TO WATCH OUT FOR

First year's RHD production sold out so may be selling at premiums which are not worth paying. 316 and 318 not powerful enough.

RECALLS

1999 (E46 from April 1998): Safety recall over failure of brake pedal clip which can allow the pedal to become disconnected and over-sensitive side airbag trigger switches.

Z1 ROADSTER

WHAT'S GOOD

Classic from day one. Groovy drop down doors. Sophisticated multi-link rear suspension. Old iron block,

single cam 171bhp BMW six.

WHAT'S BAD

LHD only. Many imported used from Germany so difficult to check history, ie may be clocked. With 'old' single cam 325i engine, needs same regular cambelt changes, can suffer same cracking of cylinder head. Panels hard to replace. Have always been around £20,000.

WHAT TO WATCH OUT FOR

Badly fitting panels hiding old accident damage. Make sure the door mechanisms work properly. Cambelts need replacing every three years or 36,000 miles. 1998: All Z1s recalled to fit new radiator cap.

Z3 ROADSTER

WHAT'S GOOD

Very compact. Snug cockpit. Doesn't buffet badly up to 80mph. 140bhp 1.9 auto available. 2.8 litre 190bhp six has bags of power. 321 bhp

3.2 litre 'M' version almost too powerful. American built. New lower engine range from Spring 1999, with 115bhp 1.9 litre 'four' and 150bhp 2 litre 'six'.

WHAT'S BAD

115bhp and 140bhp 1.9 litre fours not really enough except for cruisers. No clever roof like the SLK. Optional hardtops offer poor seal for side windows – modification kit available early 1999. Z3 'M' coupe may be fast but is aesthetically hideous.

WHAT TO WATCH OUT FOR

Many RHDs were personally imported to avoid long delivery dates and don't have UK 3-year dealer warranty. 2.8s imported from other markets may have vulnerable Nickasil lined bores rather than steel lined bores.

Z8 ROADSTER

WHAT'S GOOD

Very fast 400bhp V8 'retro' roadster, as driven by James Bond in limited production at BMW's Dingolfing plant from Spring 2000.

WHAT'S BAD

Expensive. Likely to blow your hairpiece off.

WHAT TO WATCH OUT FOR

Too soon to say.

OLD 5-SERIES (1987–96)

WHAT'S GOOD

Decent quality. Good looks. Good ride and handling. Later chain-cam, iron block 2 litre and 2.5 sixes the best engines, but powerful 535i still impresses. Touring model is a practical estate car. 3.8 litre M5 the top performer.

WHAT'S BAD

Premature bore wear in 530i & 540i V8s. Lower inertia 518i okay in town, but not strong enough for heavy motorway use and wears rapidly. Old single-cam 525i, 530i and 535i engines all need cambelt replacement every three years or 36,000 miles. 5-speed auto not liked by autobox specialists.

WHAT TO WATCH OUT FOR

Electronically 'corrected' odometer/on board computer (clockers sometimes steal one of the chips). Accident damage. Electric window problems. Faked service indicator. Whining manual gearbox can last for years but expensive to fix. Slurry autoboxes with neglected ATF and filter changes. Accident damage to M5s. Earlier model, less powerful, imported LHD M5s. Smoke from worn valve stem seals. Overheating from cracked cylinder heads. 'Problem' V8s. Duff catalytic converters. Smoking 1.8s (valve stem seals). Noisy 12-valve sixes. Misfires from faulty integrated coil units on later 24vs. Rear subframe rubbers (MOT failure point –

£200 to put right). Damage to front suspension and steering (look for uneven tyre wear). Duff ABS.

RECALLS

1998: 5s built 1988–November '94 recalled to fit new radiator cap.

NEW 5-SERIES (from 1996)

WHAT'S GOOD

Great looks. 528i provides huge feelgood factor. Decent economy from 528i and 523i. Petrol V8s overkill, but 540i can be had with 6-speed manual. Top model is 5 litre 32-valve 400bhp M5. Four Star NCAP crash test rating, but worst in group for pedestrian safety. Quiet, refined, powerful 3 litre V8 diesel automatic from Spring 1999 the best car in the range.

WHAT'S BAD

Have been some quibbles about build quality and

paint. Dodgy door seals. Engine gasket leaks. Wipers set for LHD. Diesels not significantly more economical than petrol, so best avoided. V8s not worth the extra. 2.8iSE is as far as you need to go.

WHAT TO WATCH OUT FOR

Repaired accident damage. Excessively high franchised dealer prices for over-specified cars. 523i, 528i, 530i and 540i may suffer premature bore wear due to high amounts of sulphur in some UK petrol. Solved by replacement block with steel-lined bores on sixes, 'Alusil' lined bores on V8s. Production from September 1998 fitted with 'EU3' steel or Alusil lined bores.

OLD 7-SERIES (1987–94)

WHAT'S GOOD

High mileage 6-cylinder 730i and 735iSE can be real bargains. Parts prices quite reasonable. Very luxurious.

WHAT'S BAD

V12 750 gobbles fuel. V8s may use oil.

WHAT TO WATCH OUT FOR

Avoid lower spec trim unless you like cloth interiors. Aircon system problems. Bore liner degradation in aluminium V8s. Electrical glitches. Check the on board computer carefully (see 5 Series). Suspension sags eventually. Make sure the ABS light goes on, then off at the right time. Try to find one with BMW service history; if not consistent specialist history. 1998: 7s built 1988–November '94 recalled to fit new radiator cap.

NEW 7-SERIES (from 1994)

WHAT'S GOOD

More 'modern' looking than predecessor. 728i capable of 28–30 mpg. Better ride.

Luxurious and capable.

WHAT'S BAD

Not a big improvement on predecessor. V8s re-engined – 2,997cc 730i V8 replaced by 3,498cc 735i and 3,982cc 740i replaced by 4,398cc 740i in early 1996. Premature bore wear can be a problem on the earlier engines.

WHAT TO WATCH OUT FOR

Be very wary of 730i and 3,982cc 740i V8s (the engines that were dropped in 1996). Some unsold 'P' platers still had the old engines. 728i may also suffer bore liner degradation due to high amounts of sulphur in some UK petrol. Check all electrics, computer (see 5 Series) and aircon system carefully. Check for duff cats, condensation corroded rear silencers from chauffeured cars. Chauffeured cars also most likely to suffer premature bore wear due to long periods spent idling. Automatic transmission specialists don't like the 5-speed autobox. Solved by replacement block with steel-lined bores. UK imports from March 1998 fitted with steel or Alusil lined bores, but grey imports from other markets may not be. 1998: New 7s built before Nov '94 recalled to fit new radiator cap (Very few cars involved because new 7 not launched until August 1994.)

X5 4x4

WHAT'S GOOD

BMWs own Range Rover with 3 litre petrol or diesel sixes and 286bhp 4.4 litre V8 option. First reports say it is leagues ahead of all other 4x4s as a road car.

WHAT'S BAD

Price around £27,000, and not likely to be economical. Could kill off BMW's other big 4x4: the Range Rover.

WHAT TO WATCH OUT FOR

Too soon to say.

CADILLAC

SEVILLE STS

WHAT'S GOOD

Big, squat car with reasonably restrained styling. Loaded with kit. Looks best in black. Very comfortable. Powerful, low-maintenance 305 bhp 4.6 litre V8. Not bad to drive, with strong acceleration, decent steering 'feel', good handling, nicely calculated traction control and anti-skid. Brilliant Bose stereo system (possibly the best standard in-car system available). EC fuel consumption: 13.7/27.2/19.9, so 20 mpg possible. Automatic parking brake release. 3-year, 60,000 mile warranty with 24 hour assistance. Electrically folding door mirrors.

WHAT'S BAD

Severe tyre roar. Looks a bit like a larger Rover 800 4-door. Variable-ratio steering loses 'feel' on very tight corners. Some trim not up to the standards of a luxurious European car. Garish chromed alloys. Indicator switch on the right of the column.

WHAT TO WATCH OUT FOR

Nearside suspension damage by drivers not able to judge the width. Possibility of having been pre-owned by undesirable people.

CHEVROLET

CAMARO

WHAT'S GOOD

Relatively cheap starter price of £17,950 for 3.8 litre V6 auto. 3.8 convertibles from £21,500. But 284bhp 6-speed 5.7 Z28 a much hunkier choice at £22,725 and can be surprisingly economical with 23mpg obtained by *Sunday Telegraph*'s Neil Lyndon.

WHAT'S BAD

5-speed manual box adds £1,000 to price of V6. Crude, cheapskate interiors. LHD only. Difficult to see out of and to park.

WHAT TO WATCH OUT FOR

Parking dings and donks. Lack of proper servicing.

CORVETTE

WHAT'S GOOD

Really quick and relatively cheap at prices from £36,705 on the road. (Convertible dearer at £40,605.) 339bhp and 356 lb ft torque give over 170mph and 0-60 in 5.3 seconds. Surprisingly economical with over 20mpg easy to achieve.

WHAT'S BAD

6-speed manual box costs an extra £1,150. LHD only.

WHAT TO WATCH OUT FOR

Parking dings and donks. Lack of proper servicing.

CHRYSLER

NEON

WHAT'S GOOD

Well-equipped. Good features such as electrically folding door mirrors very helpful in multi-story carparks. ABS and aircon standard on LX. Reasonably priced by UK standards. Good paint finish, especially metallics. 3-year warranty.

WHAT'S BAD

Coarse engine. Autobox has only 3-speeds but better suited to engine than manual. Huge diameter rear coil springs intrude into boot space. Rear backrests flop down crudely onto squabs. Seating material and interior plastics a bit iffy and more suited to a £7,000 car, which the Neon is in the USA.

WHAT TO WATCH OUT FOR

Kerbing damage. Damage to the mirror mechanisms (£350 + to replace). Tears in seat trim, especially flimsy backs of front seats.

NEW NEON

WHAT'S GOOD

Well-equipped and reasonably priced from £10,995 OTR with standard aircon, standard electrically folding door mirrors and standard 3-year warranty. 131bhp twin cam 16v 2 litre engine now much smoother. £13,495 LX model loaded with goodies such as leather interior trim, wood trim, cruise control (with auto), 15" alloys, ABS and Thatcham Category 2 immobiliser. Optional no extra cost auto.

WHAT'S BAD

Autobox still just three speeds.

WHAT TO WATCH OUT FOR

See original Neon.

PT CRUISER

WHAT'S GOOD

Brave, retro-styled estate car from the people who brought you the Prowler and are now in league with Mercedes Benz. Based on the new Neon with practical interior that can even take surf boards. Set to arrive in the UK in Y2K. Could be a bigger success than the new Beetle.

WHAT'S BAD

Not everyone will go for the styling.

WHAT TO WATCH OUT FOR

Too soon to say.

JEEP CHEROKEE

WHAT'S GOOD

Powerful, yet simple 4 litre straight six. European VM 2.5 litre turbodiesel. Fairly compact. Much lower than Discovery and Range Rover so better in multi-story carparks. Facelifted April 1997.

WHAT'S BAD

The model was on the LHD market for many years before it came to the UK. Small luggage area, especially with spare wheel in place. Spare wheel creates an offside rear blind spot. Have been automatic gearbox and transfer case problems. Lots came onto the market all at once, part-exchanged for Voyagers.

WHAT TO WATCH OUT FOR

Automatic transmission problems (where fitted). Old LHD imports undermining RHD values. If buying an import, make sure it had four wheel drive (they didn't all have). Look for oil leaks from gearbox, transfer case and axles. Check steering box mounting carefully.

RECALLS

1997 (January 1993–1997 model year RHD 19,200 cars): Check for stress fractures around steering box mounting. 1997: 567 cars built before Sept '96 recalled due to possibility of "inadvertent deployment of airbags". 1998: further recall over steering box mounting problem.

JEEP GRAND CHEROKEE

WHAT'S GOOD

See Cherokee. Slightly more room inside than Cherokee. New models including an RHD 4.7 litre V8 from Spring 1999, and new 5-cylinder 3.1 litre turbodiesel with 283 lb ft torque for Y2K.

WHAT'S BAD

Still comparatively small inside. Old LHD 'special order' 5,216cc (212bhp) and 5,899cc (237bhp) V8s very 'American'. Isolate the driver from what's going on. Only do 13–26 mpg. V8 values likely to fall heavily as fuel taxes increase. Lack of crumple zones means it can be severely damaged by hard impacts at speeds as low as 5mph.

WHAT TO WATCH OUT FOR

See Cherokee.

RECALLS

1997: 2,536 cars recalled due to danger of fire from a short circuit in heated seat wiring.

VOYAGER AND GRAND VOYAGER

WHAT'S GOOD

Very good looking, very 'big' MPVs from the company that has made more than anyone else. Rear seat rolls out on castors. 2.5 litre VM turbodiesel does 30mpg and has plenty of torque to pull the vast Grand Voyager body along. Excellent cruise control.

WHAT'S BAD

Inconvenient 2-2-3 seating arrangement with back three seats on a single bench which is heavy to remove. 2 litre 131bhp Neon engine + manual box not really man enough (3.3 litre autos more suited to the job). Terrible roadholding and handling on tight turns. Poor two-star performer in NCAP crash tests (0 points front impact; 14 points side impact).

WHAT TO WATCH OUT FOR

Damage from heavy use and uncontrolled children. School run kerbing damage by drivers used to Cherokees.

RECALLS

1998: Voluntary European recall of old (squarer shape) model due to possible problems with rear door latches.

CITROEN

2CV

WHAT'S GOOD

Good fun in its day, especially on empty summer country roads and in and around holiday resorts. Easy to appreciate the design. You can still have a laugh in them. 2CV experts say that all from the early 70s are happy on unleaded.

WHAT'S BAD

It's had its day. Dreadful to drive in town and to park in multi-storeys. Can suffer severe chassis rust. Body also rusts, especially around fresh air ventilator. Jobs like brakes very expensive (drive-shafts have to come off to replace front discs). Some 'beardy' and 'girlie' owners tend to neglect servicing or do it on the cheap. So flimsy, a crash in one is a terrifying thought.

WHAT TO WATCH OUT FOR

Number One: chassis rot (galvanized chassis available, but expensive). Smoking engines. Clocking (oh, yes). Loose underbonnet heater ducts. Ripped tops (but cheap to replace). Last of the line were built in Portugal and build quality of these was poor.

AX

WHAT'S GOOD

Chirpy, light to drive, economical. Cheap to run. 1.5 litre iron block diesel engine can be very long lived if well maintained with regular oil, coolant and cambelt changes. Also delivers 55–60 mpg. Front door pockets designed to take 2 litre bottles of wine.

WHAT'S BAD

Very light build so not good in a crash (especially early AXs). Offset driving position.

Fall-apart interior trim.

WHAT TO WATCH OUT FOR

Any body rot will significantly weaken fairly feeble structure. Thin body panels easily dented. Worn engines start to rattle. Oil leaks are common. Smoking usually caused by more than just valve stem oil seals. Make sure the heater is not leaking. Also check that brakes stop the car straight and true.

SAXO

WHAT'S GOOD

Bigger, better, stronger AX. Quite refined. 1.1 is very economical. 1.6 VTS very quick. Seem to be pretty good and relatively problem-free for a Citroen. Good value by UK standards. 1.5 diesel does 55 mpg. Autumn 1999 facelift includes galvanized panels, now with 12-year no perforation warranty. All now have PAS apart from 1.0

version. SXs have switchable passenger airbags. 1.1i LPG version available in Europe.

WHAT'S BAD

Twisted spine from offset driving position. 3-speed 1.6 automatic replaced by 3-speed 1.4 auto.

WHAT TO WATCH OUT FOR

Two years free insurance made them attractive to 17-year-olds who may have crashed them. See Peugeot 106 for what to watch on VTR & VTS.

RECALLS

1997: Faulty driver's seat catch on 3-door model.

BX

WHAT'S GOOD

Excellent ride and handling. Light weight. Well designed. 1.4 was under-powered, but XU engined cars good. Excellent estate. Diesel with PAS is the obvious choice. 1.9D will do 100mph and 50mpg. Height-adjustable suspension allows 'stilt effect' for floods or rough going. There was a very quick 16v version. 4x4 likely to become troublesome. Plastic bonnet and boot on all but last few years production are light and don't rust. Suspension spheres easy and cheap to replace.

WHAT'S BAD

Not all had PAS. Very light build quality. Brake pipes go. Many independent servicing agents have moved on from BXs now.

WHAT TO WATCH OUT FOR

Clocking (there are plenty of BX diesels around with well over 200,000 miles under their wheels). Make all standard XU engine cambelt, cambelt end seal, coolant and cylinder head gasket checks. Clutch cables can pull through bulkhead. Make sure the brake pipes have been replaced (replacements were better protected and longer lasting). Plastic ends of car can hide rust underneath. The last BXs had steel bonnets.

ZX

WHAT'S GOOD

Excellent ride and handling combination, second only to Peugeot 306. Comfortable and absorbs bumps well. Low used prices. 1.8 Furios can be spectacular bargains. 1.4 TU engines and diesels are the best buys. All capable of 150,000 miles plus if properly looked after. Non turbo XUD capable of 50mpg. Turbo XUD surprisingly quick. Sensible nearside-only electric door mirror.

WHAT'S BAD

1.6 is a bit of a camel. 1.8 less so. Turbo XUD not that economical – can drop to as little as 36 mpg. Boot not much bigger than Peugeot 205. Early front brake problems cured by modified callipers. Brake warning light very sensitive to low brake fluid level. If this happens with a diesel, which has a brake vacuum pump, disappearing brake fluid could leave you with no brakes Cambelts and camshaft end seals must be changed every three years and 36,000 miles. Coolant must be changed every two years to avoid cylinder head gasket problems. (Coolant is difficult to change without getting air-locks.) Petrol models may have cat converter MOT test problems.

WHAT TO WATCH OUT FOR

See above. 'J' reg ZXs could suffer front brake caliper problems cured by fitting later calipers (this will have been done to most of them). Some reports of sticking handbrakes, easily checked by seeing how easy the car is to push. Early Avantage diesels lacked power steering, as did early Avantage diesel estates which came out long after the hatch got PAS. 16v noisy, not really that quick and best avoided. Upholstery tears easily and is difficult to repair. Make sure all the electrics work. Insist on new MOT, especially if car is post-August 1992 and fitted with a cat. Check spare wheel is in its underboot cradle and not nicked.

RECALLS

1994 (Mostly Volcane May 1992–Oct 1992 and 16v 1992-1994): Brake pipe chafing. 1996 ('facelift' model from June 1994): Faulty seat belt pretensioners and, on cars so fitted, faulty airbag sensors.

BERLINGO MULTISPACE

WHAT'S GOOD

Originally designed as a van on the ZX/306 floorpan with Peugeot 405 estate rear suspension. Lots of good design points. Decent ride quality. Launched in UK as Multispace with full-length electric sunroof, bright colours and 1.8 litre 8-valve engine giving 100mph in Summer 1998. Relaunched Spring 1999 at lower prices from £10,830 on the road with 1.4i engine. Sunroof, aircon, 1.8i or 1.9D engines now all extra-cost options. Handles well for a van (though not as well as Polo Caddy Combi). Excellent for gardeners and people with dogs. Sensibly priced Brotherwood conversion available for transporting the disabled in dignity. Autumn 1999 90bhp HDI diesel introduced. Sliding rear side doors will come in 2000 (already seen in Germany).

WHAT'S BAD

It's a van-based car, not a car-based van. Brakes aren't as good as you would expect on a car.

WHAT TO WATCH OUT FOR

Nothing so far.

XSARA

WHAT'S GOOD

Bigger, more refined ZX. Much improved safety features. Ingenious (patented) side-impact protection. 3-Star above average performance in NCAP crash testing. Good 1.8 litre 16-valve engine. Excellent ride quality and bump absorption. Sharp turn-in with enhanced rear steer effect (very little understeer). 2 litre 167bhp coupe seriously quick and a fine, safe handler. Estates better than 5-door hatchbacks, with lots of room, better handling and no sacrifice in ride quality. Evergreen XUTD still good. New HDI diesel from early 1999 engine should be best in class. Three piece bumpers cheap to replace. 12-year body warranty from September 1999.

WHAT'S BAD

Nondescript looks of 5-door and coupe. Instrument bezel can reflect in screen. Only two three point rear seatbelts. Model for model lack the equipment of equivalent Astras. Depreciate more quickly than class average. Fairly steep depreciation curve.

WHAT TO WATCH OUT FOR

Check spare wheel is in its underboot cradle and not nicked.

RECALLS

1998: 14,000 owners of cars regd Sep 97–Feb '98 notified that may be a delay in airbag inflating in an accident. Also possibility of faulty seatbelt pre-tensioner.

PICASSO

WHAT'S GOOD

Xsara based and by far the best looking of the new 5-seater MPVs. Electro-galvanized body with 12-

year warranty. 90bhp 1.6i
petrol, 115bhp 1.8i 16v
petrol, or 90bhp 2 litre HDI.

WHAT'S BAD

Front window pillars can
obscure front three quarters
vision slightly.

WHAT TO WATCH OUT FOR

Too soon to say.

XANTIA (to 2000)

WHAT'S GOOD

Good looking, 'different'
hatchbacks and estates with
excellent front end grip, safe
handling, fine ride quality
out of town plus the ability
to raise themselves on their
suspension to clear
obstacles and to sink down
to the ground if required.
Good rear legroom. Estates
have three lap/diagonal rear
belts. Suspension never
goes baggy. Suspension
spheres quick, easy and
cheap to replace. 'N' reg on
16-valve 1.8 and 2 litre
engines quite sporty but can

use a bit of oil in valve stem
lubrication. Facelift Feb '98
with 3-piece bumpers.
Turbo-diesel automatic from
Spring '98 a good cruiser.
New HDI diesel engine from
October 1998 best fuel
miser in class. 12-year body
warranty from November
1999.

WHAT'S BAD

Hydraulic pumps can still go.
ABS computers fail. Parts of
more complex VSX and
Activa suspension can stick.
Average performance in
NCAP crash tests. TD auto a
bit high geared for town
work (stays in 2nd or 3rd). If
clutch cable comes off at the
pedal end, it's a long,
tedious and expensive job
to put right. Rate of
depreciation can take you
by surprise. New model due
soon.

WHAT TO WATCH OUT FOR

LX non-ABS models are the
best used buy because
there's less to go wrong. ABS
computers are a common

problem. Check spare wheel is in its underboot cradle and not nicked. Look for smoke from diesels – may be curable with a dose of injector cleaner and a fresh air filter. 1.6s likely to wear out first. If fitted with aircon, make sure it blows cold. If 2 litre petrol engine knocks, don't buy the car. (See XM for reason.)

RECALLS

1994 (May 1993–Oct 1994): Parking brake mod.

XANTIA (from 2000)

WHAT'S GOOD

Comprehensively re-thought. Galvanized body with 12-year warranty.

WHAT'S BAD

Too soon to say.

WHAT TO WATCH OUT FOR

Too soon to say.

XM

WHAT'S GOOD

Excellent ride and handling once you get to 'feel through' the steering to the front wheels. 2.1TD can be very economical and give quick journey times at 40 mpg. 2.5TD altogether more powerful, less economical. Best petrol engine is the 150bhp 8-valve 2 litre turbo. Estates are very spacious and comfortable.

WHAT'S BAD

Riddled with niggly problems and rattles prior to 'M' reg. Mark IIs from 'M' reg much better. Mk I V6 24v fast but not a success. Horrible American style foot-operated parking brake.

WHAT TO WATCH OUT FOR

Where to start? Clutch problems (best replaced at a Citroen agent), slurry automatics due to neglected ATF changes, dodgy electrics mainly due to poor contacts (solved on Mk II), ABS computer can give up, ABS pump will rust up inside if hydraulic fluid not changed frequently. Uneven tyre wear can mean serious chassis problems. Hard ride and excessive roll means suspension links have seized up. Brakes eat pads and discs will eventually wear. Make sure aircon blows cold. Listen for knocking from engines of 2 litre models (8v and 16v) due to design of piston skirts. If fault developed early, pistons were replaced FOC, but were only replaced when knocking became excessive.

SYNERGIE

WHAT'S GOOD

Good, well-planned, bright walk-through interior with dash-mounted gearshift. Nice trim colours. Compact for an MPV and easy to park. Sliding doors easy to get in and out of in tight parking spaces. Excellent,

economical 110bhp HDI diesel engine from autumn 1999. Similar Peugeot 806 was a three star performer in NCAP crash tests (7 point front impact; 15 points side impact). 12-year body warranty from September 1999.

WHAT'S BAD

Doesn't handle as well as Galaxy family. No automatics. Centre rear passenger only gets a lap belt.

WHAT TO WATCH OUT FOR

Some may be ex-rental or ex-taxis. Make sure sliding side doors open smoothly and don't stick. Check for uneven front tyre wear. Look for signs of having been overloaded. May have done a few Calais beer runs.

DAEWOO

MATIZ

WHAT'S GOOD

Styled by Giugiaro from scratch and much better looking than Move, Wagon R or Atoz. Sensible, eco-friendly city car or suburban runabout. Excellent for the school run. Good value at £6,320 including full Daewoo 3-year servicing and warranty package. Qualifies for reduced annual VED. Handles well enough given its obvious limitations. More powerful version on the way, seen testing at over 100mph.

WHAT'S BAD

800cc 50bhp engine not quite up to motorway travel. Rolled over on high speed reverse-turn by 'Autocar' magazine. Trim quality not brilliant. Terrible Neil Lyndon road test report in *Sunday Telegraph* on 4/10/98. Relatively poor performance in simulated NCAP crash tests by German TUV.

WHAT TO WATCH OUT FOR

Proper Daewoo/Halfords service history.

LANOS

WHAT'S GOOD

Rover 200 sized. Lots of standard features, including power steering, twin airbags, three-years routine servicing included in price. Better value than a Rover 200. Decent colours and paint. Doesn't look naff and cheapskate. 74 bhp 1.4 or 105bhp 1.6. £10,700 l.6 comes with standard ABS, aircon, electric mirrors and electric windows. Has sold well to private market. Average performance in NCAP crash tests.

WHAT'S BAD

A bit nondescript. Not

particularly nice to drive. Interiors not great. Smaller than Nexia, so less space for rear passengers and luggage.

WHAT TO WATCH OUT FOR

A reasonable new car buy for a certain type of owner. Questionable used car buy because why would anyone sell it before they had used up the three-year deal? Used Lanos at Daewoo 'Motor Shows' likely to be ex-rental.

NEXIA

WHAT'S GOOD

Based on the old (pre-1991) Astra with 1.5 litre 75bhp and 90bhp engines. Lots of kit as standard, including power steering and ABS on even the most basic cars. Aircon was a buyer-tempting standard fit from May 1996. 4-speed auto optional from October 1995. Used models sensibly priced for the age and specification.

WHAT'S BAD

New cars priced to include the Daewoo Deal, so initially lost value very quickly (bounced back up once the public realised what value they were). Poor ride and handling by late 1990s standards. ABS is a desirable feature, but very expensive and an MOT failure when it goes wrong. The booted version looks hideous.

WHAT TO WATCH OUT FOR

Needs frequent brake fluid changes to prevent damage to ABS. Watch out for kerbing damage. Expect trim troubles, particularly driver's door seal. Creaks and rattles are normal from ageing design. May have been bought by elderly people with no previous experience of PAS. Popular with Motability lessees, so may be holes where cars have been adapted.

RECALLS

1997 (to May '95): Check engine bay wiring harness

routing (helpline: 0800 060606).

NUBIRA

WHAT'S GOOD

Second generation Daewoo, sized between old Nexia and Espero. British designed. Usual Daewoo Deal benefits. 1.6 litre twin cam 90bhp engine or 2 litre twin cam 132bhp quite powerful for car's size. Useful, good looking estate. Standard ABS and aircon across the range. Sensibly priced by UK standards when Daewoo Deal is taken into consideration. Sells well in UK. Early bigger headlight facelift in Spring 1999

WHAT'S BAD

Engines a bit coarse. Estate car load area suffers from rear suspension intrusion.

WHAT TO WATCH OUT FOR

Not a bad new car buy for those not seeking the ultimate in refinement and handling. Used Nubiras at Daewoo 'Motor Shows' likely to be ex-rental, so check carefully for careless driver or accident damage. Watch out for uneven front tyre wear from kerbed and bent front suspension.

ESPERO

WHAT'S GOOD

Lots and lots of car for the money. Even better used value than the Nexia and much better looking. 1.8 CDi has standard aircon which will always make it a good Summer seller. Makes a perfect replacement for those who mourn the passing of the Montego saloon. May have some of its original 3-year warranty left. Not my cup of tea, but two-year-old 1.8 CDis at £5,500–£6,000 still recommended. 105bhp 2.0CDXi worth £500 more.

WHAT'S BAD

Infra dig at first, but now

accepted. Interior trim not as good as exterior of car. May suffer premature front tyre wear. Not great at fuel economy. Aircon has been known to pack up. Not worth much after 3-year warranty and service contract end.

WHAT TO WATCH OUT FOR

Why bother with base spec 90 bhp 1.5GLXi when 95bhp 1.8CDi is only a few hundred pounds more? Esperos struggled to sell at first, many went onto rental fleets where they could have suffered damage to front suspension. As a second-hand buy they have been popular as mini cabs, so watch out for clocking when buying third-hand. If it hasn't been serviced on time, why not? (The first three years routine serviced were included in the price.) Make sure the ABS works properly as this is expensive to replace. Check under oil filler cap for emulsion as expansion tank pipe has

been known to blow off leading to overheating and warped cylinder head. Bonnet catches break, so you have to ask yourself how long it has been broken and how long since anyone looked underneath. Central locking can play up. Make sure a/c blows cold.

LEGANZA

WHAT'S GOOD

Bigger than the Espero and almost in the Galant/Passat size category, but much cheaper and in UK terms a 'new car bargain'. Loaded with kit, including ABS, aircon, electric windows, height-adjustable seats. £13,800 SX better value than £15,000 CDX. New car Daewoo Deal includes three-year warranty and servicing. Daewoo's best car so far. Well taken to by public.

WHAT'S BAD

Not the world's greatest

driver's car, but how you judge it depends on what you're used to.

Very sensible new car buy for people who want a biggish motor.

DAIHATSU

MIRA (1993–95)

WHAT'S GOOD

Cheap updated Domino a useful, school run special and likely to qualify for reduced rate VED. Reliable and frugal on fuel.

WHAT'S BAD

Not happy on motorways. Very light build.

WHAT TO WATCH OUT FOR

High mileage would be quite unusual. Kerbing could damage structure as well as front suspension. Look for dings and dents and especially rust as this will seriously weaken an already weak structure. Emulsified oil under the oil filler cap a sure sign of short run syndrome.

As long as exhaust not smoking white, this should be curable with a flush and oil change. Oil is best changed every six months, but make sure it hasn't been left to more than a year. Timing belt needs changing every three years.

CUORE (from 1997)

WHAT'S GOOD

Replaced Mira. Little screamer of an engine. Prices start at £5,995 for three door 'Start' model, rise to £9,750 for turbocharged all-wheel-drive 660cc Cuore Avanzato TR-XX R4. Standard model useful for school run and likely to qualify for reduced rate VED. Reliable and frugal on fuel. Easy to steer and park. Slow depreciator both in percentage terms and money terms.

WHAT'S BAD

Handling and drivability okay, but nothing special. Transmission whines. Did not do well in German TUV/Auto Bild front offset crash tests.

WHAT TO WATCH OUT FOR

Front suspension damage and excessive tyre wear. Make sure brake servo is assisting the brakes. Uneven tyre wear on souped up Avanzato. Supermarket carpark dings and dents. Emulsified oil under the oil filler cap a sure sign of short run syndrome. Check for tears and damage to trim.

MOVE

WHAT'S GOOD

Low centre of gravity means it handled surprisingly well in *The Daily Telegraph* 'slalom' test. Little screamer of an engine. More fun to drive than bigger Suzuki Wagon R. Restyled for 1999 model year.

WHAT'S BAD

Costs less than £4,000 in Japan. Looks like a phone box on wheels. Feels like it's made out of Bacofoil (don't have an accident in one). Not much room inside. Large glass area and lots of bare metal means it suffers severe condensation in winter. Though road wheels are tiny, still has a 'space saver' spare.

WHAT TO WATCH OUT FOR

Any damage likely to be obvious, but a kerbing or serious potholing could damage the structure as well as the suspension. Has a timing belt which will need to be changed every three years or so.

SIRION

Cheap, well-built small 5-door hatchback with three-year warranty. Lots of safety kit (but see TUV test results). Optional 4-speed autobox.

Peculiar looking. 3-cylinder 989cc 54bhp engine needs working hard to deliver acceptable performance. Did not do well in German TUV/Auto Bild front offset crash tests.

Nothing specific as yet, but make sure car has proper franchise service history.

CHARADE (1987–93)

Good looking. 993cc 3-cylinder 99bhp GTti very quick and lots of fun to drive. 52bhp Charade 1.0 CXs decent enough pre-cat

superminis. PAS was available from September 1990 in CX Special and 2-speed autos. 1.3 litre 16-valve 4-cylinder 75bhp pre-cat engines were more robust. 89bhp 'cat' engine launched July 1991. 1.3s had 3-speed rather than 2-speed auto. There was an ultra-economical 3-cylinder 993cc 46bhp turbodiesel from 1987 to 93.

Light build now that the cars are getting old. 2-speed auto struggles. Plasticky interior and not great to drive. Ride and handling of all but GTti not quite up to the mark. Most diesels kicked off their lives with driving schools.

GTti very likely to have been thrashed. All models likely to be showing their age by now, could have some rust which will weaken an already light structure. GTti needs expert servicing –

can't be done by the bloke with the lock up round the corner. Only buy GTti from enthusiastic owners who have changed the oil every 3,000 miles. Timing belts need replacing every three years. Watch out for uneven tyre wear on all models and excessive tyre scrub on GTti.

CHARADE (from 1993)

WHAT'S GOOD

Much more highly rated than previous model. Grew up with starter engine now an 84bhp 1.3 litre catalysed four. Also an 88bhp 1.5, a 105 bhp 1.6 and, from February 1997, a 97bhp 1.3 GTi with lowered suspension, ABS and alloys. All light and easy to drive. All got drivers airbags from January 1988.

WHAT'S BAD

Not much boot space and still has poor ride quality.

WHAT TO WATCH OUT FOR

Lasts quite well. But check carefully for short run syndrome (mayonnaise under the oil filler and a rusty rear silencer). First GTis should have had a brake fluid change. Airbag may have gone off for no reason and the steering wheel trim panel simply stuck back on.

APPLAUSE

WHAT'S GOOD

Looks like a 3-box saloon, but is really a hatchback. Can be reliable, efficient and good value but has no image whatsoever. People may wonder what it is, but won't bother to ask. All had 1.6 litre engines: 91bhp with carb; 105bhp with injection. PAS always standard.

WHAT'S BAD

Very light 'feel-free' power steering, soggy ride, uninspiring plastic trim. Body parts likely to become hard to get.

WHAT TO WATCH OUT FOR

Worn steering, tyres and kerbed front suspension due to lightness of steering. Needs new timing belt every three years. 2nd gear can get noisy. Emulsified oil from short runs from cold lead to premature camshaft, cam follower wear. Injected models have rear discs which may be rusty from lack of use.

GRAND MOVE

WHAT'S GOOD

Charade-based tall estate car (not really an MPV). Grand Move + well equipped with standard aircon and relatively well priced by UK standards. Lots of armrests and cupholders. Optional 4-speed auto. 1.5 litre 88bhp engine. All seats recline flat to form double bed. 'Secret' compartment for valuables. A niche model appealing to an elderly niche market which wants upright seats, cupholders and reclining seats for Sunday outings.

WHAT'S BAD

Not inspiring to drive.

WHAT TO WATCH OUT FOR

See Charade 1993 on.

TERIOS

WHAT'S GOOD

Titchy but tall and narrow 4x4. 82bhp 1,296cc engine, 5-speed gearbox and 4-speed auto option. Terios + has alloys, aircon, passenger airbag and electric front windows. Very capable off road and one of the lightest 4x4s you can buy which helps enormously in snow. Starting prices under £10,000.

WHAT'S BAD

Some people might think it looks a bit silly.

WHAT TO WATCH OUT FOR

Unlikely to have seen hard off-road use, but sold by

same dealers who sell Fourtrak so could have gone to a farmer's kids.

SPORTRAK

WHAT'S GOOD

Cheap, niche, short wheelbase 4x4 with 94bhp 1.6 litre petrol engines. Hood, hardtop or both, depending on model.

WHAT'S BAD

Not much room in the back. Hard top components hard to store and quite a job to remove. Not really strong enough for serious off roading. Some of the trim is a bit flimsy. Very hard ride, not very stable at speed and a bit slow on the road.

WHAT TO WATCH OUT FOR

Probably has seen some off road use, most likely launching sailing dinghies. Do all the usual 4x4 checks and have a good look for rust from salt-water.

FOURTRAK

WHAT'S GOOD

The Yorkshire farmer's favourite. Tough as old boots. Very good at towing. Independent model from July 1993 by far the best. 2 litre 87–90bhp engine lasted from Jan 89 to July 93, otherwise all diesel. Slow 72bhp non-turbo 2.8 from Jan 89–July 93; 90bhp turbo 2.0 from Jan '90 to July '93; 101bhp turbo 2.8 TDS from July '93 also has automatically freewheeling front hubs. Power then cut to 97bhp from March '96 to meet new emissions regs. Lots of special editions include 'Timberline'. 'Anjou' and 'Riviera'. Discovery style side-facing jump seats in back okay for short trips but not for long ones.

WHAT'S BAD

Since it's a farmers' car, it has probably seen some hard use by farmers. Pre 'Independent' models have harsh ride from two solid axles. Disadvantage of only three doors makes getting into the mid-row seats difficult.

WHAT TO WATCH OUT FOR

What's it been towing? If it has a tow hook, check transmission carefully. Give it a really thorough 4x4 check. Expect bodywork, suspension, axle, steering, exhaust and general underside damage as these cars are rarely bought by townies. Look for oil smoke from worn turbo bearings, burned-out turbo oil seals.

FERRARI

F355

WHAT'S GOOD

Stunning looks. Stunning performance. Stunning handling. Low depreciation. Jeremy Clarkson bought one with his own money so it must be really special.

WHAT'S BAD

Brakes aren't as good as some race drivers expected. Enormously high maintenance costs whether you used the car or not. Frequent timing belt replacement essential.

WHAT TO WATCH OUT FOR

Repaired accident damage. Lack of maintenance (very common among little-used supercars). Flat battery. Rusted discs. Seized handbrakes. Any sign of emulsion in the engine oil. Clutch cables go (Jeremy's did). Badly worn tyres (from 'track days'). Needs new timing belts every 12,000 miles – job costs £1,000 plus.

RECALLS

1997: 120 cars recalled due to "fire risk caused by possible fuel leak". 1998:

Recall over possible fault with steering column bolt.

F360

WHAT'S GOOD

Brilliant sportscar. Even better than 355. 400bhp at 8,000rpm and 275 lb ft at 4,750rpm. Out-pointed all comers at *Autocar* magazine's 1999 handling day at Oulton Park.

WHAT'S BAD

One of the few cars selling at a significant premium in 1999 and still very hard to get.

WHAT TO WATCH OUT FOR

Repaired accident damage, etc. (see F355).

FIAT

PANDA

WHAT'S GOOD

Simple, practical, cheap car. 999cc 'Fire' engines good for well over 200,000 miles. Late Pandas had electro galvanized panels. 4x4 was best lightweight 4x4 of the lot (I found one that had done well over 200,000 miles). They're still being made (But, sadly, with the 899cc pushrod Seicento engine rather than the ohc 'Fire' engine.)

WHAT'S BAD

All but the latest Pandas rusted from new. 'Old' pushrod 903cc engine should be avoided. Selecta troublesome and dear to fix. Can suffer cold starting problems. Clutch cables snap. Wheel bearings go. Suspension bushes wear.

WHAT TO WATCH OUT FOR

Rust. Fall-apart trim. Don't pay extra for low mileage. Many low mileage cars serviced once every two years or worse. Look for wear in 4x4 drivetrain. Bounce the car on its suspension to make sure shocks are still absorbing. Mayonnaise under oil filler denotes life of short runs, never properly warmed up. Oil leaks common. Timing chain gets noisy on 903cc pushrod engine (not recommended). Make sure timing belt changed recently on 'Fire' engines. Check tyres for uneven wear. Any clunks selecting 'drive' on the 'Selecta', avoid like the plague.

CINQUECENTO

WHAT'S GOOD

Cinquecento Sporting 1.1 litre 'Fire' engine from Punto 55 is by far the best engine and the most likely to get some proper exercise.

WHAT'S BAD

Polish build quality. Not as practical as the Panda. Cinquecento 900s have the old 899cc pushrod engine which can suffer premature rocker shaft wear. Rear window can break if you shut the hatch from one side.

WHAT TO WATCH OUT FOR

Lack of maintenance and 'short run syndrome' typical of city cars. Ticking tappets. Duff cats. Signs of careless driving by inexperienced youngsters. Check trim for damage. Make sure has 'Red Key'.

SEICENTO

WHAT'S GOOD

Replaced Cinquecento in Spring 1998. Much cuter looking with optional PAS and optional citymatic autoclutch. The best model to my mind is the SX-based 'En Suite' which has a bigger, longer-lasting 1,108cc 'Fire' engine, standard PAS and aircon.

WHAT'S BAD

Most models still have 899cc version of old Fiat 903cc pushrod engine. 'En Suite' and 'Sporting' models miss out on £100pa VED by 8ccs.

WHAT TO WATCH OUT FOR

As Cinquecento. Make sure has 'Red Key'.

UNO

WHAT'S GOOD

Some panels galvanized from 1990 when all acquired plastic hatchback. 999cc 'Fire' engine good for 200,000 miles plus with proper maintenance. Good range of bright metallic colours, including a really nice metallic blue. Uno 1.0 'Start' models were well equipped and great bargains. Low insurance means they make good sense for youngsters.

WHAT'S BAD

Avoid the 903cc 'Uno 45' engine (the timing chain and valve gear rattle and it's well past its sell-by date). Unos look like refrigerators in white. Many started their UK lives on rental fleets. Privately owned Unos used for shopping and the school run never warm up, contaminate their oil and suffer premature engine wear.

WHAT TO WATCH OUT FOR

Rust by the bucket load in pre-1990 facelift models. Duff catalytic converters. Kerbing damage. Bonnet catches break, so you have to ask yourself how long it has been broken and how long since anyone looked underneath. Selecta best avoided due to potentially expensive problems.

PUNTO (to Autumn 1999)

WHAT'S GOOD

The best designed small car in the world and a worthy 'Car of the Year' award winner. Excellent upright seating. 4-door SX and ELX versions have height-adjustable seats and steering wheels and are the easiest cars for the elderly to get in and out of. Best of the range are basic 55 or 60 three door models with sunroofs 85 SX 5-doors with standard PAS. Galvanized bodies won't rust unless accident damaged. Cheap 'nearly-new' because most start their lives on rental fleets. Amazing range of bright and attractive metallic colours best of which is 'Rialto' blue and adds £200 to the used price. Recommended.

WHAT'S BAD

Choppy ride quality. Handling and roadholding not as good as the latest Fiestas. Rear brake adjusters a bit gimpy. Selecta CVT auto is excellent in theory and practice, but can become troublesome. Diesels not brilliant. Bonnet releases break (see Uno).

Hydraulic clutch slave cylinder may develop a leak. Franchised agents are becoming thin on the ground.

WHAT TO WATCH OUT FOR

Accident damage. Silly damage from careless renters and their kids. Rear suspension arm bushes wear and are expensive to replace (check for uneven rear tyre wear). If test driving a Selecta, make sure the electromagnetic clutch is 100% (there should be no jerk when you put the lever in 'drive', no jerk when you drive away, and no 'creep' at idle). Make sure has 'Red Key'.

RECALLS

1998 (March '97–Nov '97 build): Faulty seat belt pre-tensioner.

PUNTO (from Autumn 1999)

WHAT'S GOOD

Fiat has improved the Punto

in every area where the old model was criticised. The car has a sharp new look that could tempt Polo buyers. New torsion beam rear suspension helps handling and comfort and eliminates the bearing wear problem of the old model. Galvanized bodies won't rust. Amazing range of bright and attractive metallic colours. Height-adjustable steering wheel and drivers seat. Roomy inside. Engines now:- 60bhp 1.2 8v; 80bhp 1.2 16v; 130bhp 1.7 16v; 1.9 60bhp diesel; 1.9 80bhp JTD common rail diesel. 6-speed manual box available with 80bhp 1.2 in 'Sporting' model. 7-speed CVT available with 80bhp 1.2 in 'Speedgear' model or plain CVT with 60bhp 1.2.

WHAT'S BAD

Interior not quite as pleasingly well designed as old model.

WHAT TO WATCH OUT FOR

Make sure has 'Red Key',

otherwise oo soon to say.

TIPO

WHAT'S GOOD

Brilliant, practical design, more roomy inside than any other car in the class before or since. Cheap to buy. Electro galvanized bodies won't rust unless accident damaged and badly repaired. Evocative 'Sedicivalvole' (16-valve) version a bargain performance buy. 1.9 TD quick, economical and cheap to buy once the miles pile on.

WHAT'S BAD

Shape and design qualities not generally appreciated. Dodgy cost-saving digital dash on early 'DGT' versions. 1.6 not much quicker than 1.4. 1.8 not a good engine. Most 1.4ies began their lives on rental fleets. Some reports of non-galvanized subframes rusting prematurely.

WHAT TO WATCH OUT FOR

Leaks between cam carrier and cylinder head of modular 1.4 and 1.6 engines. All need coolant changed every two years, particularly iron block, alloy-headed diesel. Electrics develop problems. Make sure all the lights work. All too easy to cross the threads in the alloy head when replacing spark plugs. Bonnet catches break, begging the question how long since anyone looked underneath.

BRAVO/BRAVA

WHAT'S GOOD

Bravo (three door) styling. Brava (five door) practicality. Particularly good, sharp steering. Easy to use dash-top radio/cassette. Excellent, fully-adjustable seats and steering wheels throughout the range. (Designed by Professor Mark Porter's Ergonomics group at Loughborough University.) 5-cylinder HGT is a powerful, well-balanced 'hot hatch'. Used prices came down sharply in 1998/99. Diesel Bravas particularly well priced at 6 months old with 12,000–16,000 miles (just over £8,000 from a nearly-new specialist). Even better range of metallic colours than Punto. 'Ink Black' and 'Juvarra Ivory' best of the lot.

WHAT'S BAD

Many UK cars begin their lives on rental fleets. First thing that breaks is the cassette lid. Bravos (three door) about £1,000 dearer than more practical (five door) Bravas. Bravas can be affected by side winds. Two Star below average performance in NCAP crash tests. Small number of cars have suffered from faulty engine speed sensor leading to erratic running and cut-outs.

WHAT TO WATCH OUT FOR

Cassette lid. Silly damage from careless renters and their kids. Check aircon on cars so fitted. Check operation of electric sunroof and windows if fitted. Have had reports of premature HT lead failure which could, in turn, spike the catalytic converter. Bonnet catches break (see Tipo). Plastic timing belt tensioner pulley can shatter without warning. Best to change timing belt and tensioner every three years/35,000 miles. Make sure has 'Red Key'.

RECALLS

1997 (1996–97 build: 17,000 cars): Petrol may contaminate brake vacuum diaphragm leading to loss of power assistance to brakes. 1998: Fiat Bravo/Brava 1.4 and 1.6 with ABS built before Oct '97: Check for chafing of brake hoses.

MAREA

WHAT'S GOOD

As Bravo/Brava. Useful 'Weekend' estate. Tremendous 125bhp diesel followed by even better 130bhp JTD.

WHAT'S BAD

Ugly.

WHAT TO WATCH OUT FOR

As Bravo/Brava. Make sure has 'Red Key'.

RECALLS

1998: 1.6 16v, non-ABS: Check for chafing of brake hoses; 1999: 1.8, 2.0 and 1.9TDS (1993–96 build): Front coil springs

BARCHETTA

WHAT'S GOOD

Cute, 1,800cc twin-cam, front wheel drive sportscar with some nice design touches.

WHAT'S BAD

Left-hand drive only. Most will have been personally imported from Europe where they can cost as little as £10,000 new.

WHAT TO WATCH OUT FOR

Imports with the wrong lights and speedos being re-sold as UK market cars at UK car prices. Make sure has 'Red Key'.

RECALLS

1999: Problem of sticking control valve for engine variable valve timing – makes engine sound like a diesel. Announced on BBC Watchdog 21/1/99.

COUPE

WHAT'S GOOD

Great looking coupe, initially with twin cam 2 litre 4-cylinder 16v injected or turbo engines, then with 2 litre 5-cylinder 20-valve injected or turbo engines. 6-speed gearbox from 2000.

WHAT'S BAD

Back seat only suitable for dwarfs and pre-teen children. Quality/assembly problems.

WHAT TO WATCH OUT FOR

Signs of being hard driven or badly driven. Avoid any cars with kerbed wheels.Make sure has 'Red Key'.

MULTIPLA

WHAT'S GOOD

Bravo-based, but shorter. Six seats in two rows of three, all with proper three-point belts. Funky interior styling. Dashboard gearshift, so no obstructions in the floor. Excellent 105bhp 1.9JTD engine pulled it to 115mph on the Millbrook bowl, so must be more aerodynamic than it looks. Bright range of colours.

WHAT'S BAD

Controversial looks. Roll understeer on tight bends. A long step up to the seats and down from them for the elderly or infirm (though less-so from a high kerb). Comparatively poor performance in TUV/Auto

Bild front offset crash test.

WHAT TO WATCH OUT FOR

Make sure has 'Red Key', otherwise too soon to say.

ULYSSE

(See Citroen Synergie. Has PSA XUD diesel rather than Fiat engine.)

FORD

KA, KA², KA³

WHAT'S GOOD

Like it or lump it styling. Flexible edges good for parking bumps. Good ride comfort. Great handling. With PAS, nice to drive, easy to park. Aircon available.

WHAT'S BAD

Endura E 1.3 pushrod engine very long in the tooth, can develop camshaft trouble. Not much space in the back. Doors unprotected from parking damage. Have been complaints of over-servoed brakes.

WHAT TO WATCH OUT FOR

Flaking paint. Suspension damage from kerbing.

Hidden damage underneath deformable ends. Kids sweets, etc.stuck to carpet and seats. Aircon much better than an aftermarket sunroof.

RECALLS

1998 Kas with ABS (Mar '98–Sep '98): Brake master cylinder may fail.

FIESTA (1977–89)

WHAT'S GOOD

Low insurance groups. Cheap and simple. 'Valencia' pushrod engines are long-lasting as long as the cars get driven. Spares cheap and second-hand parts plentiful. Larger 1.3 and 1.4

CVH engines best avoided apart from 1.6 CVH in XR2. CTX auto could be reliable in 84–89 cars.

WHAT'S BAD

Too light. 'Square front' (pre-1984 model year) very rust-prone, particularly front inner wings just above strut top mountings. A rust-weakened light car is a disaster waiting to happen, particularly with young people aboard. 'Round front' 1984-89 Fiestas has improved anti rust treatment, but nearly all these cars are now more than ten years old and need checking carefully.

WHAT TO WATCH OUT FOR

Rust. 'Short run syndrome' because many were used for shopping by elderly ladies and never got properly warmed up. A 10-year-old Fiesta with 25,000 miles will be close to needing a new engine and clutch. On the other hand a white socks and back-to-front baseball cap XR2 might have been surprisingly well cared for apart from huge holes in the parcel shelf for oversize speakers.

RECALLS

(None known 1994–98, but check seatbelt inertia reels.)

FIESTA (1989–95, continued as CLASSIC to Jan 1997)

WHAT'S GOOD

A bigger, better Fiesta with more than a hint of the Peugeot 205 about it. The cheapest, most basic ones seem to be the best. Some 1.3s had power steering.

WHAT'S BAD

Roadholding and handling a far cry from 205s higher standards. Fiestas suffered badly from catalysation in 1992. 1.3s from this date on were almost unbelievably slow. CTX autoboxes became troublesome due to oil leak.

WHAT TO WATCH OUT FOR

Front suspension bushes wear and suspension likely to have been 'kerbed'. Be very wary of uneven front tyre wear. Brake discs don't last long and can start to judder after 20,000 miles. CVHs need regular timing belt changes. Timing chains of 1.1 and 1.3 pushrod engines can start to rattle. Engines suffer badly from sludging up due to short run syndrome and insufficiently frequent oil changes. More than its fair share of recalls, so satisfy yourself that the recall work has been carried out. Make sure nylon timing belt idler gear in diesel engine has been replaced with a steel idler. 1.4CVHs with ECUs may suffer starting and running problems due to the flywheel sensor connector becoming loose.

RECALLS

1995 (VIN: SK, SD): Tyres may be incorrectly fitted. 1995 (VIN: SE): Brake lights may not work. 1995 (Ford Fiesta diesels: VIN: SIGHS, ST): Brake vacuum pump may not create enough vacuum for servo. 1996: (March 1989F–Sept 1990H build: Check for possibility of front seatbelt inertia reel locking mechanism failure.

NEW FIESTA 1995–99

WHAT'S GOOD

Zippy 1.25 Zetec 'S' engines. Nice power steering. Vastly improved chassis offering excellent ride, handling, and roadholding. Good fun to drive. Came out well in NCAP crash tests. Favourable insurance ratings due to reduced damageability and improved reparability. (NEW, HEAVILY REVISED FIESTA DUE YEAR 2000, CHECK FRANKFURT SHOW.)

WHAT'S BAD

1.3 'Endura' pushrod engines starting to show their age. Cabin lower and not as roomy as Punto, Ibiza, Polo. Water ingress via ventilation system.

WHAT TO WATCH OUT FOR

Have been a number of recalls. Double recall over front brake pipes because original recall failed to remedy the problem. Make sure these have been carried out.

RECALLS

1995 (VIN SE): Brake lights may not work. 1995 (VIN SY, SS, ST): Brake vacuum pump may not create enough vacuum for servo. 1996 (Fiesta and Courier van 1996 model year – 47,500 cars): Check for faulty piston seal in hydraulic clutch master cylinder. Check for contamination of brake fluid and incorrect front brake hose routing. 1997 (5-door models built Oct '95–May '96): may have faulty rear door latches. 1998 (July 1995–June 1996 build – 67,000 cars): Possibility of brake failure due to front brake pipe chafing on bracket. Modified pipe and bracket to be fitted to both front brakes. (Repeat brake pipe recall announced on radio 12/2/98). Fiestas with ABS (Mar '98–Sep '98): Brake master cylinder may fail. Fiestas with passenger airbags built Aug '96–Feb '97: passenger airbag may go off while car is stationary.

NEW FIESTA (from 2000)

WHAT'S GOOD

New face to old favourite. 104bhp Zetec S should be fun and a good substitute for the old Peugeot 205GTi. There will be a sub-1.1 litre Zetec 'S' engine to qualify for reduced-rate VED.

WHAT'S BAD

It is an OLD favourite as basic bodyshell dates back to 1989.

WHAT TO WATCH OUT FOR

Too soon to say.

PUMA

WHAT'S GOOD

Highly rated, brilliant handling Fiesta-based coupe. Yamaha developed 125bhp 1.7 litre Zetec S engine supplemented by 90bhp 1.4 Zetec S in February 1998.

WHAT'S BAD

There was quite a waiting list. Could suffer similar brake problems to Fiesta. Long-term life of special bore linings of 1.7 unknown in day-to-day use, though no problems to date.

WHAT TO WATCH OUT FOR

Possibility of having been thrashed. Check the oil level as well as oil colour of 1.7s. 5,000 mile oil changes far more sensible than Ford recommended 10,000 mile intervals. Don't switch to fully synthetic oil without written approval from Ford as may affect bore liners. Kerbing will throw out critical front suspension alignment. Uneven front tyre wear should put you on your guard. Don't pay too much just to get one.

RECALLS

1998 (built Mar '98–Sep '98): 4,500 Pumas recalled to have brake master cylinder replaced.

ESCORT (1983–91)

WHAT'S GOOD

Popular.

WHAT'S BAD

They rust badly underneath. CVH engines choke themselves to death with black sludge.

WHAT TO WATCH OUT FOR

Crash repaired, cloned, clocked, stolen in their thousands. An Escort bought in 1998 may have been stolen and ringed ten years ago and never been noticed. Often fail the MOT on structural rust before 10 years old.

ESCORT (1991–99)

WHAT'S GOOD

Popular. Bland, but not bad looking. Handling and roadholding improved through the car's model life and 'wide mouth' cars from 1995 model year on by far the best. Almost all of these later models from LX up have power steering.

WHAT'S BAD

Had a terrible start. Early cars were a disgrace with awful handling, terrible steering and suspect body-shells which rotted in the bulkhead and around the rear window. Early diesels had overstrength valve springs which caused them to snap their cambelts. Early Zetec engines from 1992 suffered sticky valves (see Mondeo). Rear trailing arms of suspension up to 1995 were too weak and twist when they're not supposed to. Mid-life 'oval grille' facelift looks terrible and very dated. Fuse boxes rust out. Two Star below average performance in 1999 NCAP secondary safety tests.

WHAT TO WATCH OUT FOR

Bodged rust repairs on early cars. Clocked mega-mile ex-fleet cars. Inadequate 'home servicing'. Poor quality aftermarket parts – especially brake parts. Check for uneven tyre wear due to suspension damage from kerbing. Electrics may play up (check for damp and/or rusting inside fusebox). Rear suspension arms flex too much and may weaken as a result (16vs were strengthened with rear anti-roll bar). Some 1992/93 Escorts came out of the factory with misaligned front suspension which caused the insides of the front tyres to wear excessively. Diesels should have had nylon timing belt idler replaced with a steel idler. These should both have been sorted out 'in service', but if the car was maintained 'in house' by a fleet or by a private owner, it may not have been done.

RECALLS

1994 (1.3 and 1.4CFi – 92 VIN NE, NL, NY, NS, NT; 93 VIN PJ, PU, PM, PP, PB, PR, PA, PG, PC, PK): Electrical check. 1995 (VIN: SE): Brake lights may not work. 1995 (Escort diesels: VIN: SY, SS, ST): Brake vacuum pump may not create enough vacuum for servo. 1995 (VIN: SE, SL): Loose rear brake cylinders. 1995 (VIN: SC, SK, SD): Possible damage to seat belt webbing. 1998 Escorts with passenger airbags built Aug '96–Feb '98: passenger airbag may go off while car is stationary.

ORION (1983–93)

WHAT'S GOOD

As for equivalent Escort, but with a boot.

WHAT'S BAD

As for equivalent Escort. Diesels more likely to have once been taxis. Orion name dropped in 1993 in favour of 'Escort 4-door' – helped to boost 'Escort' sales figures.

WHAT TO WATCH OUT FOR

As for equivalent Escort.

RECALLS

As for equivalent Escort.

FOCUS (from Oct 1998)

WHAT'S GOOD

1998 Car of the Year and cars in its class come no better. Brave all-new styling. Different from the mainstream. Proper independent rear suspension. Excellent roadholding/handling and ride quality combination on optional 15" wheels fitted with 195/60 tyres. Plenty of leg and headroom inside. Good seats. Multi-adjustable steering wheel. Nice deep door pockets. Close gearbox ratios and precise shift quality (60mph @ 6,500rpm in 2nd). Galvanized body with 12-year anti perforation warranty. Joint top of the class for secondary safety in NCAP tests. Should appeal to the public as well as the fleets. 1.4 and 1.6 16-valve Zetec 'S' engines; same 2 litre 16-valve Zetec engine as Mondeo. You get the feeling that everything has been very carefully thought through. The best Ford ever built. Highly recommended.

WHAT'S BAD

Sharp edges of rear hatch. Bonnet opened by key-lock in grille badge which could be vulnerable to road salt. ABS, aircon etc.all extra bundled in £500 'extras' packs. 1.6 is overgeared at 23.35mph/1,000 rpm

(3,000rpm = 70mph and 6,500rpm would equal 152mph) which gives flat performance at motorway speeds. High price for a car with just a 12 month warranty. Saloon and estate car nothing like as good looking as hatchback.

WHAT TO WATCH OUT FOR

Too new to say.

RECALLS

61,000 cars built September '98–March '99 recalled in July 1999 for better waterproofing of alternators to prevent short-circuits. Announced *Daily Telegraph* 16/7/99. Cars built September–November '98 recalled in October 1999 to cure possible failure of door latches.

SIERRA

WHAT'S GOOD

All independently sprung successor to the Cortina, sold as "man ands machine in perfect harmony". Early 2.0 lire versions were fast cars with 9 second 0-60 and 120 mph max.

WHAT'S BAD

Front suspension wears out and makes it terrible to drive. Sierras are one of the few cars better bought after accident repairs to the front which can make them feel new again. But make sure damage has not crumpled transmission tunnel, severely weakening the shell.

WHAT TO WATCH OUT FOR

Every single trick in the book. Clockers. Cloners. Cut & Shuts. Rust traps in doors. Warped front discs. Cracked heads and oil leaks on two litre twin-cams. Treat all 4x4s and Cosworths with particular suspicion. This is just the tip of the iceberg, so check everything.

MONDEO (to 2000)

WHAT'S GOOD

Decent build, decent handling, tremendous 'feelgood' factor, multi-adjustable steering (in, out, up, down). Hugely improved from 1997 model year facelift, which made the 5-door much better looking than rather dowdy 93K–96N Mk Is; three lap/diagonal rear belts now standard. Problem-free from '97 model year. Very strong bodyshell at the front. Comparatively good performance in NCAP crash tests. Easy and cheap to repair body damage. 1997 MY on recommended.

WHAT'S BAD

Subframe needs dismantling to change the clutch, making it a £500–£600 job. Incorrect reassembly leads to tracking problems. Sticking valves on 1.6s, 1.8s and 2.0s run short distances on cheap petrol (most have now been cured by 'in-service' modifications which cause engine to use a bit more oil.) Engine management problems on 2.5 24v V6 can burn out catalytic converters (the car has three). 1.8 diesel engine very antiquated. ST 200 has short gears and traction problems. New car due Y2K.

WHAT TO WATCH OUT FOR

Slipping clutch. Baggy suspension. A bang on a speed bump can knock out the otherwise well protected catalytic converter on 4-cylinder cars. Infamous 'pulling to the left' caused by kerbing damage, by worn track control arm bushes, by misaligned reassembly of front subframe after clutch replacement or by failure to re-track properly after replacing track control arms. Look for uneven tyre wear (outer shoulder wear normal). Early (1993) Mondeos prone to starter motor failure. If ABS fitted, make sure light goes out

after 3 seconds or new pump or ECU may be needed. Shafts of front electric window winder mechanism can go: make sure both work. More than its fair share of recalls. The Mondeo is a bigger, heavier, wider car than the Sierra. May not fit your garage. If automatic, make sure shifts are smooth and check ATF. Should be red, not black. Timing belts on Zetec petrol engines last five years or 80,000 miles, but belts on diesels only good for three years or 36,000 miles. Suspension bags out after 120,000 miles.

RECALLS

1994 (92 VIN NY, NS, NT; 93 VIN PJ, PU, PM, PP, PB, PR, PA, PG, PC, PK, PD, PE; 94 VIN RL, RY, RS, RT, RJ, RU, RM): Headlamp failure. 1995 (Mondeo diesels: VIN: SY, SS, ST): Brake vacuum pump may not create enough vacuum for servo. 1995: Fuel pipe. 1995: (VIN: RP, RB, RR): Static sparks may occur when refuelling. 1996: "Free recall" (per 'What Car?' 9/96 p. 132) to sort out problem of sticking valves – work will usually be carried out when car is in for a routine service. 1996 (1996 model year with hydraulic clutch – excluding V6): Check, replace if necessary clutch master cylinder/slave cylinder. Check front brake callipers. 1997: (24v built 1/8/94–14/6/96 – 9,000 cars): Free official recall to replace catalytic converter closest to exhaust manifold. 1998 Mondeos with passenger airbags built Aug '96–Feb '97: passenger airbag may go off while car is stationary. Ford Mondeo V6 with ABS(Dec '97–Jan '98): ABS System may fail. Cars built September–November '98 recalled in October 1999 to cure possible failure of door latches.

MONDEO (from 2000)

WHAT'S GOOD

Too soon to say.

WHAT'S BAD

Too soon to say.

WHAT TO WATCH OUT FOR

Too soon to say.

GRANADA/ SCORPIO

WHAT'S GOOD

Big, soft, comfortable overgrown Sierra. 2 litre twin cam petrol is reasonably economical.

WHAT'S BAD

Dropped from Ford line-up in April 1998. Autobox problems common from 60,000 miles. ECU problems common, leading to catalytic converter problems. Fuseboxes vulnerable and contacts rust. Standard ABS costs a fortune to fix. Timing chain of 24v only lasts 60,000 miles. Cracked heads and oil leaks on two litre twin-cams.

WHAT TO WATCH OUT FOR

Oil leaks caused by cracked head on 2 litre 16v. Smoking V6s. ABS failure. ECU failure. Fusebox failure. Cat failure. Alternator failure on 2.5TDs (instead of 120 amp alternators, some Turbodiesel models were fitted with 75amp alternators which are not up to the job and cost £900 to replace with 120amp units). 24-valve needs a new timing chain and associated tensioners every 60,000 miles. Autoboxes only last 60,000–80,000 miles. Clocking rife on these cars. Avoid 4x4.

RECALLS

1996 (Aug '94–Jul '96): Check for sticking throttle due to corrosion by road salt. 1996 (Feb '96–March '96): Rear axle mounting may loosen. 1997: TSB 21: replace 75amp alternators with 120 amp alternators on 2.5 litre Turbodiesel models. 1998 Scorpios with passenger airbags built Aug '96–Feb '98: passenger airbag may go off while car is stationary.

GALAXY

WHAT'S GOOD

Good styling, low wind noise, decent handling, nice to drive. Up to seven proper seats. TDI 90 takes 10,000 miles to run-in, then goes quite well and delivers 38 mpg fuel economy. Similar VW Sharan was a three star performer in NCAP crash tests (6 points front impact; 15 points side impact).

WHAT'S BAD

Hard to park. 2.8 VR6 okay in manual form but VR6 autos gobble fuel. Below average 'customer satisfaction'. You have to open the doors to turn the GLs front seats right round. Lots of quality problems and falling sales led Ford to pull out of the joint production venture in Portugal and values then fell heavily.

WHAT TO WATCH OUT FOR

Make sure 7-seaters are genuine seven seaters with rearmost area heating and not just 5-seaters with two extra seats clipped in. Make sure recall work carried out.

RECALLS

1996 (April '96–July '96): Check for overheating of brake system. 1996 (2-litre with air-conditioning – Jan '95–Feb '96): Aircon compressor may seize up. 1997 (built Jan '96–Apr '97): check optional child seats.

PROBE

WHAT'S GOOD

First fruit of Ford's gradual buying into Mazda. launched in the USA in 1992. Essentially a re-styled Mazda MX6 with the same smooth and revvy quad-cam 163bhp V6, but also offered with a 2 litre 128bhp four from the 626. Only started to sell once it dropped to a sensible price on the used market and actually bounced back for a year or so.

WHAT'S BAD

A model Ford would prefer to forget. Huge and variable panel gaps. Not enough rear legroom. Harsh ride. Far too expensive new. A Ford agent even tried to pre-interest the trade with a UK 'K' registered 3,000 mile LHD 24v. Between December 1992 and January 1993 it dropped from a top 'bid' of £14,800 to £12,700, clearly showing that a list price of £19,350 was pie in the sky.

WHAT TO WATCH OUT FOR

Accident damage. And the sort of deterioration that results from sitting around unsold in compounds (rusty discs, rusty exhaust, flat battery, a/c u/s, etc.) 2 litre best avoided. V6 may need a new timing belt.

COUGAR

WHAT'S GOOD

Sharp-suited Mondeo coupe with Mondeo 2 litre and 2.5 litre engines. Good looking and different. Low wind noise. 2.5 V6 recovers lost speed extremely well. Handles and holds the road well nicely without much understeer. Effective 'eyeball' vents. Sensible boot. Fold-down rear seats ideal for golf clubs. Rear view mirror well placed for motorways and heavy traffic. Sounds a bit like an Alfa 156 2.5 V6. 30mpg possible from 2.5 litre; 36 + from 2.0.

WHAT'S BAD

Hopeless rear headroom. Harsh, crashy ride. Quite a few rattles, even when new. Console straight out of Mondeo. 2.5 V6 lacks low-down torque and needs to be revved for maximum effect (red-line only starts at 7,000rpm). Short-range tank only good for 300 miles at a push. Odometer under-reads by 2%.

WHAT TO WATCH OUT FOR

Too soon to say

RECALLS

Cars built Sept– Nov '98 recalled in October 1999 to cure possible failure of door latches.

MAVERICK

WHAT'S GOOD

Nissan Terrano II with Ford badge. Reasonably effective off road. LWB 5-door model has 7-seat option. High driving position. High and low range gears. 2.7 TD got power boost from 100bhp to 125bhp in July 1996 and this is the best engine to go for. 3-year dealer warranty to match Nissan's for Terrano II.

WHAT'S BAD

Dropped from Ford line-up April 1998. 4x4 on-road handling. Dropped from Ford line up in April 1998 along with Scorpio. Very high and narrow looking, so not bought by suburbanites as a style statement.

WHAT TO WATCH OUT FOR

Make all usual 4x4 hard usage checks, especially if fitted with a tow hook. Tends to suffer premature wheel bearing wear. TD needs oil changes at least every 5,000 miles to protect turbo from coking up and rest of engine from burned out oil. be very wary of blue oil smoke from burned out turbo oil seals.

RECALLS

1995 (Maverick with Michelin 215/80 R15 tyres – VIN: PM, PP, PB, PR, PA, PG, PK, PD, PE, RL, RY, RS, RT, RJ, RV, RM, RP, RB, RA): Tyres may lose pressure.

EXPLORER

WHAT'S GOOD

Starred along with the other dinosaurs in 'Jurassic Park'. American alternative to the Range Rover and Jeep Grand Cherokee. Quite a good towcar for people with twin-wheel 20' caravans.

WHAT'S BAD

Oversize and over here. Not as well rust-proofed in body cavities as you might expect. Fuel consumption difficult to justify.

WHAT TO WATCH OUT FOR

More of a suburban status symbol than a serious off roader. Look for damage due to underestimated vehicle size.

RECALLS

Oil pump recall notice issued January 1998. Explorer TSBs (Technical Service Bulletins) include curing a transmission shudder. Warning in May 1998 that accelerator may be jammed open by the driver's floormat.

HONDA

LOGO

WHAT'S GOOD

Worthy, perpendicular small three-door hatchback sold in Europe for more than a year finally reaches UK in Y2K. 1,343cc 64bhp engine with 80 lb ft torque. Did reasonably well in German TUV/Auto Bild front offset crash tests.

WHAT'S BAD

Styling isn't exactly inspired.

WHAT TO WATCH OUT FOR

Too soon to say.

UK CONCERTO

WHAT'S GOOD

Smooth Honda engines: Pre-cat 88bhp 1.4; 106bhp 1.6; 130bhp twin cam 1.6 to August 1991. Post-cat 89bhp 1.5; 110bhp 1.6; 121bhp 1.6i-16 from August 1991. Twin-cam 16-valve cars were quick. Smooth 4-speed autos. Decent UK build quality formerly from Rover, latterly from new Swindon factory. 'Blaise' run-out 1.6i-16v well liked.

WHAT'S BAD

Same body problems as old Rover 200. Honda engines require more maintenance than Rovers. Honda agent labour rates can be high. Expensive ignition igniters tend to go at 50,000 to 60,000 miles and resulting misfire could hot spot the cat.

WHAT TO WATCH OUT FOR

Rust around windscreen. Rusty sunroof surrounds. Frequent oil changes important – vital with twin cam 16-valve cars. Ignition ignitor problem. High incidence of ABS pump failures when the brake fluid had not been changed regularly.

UK CIVIC

WHAT'S GOOD

'Swindon' 5-door hatchbacks and estate on floorpan shared with Rover 400. 89bhp 1.4, 89 bhp 1.5 VTEC-E, 111bhp 1.6 from 95–97; 112bhp 1.5 VTEC, 114bhp 1.6 and rip roaring 167 bhp 1.8 VTEC from 97 on. Smooth 4-speed autos. 1.5 VTEC-E was capable of 45–50 mpg, but at a price. Very nicely built, under-bonnet looks like Honda motorcycle high tech. VTEC-E replaced by 85 bhp Rover 2.0 DI engine. Average performance in 1998 NCAP safety tests. Two-year warranty grew to three.

WHAT'S BAD

1.5 VTEC-E sometimes seen at head of long traffic queue as elderly driver tries to keep in economy range. 5-door range did not sell as well as Honda might have hoped as still some anti- Japanese ill feeling and 'True Brits' go for the Rover equivalents.

WHAT TO WATCH OUT FOR

Quite a few 1.5 VTEC-Es were laundered into second hand cars via the rental fleets. All 'Swindon Civics' appreciate frequent servicing and clean oil. Some complaints of poor reverse gear selection, so check this on test drive.

JAPANESE CIVIC (1991–96)

WHAT'S GOOD

3-door hatchback with split tailgate; four door saloon. Impressive engines: 74bhp 1.3; 89bhp 1.5; 123bhp 1.6 and 158bhp VTi. 4-speed autos available on 89bhp 1.5 and 123bhp 1.6.

WHAT'S BAD

Very small luggage area in split tailgate hatch. Saloon not as roomy inside as exterior dimensions suggest because roofline is quite low. Honda servicing is usually pricey. Ride not very smooth. Suits the small rather than the tall.

WHAT TO WATCH OUT FOR

Needs to have been regularly serviced, preferably with six monthly oil changes. VTECs must have clean oil and are particularly vulnerable to extended service intervals.

RECALLS

1994: Honda Civic 3-door, 4-door, CRX automatics: auto gear indicator may show wrong transmission mode.

JAPANESE CIVIC (from 1996)

WHAT'S GOOD

Restyled slightly bigger, quieter Civics. 3-door now has conventional hatchback and more luggage space. Engine range now 90bhp 1.4, 114bhp 1.5, 116bhp 1.6, 158bhp VTi. Normal 4-speed auto or option of CVT auto in 116bhp 1.6ES 3-door only. Two-year warranty grew to three.

WHAT'S BAD

Average NCAP crash test results. Goggle-eyed restyle not wholly successful. 3-door side doors very long, so difficult to emerge in tight parking spaces with any dignity.

WHAT TO WATCH OUT FOR

Still quite new and should still be in the hands of Honda agents for servicing. The last thing you want to see in a Honda is dirty oil on the dipstick.

USA CIVIC

WHAT'S GOOD

2-door coupes, launched as 100bhp 1.5s in February 1994 and ran through to January 1996. Then relaunched with same goggle eyed front as Japanese Civics in January 1996 as LS with 103bhp 1.6 or SR with 123bhp 1.6, ABS and alloys. 4-speed auto optional. Aircon optional from June '97. Praised for much softer ride than other Civics. Reasonable rear head and legroom.

WHAT'S BAD

Not much.

WHAT TO WATCH OUT FOR

Same as Japanese Civics.

ACCORD (1989– May 1993)

WHAT'S GOOD

Extremely well regarded, reliable Japanese built saloon cars give ten years fault-free service as long as serviced on time. Badged Acura, have been the USA's top selling car. Healthy 135bhp 2 litre catalysed down to 131bhp from December 1991. Alternative engine was always catalysed 148bhp 2.2. Excellent 4-speed autoboxes. Beautifully built.

WHAT'S BAD

Steering a bit light. Bonded windscreens very difficult to replace and this usually leads to scratches, rust and water ingress around screen area. Sheet metal not as thick as German cars.

WHAT TO WATCH OUT FOR

Tend to be entirely trouble free as long as serviced on time. Check screen area for rust. Make sure aircon blows cold. Aircon may still contain environmentally unfriendly R12 refrigerant. Needs to be recharged with CFC-free 134A refrigerant. Look for uneven tyre wear as a result of kerbing. Check under oil cap for emulsified oil due to short runs from cold stars – also likely to have rotted out rear silencer box.

UK ACCORD (1993–98)

WHAT'S GOOD

Accord saloons built in Swindon. Smooth Swindon built engines: 113 bhp 1.8 from March '96; 129bhp 2.0 from May '93; 148bhp

2.2iVTEC from March '96; 156bhp 2.3iSR from October 93 to March '96. Decent roadholding and handling, especially 2.2 and 2.3. Excellent 4-speed autoboxes. Recommended. Two-year warranty grew to three.

WHAT'S BAD

Steering a bit light. Exhaust rear silencer boxes rot out on low mileage 'short run' examples. New 1999 model instantly 'dates' a 98R old model.

WHAT TO WATCH OUT FOR

Tend to be entirely trouble free as long as serviced on time with regular changes of coolant and brake fluid. Look for stone and screen chips on the quicker versions.

UK ACCORD (from Oct 1998)

WHAT'S GOOD

Re-engineered and rebodied Swindon Accord. Very well received and a good alternative to the VW Passat. 5-door hatch supplemented 4-door saloon from Summer 1999. 136bhp 1.8 and 146bhp 2.0 powerful enough. Fire breathing 210bhp Type R very fast indeed. Rover-engined diesel dropped from line-up. Three-year warranty.

WHAT'S BAD

Too soon to say.

WHAT TO WATCH OUT FOR

Too soon to say.

HONDA USA ACCORD (1994–1997)

WHAT'S GOOD

Good-looking American built 'Aerodeck' estate cars and two-door coupes., badged Acura in the States. High specification includes aircon. 131-134 bhp 2 litre engine, 150bhp 2.2 litre (same as Shuttle). Two-year warranty grew to three.

WHAT'S BAD

Load area compromised by suspension intrusion. Honda servicing can work out expensive.

WHAT TO WATCH OUT FOR

Aircon needs recharging every three years with CFC-free 134A refrigerant. Must have regular servicing to remain reliable.

USA ACCORD COUPE

WHAT'S GOOD

New coupe from Summer 1998 with choice of 145bhp 4-cylinder engine man/auto or 197bhp V6 auto only. Understated good looks. Three-year warranty.

WHAT'S BAD

A bit 'too American' for some European tastes.

WHAT TO WATCH OUT FOR

Nothing yet.

SHUTTLE MPV

WHAT'S GOOD

Air-conditioning standard. Excellent, obedient 4-speed autobox with good column shift as standard. Powerful 2,156cc 150bhp engine also standard (grew to 2,258cc from early 1998). Handles very well for an MPV. Called the 'Odyssy' in the USA where it is far and away the most reliable MPV of the lot. Late model LS offered with seven seats at new low £18,000 price. Rear pair of seats fold away into the floor. Not too juicy (25–28 mpg). Looks more like a big car than a van. Recommended.

WHAT'S BAD

Not as versatile as Galaxy/Alhambra/Sharan or Renault Espace. Lap belt only for centre mid-row seat.

WHAT TO WATCH OUT FOR

Look for a proper Honda service history. Buy on basis of current £18,000 LS model rather than previous, overpriced £24,000 six-seater ES. Aircon needs servicing and recharging every two years with CFC-free 134A refrigerant – costs around £150.

HRV

WHAT'S GOOD

Be-spoilered suburban style wagon with part-time four wheel drive. Slightly cheaper than CRV with smaller 1.6 engine offering 104 or 123bhp. 5-door version added from AUTUMN 1999.

WHAT'S BAD

Why? But if there's a niche, Honda might as well exploit it.

WHAT TO WATCH OUT FOR

Will look silly when the joke wears thin.

CRV

WHAT'S GOOD

The best 'supermarket' 4x4 yet. Rear drive only cuts in when front wheels slip. The most car-like 'multi activity vehicle' to drive. Lots of useful knick-knacks. £3,000–£4,000 cheaper than equivalent Land Rover Freelander. Honda three-year warranty.

WHAT'S BAD

Not much. Okay, you can't drive at much more than 40 mph with the centre sunroof open unless you also open a few windows or fit a Clim Air deflector. The seats are quite a bit lower than in a Freelander – fine if you have a long back, but not if you're little and want to look over the tops of hedges.

WHAT TO WATCH OUT FOR

Signs of severe usage. Tow hooks (what's it been towing? can lead to wear in both front and rear clutches). But this is the most suburban friendly 4x4 of the lot and therefore the least likely to have led a hard life.

LEGEND (from 1991)

WHAT'S GOOD

A Quentin Willson favourite – four door saloon or plush two door coupe. Grew up once it shook off Rover 800 association, first with 201bhp 3.2 V6, then with 202bhp 3.5 V6 from June 1996.

WHAT'S BAD

Any problems tend to be expensive.

WHAT TO WATCH OUT FOR

Treat like a Lexus, so must have full agent service history with frequent ATF, brake fluid, coolant, aircon refrigerant changes. Check carefully for any signs of uneven tyre wear. Look for oil leaks on ground where car has been standing.

Give it some heavy braking on the test drive to check for warped discs caused by drivers holding the car on the brakes after a heavy stop.

PRELUDE (1992–96)

WHAT'S GOOD

Old Prelude turned from a glassy coupe into a more serious looking car altogether. Great shark-nose 'mini XJS' styling. Useful range of engines include 131bhp 2 litre; 158 bhp 2.3 and 183bhp 2.2 VTEC. VTEC is the enthusiasts choice, but they're all good.

WHAT'S BAD

Honda maintenance is expensive, particularly VTEC. Aircon may play up (best serviced and recharged with CFC free 134A refrigerant by an aircon specialist). Not much room in the back seat. Paint may flake, particularly silver.

WHAT TO WATCH OUT FOR

Rusty or damaged exhausts and blown cats. Look for mismatched paint and check if due to flaking or accident damage. Check for kerbed alloys, uneven tyre wear, suspension damage. Has the car left Honda agent servicing fold? If so, who's been servicing it?

PRELUDE (from 1996)

WHAT'S GOOD

American styling not as interesting or original as predecessor. 132bhp 2 litre or strong 185bhp 2.2 VTi. 4-speed auto has 'Tiptronic' type manual control. Motegi kitted 132bhp 2.0 and 183bhp 2.2 from Summer 1998. Aircon standard on all. One of the few cars the look of which is improved by lowered suspension and a factory body kit. Best colour: dark metallic blue.

WHAT'S BAD

Autobox manual control the wrong way round (should be back for upshifts and forward for downshifts to match laws of physics).

WHAT TO WATCH OUT FOR

Watch out for kerbing damage to big alloys and front suspension. Check for uneven tyre wear. Engine oil should be clean. Honda agent service record should be complete.

NSX

WHAT'S GOOD

Surprisingly civilised supercar. As easy to drive as a Honda Civic, but has storming VTEC V6 with 271bhp that sounds wonderful. Early 5-speed models did not have standard PAS and were better for it (optional PAS was electric). Aircon standard, naturally. Auto optional. Targa came along in July 95 with standard PAS and optional F-Matic auto or 6-speed manual. Far more reliable and easy to live with on a day to day basis than a Ferrari.

WHAT'S BAD

Tends to understeer quite a lot rather than catch you out with snap-oversteer. Power-steered cars lack steering feel. Eats rear tyres (6,000–8,000 miles).

WHAT TO WATCH OUT FOR

Must have full agent service history with super-clean fully synthetic oil, frequent ATF, brake fluid, coolant, aircon refrigerant changes. Check carefully for any signs of uneven tyre wear. Alloy suspension is vulnerable to off road (or off track) excursions.

HYUNDAI

ATOZ

WHAT'S GOOD

Quite good tall 5-door micro competes hard against Daewoo Matiz. Name springs from 'A to Z'. Power steering and three-year unlimited mileage warranty standard in £6,999 price. Another £1,000 brings air-conditioning, driver's airbag, alloys and central locking. Auto option. Makes much more sense for the school

run than a Grand Cherokee. Fits tiny parking spaces or a short, narrow pre-war garage. Likely to benefit from reduced annual VED. 55bhp, 90 mph and 45mpg. Had good write-ups on launch, especially by Neil Lyndon in *Sunday Telegraph* and 'Telegraph Motoring' ran one for several months out of choice.

WHAT'S BAD

Snobs driving their offspring

to school in Grand Cherokees will look down their noses at you. Build quality a bit light. £4,750 in Spain.

WHAT TO WATCH OUT FOR

Kerbing damage. Damage to thin body panels. Damage to trim by children.

AMICA

WHAT'S GOOD

New 5-door hatchback on Atoz platform, but radically different and lower-priced.

WHAT'S BAD

Too soon to say

WHAT TO WATCH OUT FOR

Too soon to say

PONY X2 (1990–94)

WHAT'S GOOD

Cheap and fairly reliable if properly serviced. 1.3 litre had 72bhp; 1.5 had 83bhp.

1.5 has PAS. Not overly complicated so not too much to go wrong.

WHAT'S BAD

Ugly. Cheap trim. Sunroofs leak. Power outputs of both engines fell sharply when catalysed from August 1992. 'Pony and trap' is Cockney rhyming slang for something not very nice. Automatic gearboxes can start to give trouble after 6–7 years.

WHAT TO WATCH OUT FOR

Inadequate or incompetent kerbside home servicing. Could have sat around for a long time before being first registered. Cheap new so should be very cheap by now.

ACCENT (1994–99)

WHAT'S GOOD

Replaced Pony X2 and a much better car with something akin to sporty handling. Engines include

83bhp 1.3, 87bhp 1.5 or, from Jan 97, a 98bhp 1.5. PAS standard on 1.5s. 4-speed auto optional on 1.5 saloon and 5-door hatch. Quite well screwed together and generally cheap. Proper three-year warranties.

WHAT'S BAD

Comparatively poor 1.5 Star NCAP crash test results. Base 1.3s don't have PAS. Styling of front valence is dubious.

WHAT TO WATCH OUT FOR

Some did go onto leasing, rental and particularly Motability fleets. If less than three years old, make sure has not disqualified itself from 3-year warranty. With older cars watch out for same inadequate or incompetent kerbside home servicing as Pony. Front tyres tend to wear badly. Must have regular cambelt changes every three years or 36,000 miles.

RECALLS

1998 (built 1994–1997): Possibility of road salt corrosion to front coil spring causing spring to damage tyre.

NEW ACCENT (from 2000)

WHAT'S GOOD

New model looks 'all new' and takes the car up half a class – bigger than a supermini, but smaller than a Focus/Golf. Slots into Hyundai/Kia range between Kia Pride and Kia Shuma. 3-door hatch, 5-door hatch and 4-door saloon. 1.3 manual has 55bhp; 1.3 auto has 63bhp; and 1.5 man/auto has 65bhp with 97lb ft torque. All models now have pas. All autos 4-speed. All can do over 100mph. Average fuel consumption: 36.22mpg to 44.14mpg. Price competitive.

WHAT'S BAD

Grille styling won't appeal to everyone.

WHAT TO WATCH OUT FOR

Too soon to say.

LANTRA (1991–95)

WHAT'S GOOD

Not bad Orion-sized four-door with Mitsubishi derived power trains. 84bhp 1.5, 112bhp manual 1.6, 104bhp 1.6 auto, 124bhp 1.8. All had standard PAS. 1.6Cdi and all 1.8s had standard aircon. 1.8Cdi got standard ABS from October '93.

WHAT'S BAD

Danger of being seduced by high spec of CD version. This is a reasonable car, but it's no BMW.

WHAT TO WATCH OUT FOR

Must have regular cambelt changes every three years or 36,000 miles. ABS needs frequent brake fluid changes. Aircon needs recharging with CFC free 134A refrigerant every three years.

RECALLS

1996 (1991–1996): Check for fracture of rear suspension bolt.

LANTRA (1995–2000)

WHAT'S GOOD

Quite nicely styled saloon or 5-door estate. Grown up engine range of 112bhp 1.6, 126bhp 1.8 or 137bhp 2 litre. PAS standard on all; ABS either standard or optional. Aircon standard on CDs; optional on 1.8Si and 1.6s.

WHAT'S BAD

Advertised as 'the curvy car', which was an odd way to attract customers. Dealers try to sell them as more upmarket than they are.

WHAT TO WATCH OUT FOR

Must have regular cambelt

changes every three years or 36,000 miles. If less than three years old, make sure has been regularly serviced and still qualifies for warranty.

LANTRA (from 2000)

WHAT'S GOOD

New model due mid-2000.

WHAT'S BAD

Too soon to say.

WHAT TO WATCH OUT FOR

Too soon to say.

COUPE

WHAT'S GOOD

If the Lantra is 'the curvy car', then this is 'the swoopy coupe'. Good looking and a lot of coupe for the money. 112bhp 1.6 the entry level at a reasonable £14,000. 137bhp 2 litre a more serious car with standard alloys. Aircon optional on 1.6 and 2.0i; standard on 2.0iSE which also comes with leather seats. FI has big alloys and low profile tyres. Will impress those who don't know what it is and is not a bad car in its own right. Handles quite well. Sells well.

WHAT'S BAD

OTT launch advertising campaign compared the look of it to a Ferrari. Will not confer quite the same status on driver as a 3-Series, a Corrado, a Celica or even a Prelude. Dubious restyle for Y2K.

WHAT TO WATCH OUT FOR

Cars that are flash for not much cash can be prime candidates for the repo man, so used examples may be missing service books and some of the keys, and definitely warrant an HPI check. Still young enough to want to see full agent service history.

SONATA
(from 1994)

WHAT'S GOOD

Biggish cheap car. Reliable enough. Surprise restyle in September 1996 gave it a new begrilled nose. 1994 – 96 2 litre had a reasonable 136bhp. 5-speed manual or 4-speed auto. ABS standard on 2.0CD and 3 litre. CDs and V6s also have aircon, while V6 offers cruise control and leather.

WHAT'S BAD

Ride and handling not up to European standards for the class. Power of 2 litre dropped to 122bhp after the 1995 re-style. 3 litre V6 only ever had 143bhp and a sluggish autobox.

WHAT TO WATCH OUT FOR

Though it may be out of warranty, you still want to see a proper agent service history showing regular brake fluid, ATF, coolant, timing belt and aircon refrigerant changes. Don't buy an ex-taxi that's been serviced on the taxi rank.

TRAJET MPV

WHAT'S GOOD

New for 2000 and to be well priced from £14,000. 2 litre 4-cylinder and 2.7 litre V6 petrol engines plus a 2 litre common rail direct-injected diesel. Seats in 2–3–2 pattern.

WHAT'S BAD

Rather anonymous. Yet another 7-seat MPV, curiously from the same company that builds the new Kia Sedona.

WHAT TO WATCH OUT FOR

Too soon to say.

ISUZU

TROOPER (to 1992)

WHAT'S GOOD

Square, 'honest' and quite well thought of 4x4s with petrol or diesel engines and short 3-door or long 5-door bodies and the option of 7 seats in the 5-door. Engines: 2,254cc 109 bhp petrol four; 2,559cc 111bhp petrol four; 2,238cc ohc 74bhp diesel four to Jan 1988, then much better 2,771cc 95bhp TD from Jan 1988. 'Duty' pack offers better kit and, from Jan 1988, a limited slip diff.

WHAT'S BAD

They do rust, quite badly. Older ones are likely to have had a hard life and may well be simply worn out.

WHAT TO WATCH OUT FOR

Rust, signs of hard usage such as a battered floor, scrubs on bodywork, oil leaks from powertrain, inadequate servicing, broken springs, shocked out shocks, uneven tyre wear, excessive smoke from turbodiesel, crunchy gearchange, make sure four wheel drive engages properly. Some reports of cracks developing in cylinder heads of petrol models. The car could easily be an older 'grey import' offering no means of checking on its past.

TROOPER (1992–98)

WHAT'S GOOD

3.1 litre 113bhp TD or 3.2 litre 174bhp petrol V6 in two wheelbases – short with 3 doors or long with 5 doors and the option of 7 seats. 3-year warranty. 'Duty' pack takes trim up one stage from basic. 'Citation' takes it up another stage.

WHAT'S BAD

Brick-like styling. The last two years worth sat around for a long time waiting to be sold – which delayed the UK launch of the new model. Not quite as reliable as you might expect – possibly due to long wait for a buyer. Re-incarnated (disastrously) as the Vauxhall Monterey.

WHAT TO WATCH OUT FOR

Rust, signs of hard usage such as a battered floor, scrubs on bodywork, oil leaks from powertrain, inadequate servicing, broken springs, shocked out shocks, uneven tyre wear, smoke from diesel's turbo, crunchy gearchange, make sure four wheel drive engages properly. If it has a tow hook, what has it been towing – and where? Could have been pulling a livestock trailer over a Welsh mountain. Not quite the same 'green welly' appeal as a Discovery or a Shogun, so

more likely to have been a working vehicle.

TROOPER (from Spring 1998)

WHAT'S GOOD

New 159 bhp twin-cam 16-valve direct-injected common rail diesel engine gives stump pulling 246 ft lb torque at just 2,000rpm. Combined fuel consumption figure of 31.6 very good for this type of vehicle. (Also a 215 bhp 3.5 litre petrol V6.)

WHAT'S BAD

Essentially, the old body with a more rounded front – and we had to wait for it while stocks of the slow-selling old model got shifted.

WHAT TO WATCH OUT FOR

Shouldn't be troublesome yet but problem areas likely to be same as old model. First common rail DI in the UK, so first test of individual electronically controlled injectors.

JAGUAR

X-400 (from 2001)

WHAT'S GOOD

New baby Jaguar should do very well.

WHAT'S BAD

Too soon to say.

WHAT TO WATCH OUT FOR

Too soon to say.

S-TYPE (launch Spring 1999)

WHAT'S GOOD

New small Jaguar with design cues from 1960s Mk II. Choice of 240bhp Duratec V6 or 280bhp Jaguar V8 engines. Manual (V6 only) or Ford auto. CATS option of adaptive damping and 17" wheels worth having. Prices start at £28,300 OTR. Good to drive, with enough steering feel, decent handling and good ride quality. Manual much better than auto. A success from day one. Six-cylinder manual model the recommended choice.

WHAT'S BAD

Automatic 'J' change can be sloppy and apt to drop a gear unasked when you're half way round a corner.

WHAT TO WATCH OUT FOR

Too soon to say.

XJ6 SIII (to Oct 1986)

WHAT'S GOOD

Last of the classic 'feline' shape XJ6 and prices of good late examples have been rising. 4.2 had 205 bhp. 5.3 V12 had 299bhp and carried on alongside XJ40 to September 1989.

WHAT'S BAD

The dashboard is a mess.

Rust may have set in.

WHAT TO WATCH OUT FOR

Buy carefully from an expert specialist such as Robert Hughes (01932 858381) to avoid pitfalls. The coolant needs to have been changed every two years without fail or the block will sludge up at the back, overheat, blow its head gasket and possibly warp its cylinder head. Rust first appears under rear valence, under the front wings behind the headlamps and along the top of wing seam. Use a magnet. Otherwise, see XJ40 below and be very wary if the car overheats.

XJ6 XJ40 (1986–94)

WHAT'S GOOD

Less likely to have build faults than previous Jaguars. Quiet and quick, nice ambience inside a Sovereign. Non cat 3.6 has 221bhp. Catted 3.2 AJ6 has 200bhp. Pre-cat 4.0 has 235bhp, sinking to 205bhp with cat. 4.0 XJR has 248bhp. Catalysed 5.3 V12 has 264bhp. All should take unleaded.

WHAT'S BAD

Styling the most boring of any XJ. Lack of steering 'feel'. Too low for some. Not as much rear legroom as length implies. 165bhp 2.9 litre version best avoided unless really cheap (less than £1,000).

WHAT TO WATCH OUT FOR

Must have leather seats (or at least leather seat facings) – a £750 trimming job. Aircon more desirable than sunroof. Make sure aircon blows cold. Good news if has been recharged with CFC-free 134A refrigerant instead of old R12. Will rust – the first place is around number plate lights in the boot lid, but if there's rust in the wings, sills and inside the boot, walk away. Light reflectors also let in water and rust. Listen for timing chain rattle – a sign of age and insufficiently frequent oil changes. The coolant needs to have been changed every two years without fail or the block will sludge up at the back, overheat, blow its head gasket and possibly warp its cylinder head. If the brake fluid isn't changed every two years, the ABS pump could rust up inside, so make sure the ABS light goes on when you switch on and off a few seconds after start up. Check all electrics. Check for uneven tyre wear signifying suspension or steering damage. If tyres are worn, they're costly to replace. Listen for clonking from the rear axle on gearchanges, which should be smooth. Manuals are rare and early ones had a clutch problem but all should have been sorted by now. If fitted with self-levelling suspension, make sure it self-levels. Try and feel the discs for scoring, lipping and wear.

Brake callipers can seize and are expensive, so be very suspicious of uneven braking on test drive.

XJ6 and XJR (1994–97)

WHAT'S GOOD

Gained an impressive reputation for reliability both on the fleets and in private hands. Better even than Mercedes or BMW. Well liked by owners. 216bhp 3.2 litre straight six; 245bhp 4.0 straight six; 322bhp 4 litre supercharged straight six. Good 5-speed manual or less good 'J-change' 4-speed ZF automatic. Three-year 60,000 mile warranty.

WHAT'S BAD

A glut of these were p/x'd for XJ8s by status seekers when the XJ8 came out and prices fell. They climbed back up once the market realised how good the sixes were.

WHAT TO WATCH OUT FOR

Less than pristine examples are worth a lot less – pay no more than Parker's Guide 'Fair' prices for scruffy XJs. Also check the spec, because you don't want a standard model with cloth seats and no aircon. Still new enough to insist on a proper Jaguar agent service record. Bodies may flex and crack windscreens. Alloys oxidise easily. Rear bumper protector falls off. Check all electrics, particularly the dashboard computer. Feel the discs for lipping or scoring and watch out for uneven braking on the test drive. Brake judder may be due to drivers sitting on the brakes after a hard stop which causes localised overheating and warps the discs. For older cars, see tips for previous model XJ 40 above.

XJ8 and XJR8 (from 1997)

WHAT'S GOOD

Same car with new 240bhp 3.2 V8, new 290bhp 4.0 V8 and stonking 370bhp supercharged 4.0 V8. 5-speed automatic only. Climate control on all models. Three-year 60,000 mile warranty. The XJR8 is the best car you can buy for £50,000 bar none.

WHAT'S BAD

Painted front bumper looks organic and is easy to scratch. No means of checking 5-speed ZF autobox oil level or refilling it. Jaguar says, "sealed for life", but no oil changes could mean a 'life' of just 10 years. (XJR8 has a stronger, much better Mercedes box.) No manual option.

WHAT TO WATCH OUT FOR

Must have a full Jaguar agent service history (without it, you lose the 3-year warranty) and must be immaculate to command top money.

RECALLS

Jaguar XJ8 (July–October 1997 – 11,221 cars): May

suffer sudden deceleration due to weak retention bracket on accelerator cable. Extra clip "costing pennies" solves the problem. (Announced on radio 7/2/98)

XJS 3.6 AND 4.0

WHAT'S GOOD

3.6s didn't have cats and did have 225bhp. Roll-bar cabrio from 1986–87 was stiffer than later convertible. Convertible 4 litre from 1992 was much better looking. Always the option of a 5-speed manual or 4-speed autobox.

WHAT'S BAD

Early 1986–87 AJ6 3.6s don't like unleaded and had dodgy engine management systems. 4 litre came with a cat so, despite an extra 390ccs, is down on power to 223bhp.

WHAT TO WATCH OUT FOR

Fairly apt to suffer front suspension and steering damage, so check this carefully. Any signs of uneven tyre wear – either avoid the car or budget for a big bill. The coolant needs to have been changed every two years without fail or the block will sludge up at the back, overheat, blow its head gasket and possibly warp its cylinder head. Check that standard aircon blows cold. Good news if has been recharged with CFC-free 134A refrigerant instead of old R12. Look for rust in the flying buttresses at the back, sills and wheelarches. Otherwise, see XJ40 above.

XJS V12

WHAT'S GOOD

Monster 5.3 litre 299bhp lost 20 bhp to catalyser, but 6 litre V12 from May 1993 was back up to 308 bhp. Only a few early versions were manual. Rest automatic only and all are oilwell emptiers.

6 litre pre-cat XJRS from Sept '89 had 318 bhp, boosted to 333 bhp in October 1991. Can be very reliable, but see below.

WHAT'S BAD

Ask yourself if you really need all this power in a soft car with overlight power steering which lacks 'feel'. I know of two XJS single-car accidents within half a mile of each other on the same stretch of road.

WHAT TO WATCH OUT FOR

The rearmost pair of spark-plugs are hidden by plumbing, take hours of dismantling to get at and consequently are rarely changed. Contrary to the horror stories, these big, unstressed V12s can be very reliable and trouble-free if treated and maintained with respect. This means 3,000 mile or six month fully synthetic oil changes (no later), annual transmission oil changes, new brake fluid and coolant every two years

without fail. Fairly apt to suffer front suspension and steering damage, so check this carefully. Any signs of uneven tyre wear – either avoid the car or budget for a big bill. Otherwise, see comments on XJS 3.6/40 and XJ40. If it overheats, it's going to be trouble so leave it alone.

XK8 and XKR

WHAT'S GOOD

Much better looking, more 'Jaguar-like' than XJS. Tried and tested styling seen before on Aston Martin DB7. Convertible looks lovely. Says you're rich, British and proud of it. 290bhp in standard form. Supercharged XKR has 370bhp and 387 ft. lbs torque – and there is an XKR convertible. 0–60 5.2 seconds. Three-year 60,000 mile warranty.

WHAT'S BAD

May suffer from infuriating

build quality problems. No easy means of checking 5-speed autobox oil level or refilling it. Jaguar says, "sealed for life", but no oil changes mean a 'life' of 10 years tops. (XKR has a stronger Mercedes box.) These cars gulp gas, of course. Rear passengers need to be legless.

WHAT TO WATCH OUT FOR

Vital to buy the right trim combination – the 'Classic' rather than the 'Sport' or the base model.

RECALLS

1997: Rear suspension. 1998 (July–October 1997 build – 11,221 cars): May suffer sudden deceleration due to weak retention bracket on accelerator cable. Extra clip "costing pennies" solves the problem. (Announced on radio 7/2/98)

KIA

PRIDE

WHAT'S GOOD

Old Mazda 121 re-incarnated, built in South Korea. Helped Kia establish UK foothold. 1,324cc model relaunched at lower price in Summer 1999 after company taken over by Hyundai. Standard 3-year warranty.

WHAT'S BAD

Kia got into bad financial trouble in early 1998. The company has been taken over by Hyundai.

WHAT TO WATCH OUT FOR

Uneven tyre wear signifies worn front suspension bushes. Catted versions may have problems. Treat only as a cheap buy offering decent reliability.

MENTOR

WHAT'S GOOD

Quite well made and quite reliable. Owners seem to like them. Available as 4-door saloon or 5-door hatch.

WHAT'S BAD

Zero image, completely ordinary, fairly small 4-door saloon (slightly smaller than an Orion) or 5-door hatch. Lacks specification (sun roofs are cheap aftermarket 'pop-up' add-ons). Strange engine line-up on earlier models. 1.5 litre had 80bhp and 88 ft. lbs torque; 1.6 litre had 79bhp and 92 ft. lbs torque. But peak power and torque figures closer in rev range on 1.6.

WHAT TO WATCH OUT FOR

Hard to match damaged body panels. Likely to have been privately owned by the over-50s and frequently parked facing the sea.

MENTOR II / SHUMA

WHAT'S GOOD

New 4-door saloon and 5-door hatch, more modern and much better looking than previous model. 1.5 litre 88bhp and 1.8 litre 110bhp engines. Mentor II saloon has more restrained styling. Shuma 'Fastback' goes for twin headlight look. Optional 4-speed auto. Three-year mechanical and six-year body warranties. Low prices (from £8,500 OTR).

WHAT'S BAD

Too soon to say.

WHAT TO WATCH OUT FOR

Too soon to say.

CARENS

WHAT'S GOOD

Strangely styled multi-purpose estate car based on Kia Shuma. 110bhp 1.8 litre engine. ABS standard.

3-year warranty.

WHAT'S BAD

Just look at it. May not come to UK.

WHAT TO WATCH OUT FOR

Too soon to say.

CLARUS

WHAT'S GOOD

Mondeo sized 4-door saloon and estate, but much cheaper. 116bhp 1.8litre SX priced close to new Neon at £10,995; 133bhp 2 litre Executive top model with a/c, alloys, ABS and leather just £13,495, or £14,295 with 4-speed autobox. Station wagon also available with huge lights set high in rear 'D' pillars. Standard 3-year warranty.

WHAT'S BAD

Zero image.

WHAT TO WATCH OUT FOR

Too soon to say.

ROADSTER

WHAT'S GOOD

Effectively a re-working of the much sought after front-wheel-drive Lotus Elan, now with 136bhp 1.8 litre engine. Standard 3-year warranty.

WHAT'S BAD

Not quite the car it looks to be. Top speed only 123mph with 0-60 in 9 seconds. May not come to UK.

WHAT TO WATCH OUT FOR

Too soon to say.

JOICE

WHAT'S GOOD

7-seater 'carlike' MPV. 2 litre 139bhp engine. Standard ABS. based on Kia Shuma. 110bhp 1.8 litre engine. Standard 3-year warranty.

WHAT'S BAD

Utilitarian external looks. May not come to UK.

WHAT TO WATCH OUT FOR

Too soon to say.

SPORTAGE

WHAT'S GOOD

Cheap alternative to Vitara, RAV 4, Honda CRV and Land Rover Freelander. Lively enough, with 128bhp (more than any Freelander so far) and 88bhp turbodiesel. Re-launched Summer 1999 to include longer wheelbase "long version" five-door and a retro styled short-wheelbase 'Sportage Classic' as well as the standard SWB three-door. Standard 3-year warranty.

WHAT'S BAD

Not exactly sophisticated. Or very roomy. Not as good as any of the expensive alternatives. Can be troublesome and, when they are, the agents may not be very accomplished in getting them right.

WHAT TO WATCH OUT FOR

Evidence of off-road use. Has the upholstery been 'crocodiled'? (eaten by dogs). Better to buy a town car than a country car.

RECALLS

(None known 1994–98, but some cars have been riddled with faults.)

SEDONA

WHAT'S GOOD

Big, heavy Voyager sized 7-seater MPV with side sliding doors and either a 126bhp 2.9 litre 16-valve TDI diesel engine with 249 lb ft torque or a 165bhp 3 litre petrol V6 with 164 lb ft torque. Top speed of manual V6 is 116mph with 13.5 second 0-60; diesel does 105mph with 17 second 0-60 and 34.03 mpg. Autobox available with both engines but slower. 'Slide through' driving compartment with high mounted gearlever. Centre row seats of LS version swivel to face rear seats. Aircon standard in LS. RS base models priced from around £14,000, undercutting even the cheapest Zafira. Standard 3-year warranty.

WHAT'S BAD

Bland looking, with no personality or image. Inconvenient 2-2-3 seating arrangement with back three seats on a single bench. A bit slow for the power outputs.

WHAT TO WATCH OUT FOR

Too soon to say.

LADA

RIVA

WHAT'S GOOD

Based on 1960s Fiat 124. Very tough. They give you a full set of tools to fix it when it goes wrong. Kids don't steal them for joy rides. Made infamous by 'Driving School's Maureen and Dave Rees. Owners display their own brand of inverted snobbery. Quite a few 'catless' cars legally took advantage of extended 1993 'cat' deadline. Estate cars make the best sense. Dealers and parts specialists can be 'salt of the earth'.

WHAT'S BAD

Appalling build quality. Very basic. Noisy, thirsty and lumpy to drive (nothing like a real Fiat 124). Spare parts supply not guaranteed to last indefinitely. Factory infiltrated by the Russian Mafia. Post August 1992 models fitted with cats have severe trouble passing MOT advanced emissions systems test.

WHAT TO WATCH OUT FOR

Where do you start?

Conscientious owners like Dave Rees look after them properly. People who buy them for £100 at an auction don't bother and simply run them into the ground. Listen for signs of big ends going. Expect some gearbox whine, but not too much. Unscrew a spark plug to see if it's burning oil. Trim may have fallen apart of its own accord under the inevitable seat covers. Electrics play up (fusebox shorts, distributor wear). If you're paying a proper price, make sure the tools are all there.

SAMARA

WHAT'S GOOD

Engines and gearboxes not that bad. Body reasonably robust. Cheap.

WHAT'S BAD

Usual dreadful Lada build quality. Slothful suspension. Horrible handling. Rickety ride. Terrible trim. Eccentric electrics. May not pass MOT 'advanced emission control system' test.

WHAT TO WATCH OUT FOR

Depends who's had it before (see 'Lada Riva'). Check all electrics. 'Reverse-turn test' driveshaft joints for clonks.

NIVA

WHAT'S GOOD

Lada's 4x4. Dates back to the 1970s, but quite good if your need is for a tough, basic 4x4. Usual Lada full tool kit supplied. Reasonably competent off road. Latest cars have Suzuki like front.

WHAT'S BAD

Very noisy, slow and thirsty. Quite a small cabin (looks like a Fiat 127 on stilts). Trim not up to the job. Horrible to drive on the road (swaps ends in the wet). Obstructive gearbox.

WHAT TO WATCH OUT FOR

Make all the usual working 4x4 checks as these aren't

bought for status and are bound to have been hammered off road. Look for leaking gaskets and seals in the axles, gearbox and transfer case. Check the hub bearings and steering bushes carefully. Look for rock damage to sump and axles. Expect the seat trim to have fallen apart. Expect some rust. If there are holes on the surface panels, check the structure very carefully with an old screwdriver. Be highly suspicious of fresh underseal.

LANCIA

Y10 (1985–92)

WHAT'S GOOD

Fiat Panda-based upmarket mini. Range included excellent, long-lived 45bhp 999cc 'Fire' engine, 55bhp ohc 1,049cc Brazil engine; 85bhp 1,049cc Turbo Brazil, 57 bhp 1,108cc 'Fire' engine and 1,301cc ohc from Strada with multipoint injection giving 78bhp to GTie. 1,108cc 55bhp 'Selectronic' CVT auto also available. Size always a benefit for parking. GTie best model.

WHAT'S BAD

Rust, citycar abuse, handling abilities strictly limited.

WHAT TO WATCH OUT FOR

Look for oil and coolant leaks, accident damage, rust, damaged trim.

DELTA HF and INTEGRALE

WHAT'S GOOD

Sensational performance. 165bhp 8v HF from May 87 to Dec 87; 185bhp 8v Integrale from Feb 88 to March 89; 196bhp 16v from

Sep 89 to Jan 92. Special order only last of the line 210bhp Evo 2 from Jan 92 is a collector's item and if kept immaculate will hold its value.

WHAT'S BAD

Left hand drive only. May be an expensive performance car, but is still based on the Delta which itself is based on the Fiat Ritmo/Strada. So will rust. Will have iffy electrics (dash, rear wash wipe, heated rear screen, central locking. electric door mirrors).

WHAT TO WATCH OUT FOR

First, decide if you want a competition car for rallies or track days, or a flash road car with air and leather. A used competition car will have had offs and will have suffered damage. Uneven tyre wear could be due to suspension misalignment, suspension damage or a distorted shell and is a big job to set up correctly. Timing belts must be changed every 36,000 miles or three years, whichever comes first. Brake fluid needs changing every year on ABS systems. Coolant needs changing every two years. look for coolant and oil leaks. Don't buy one that smokes. Check the condition of the very expensive brake discs. You really need an Integrale specialist to go over one of these over for you.

DEDRA

WHAT'S GOOD

Galvanized Tipo/Tempra based Lancia saloon, so won't rust like a Beta. 165bhp 2.0 turbo is a bit of a tyre shredder, but will give BMW 318i drivers a nasty shock. 2.0ie has 120bhp which sank to 115bhp with cat. SE has automatic suspension control. 1.8ie has 110 bhp – down to 107bhp with cat; 1.6ie has 90bhp, down to 80bhp with cat. Good ride quality, decent handling. Alcantara trim is nice, but not everyone likes the colours. These cars are cheap and can be bargains.

WHAT'S BAD

Ugly, especially from rear.

WHAT TO WATCH OUT FOR

Check for uneven and excessive front tyre wear (especially turbo) – may be suspension damage. Heater may be u/s. Look for exhaust smoke from turbo oil seals. Satisfy yourself that performance of turbo is up to the mark. Check all electrics (of course). Expect the odd oil leak, especially from gasket between two-piece head and cam carrier. Need regular 35,000–40,000 mile timing belt changes.

THEMA (to 1989)

WHAT'S GOOD

Decent handling, decent performance. The 8.32 of 1988 even had a 215bhp Ferrari V8 engine, but 165bhp 2.0 Turbo probably the best performance buy. Normal 8-valve 2 litre 120bhp, 2.8 V6, 150bhp. Lots of room inside cabin. Big boot. (See Thema from 1989.)

WHAT'S BAD

Tainted by Lancia's UK reputation for unreliability and rust and not entirely immune from either.

WHAT TO WATCH OUT FOR

Urgently need new timing belts every three years or 36,000 miles. Benefits from fully synthetic oil with regular changes (particularly 8.32 and Turbo). 8.32 often low mileage and doesn't take well to sitting around. Will need expensive timing belt change before you drive it anywhere (this work could cost £1,000.) Look for mayo under oil cap – usually indicates cylinder head problems. Check turbo exhaust for oil smoke. Gearbox synchromesh gets worn. Do a reverse-turn driveshaft test and listen for clonking. Check condition of discs. Check all electrics – some are bound to be u/s so use your judgement and adjust your price. Rattles and squeaks are normal. Do look for rust. If front tyre wear uneven, look carefully for signs of accident or suspension damage.

THEMA (1989–94)

WHAT'S GOOD

Range rationalised from 1989. 2 litre 16valve now has 150bhp; turbo 185bhp. Turbo SE best Thema ever on sale in UK, though Italians had an estate car version and a diesel. Cats from August 1992 strangely brought yet another power hike: to 155bhp and 205bhp. To help curb torque steer, Turbo got Viscodrive diff. Late models are a lot of car for not much money.

WHAT'S BAD

Lancia's UK reputation. Turbo has high insurance group. Market doesn't like them. No Lancia agents, just specialists.

WHAT TO WATCH OUT FOR

As 85–89, but exclude notes about 8.32. Smoky exhaust, excessive oil consumption may be turbo, may be valve stem seals.

LAND ROVER

FREELANDER

WHAT'S GOOD

The best-built product from Solihull ever. Good styling. Comfortable. Likeable. Plenty of room for four or five passengers. Kids enjoy the high back seat and proper three-point centre belt. Useful underfloor lockable cubby-safe. The hill descent control works well. The more you drive it the more you like it. Longer 3-year warranty inclusive from Spring 1998. Low depreciation. Fairly damage-proof at the front because even the wing-tops are plastic.

WHAT'S BAD

More ponderous than Honda CRV and £3,000 to £4,000 more expensive, spec for spec. Not as economical as expected, but diesel can average 35 mpg at a 70 mph cruise. Becoming increasingly expensive with Freelander 50th 5-door diesel listed at £24,995. Began to have some quality problems despite promising start. Several recalls.

WHAT TO WATCH OUT FOR

Signs of severe usage. Tow hooks (what's it been towing? – neither the 1.8 or the diesel is really powerful enough). Underside damage. Drivetrain leaks. Make sure everything works,

especially the 'hill descent control', if fitted.

RECALLS

TSBs (Technical Service Bulletins) over some part-time four wheel drive clutch systems failing due to fluid leaks and replaced 'in service' by Land Rover agents. Also failures of hill descent control, driveshafts and gearboxes and blocked ventilation slots (Sunday Times' 6/3/99). Official November 1998 (build June '97–June '98): Recall to check welding on joints of rear suspension arms. 1999 Official note to owners to reduce tyre pressures from 2.1 bar to 1.8 bar when not fully loaded.

DISCOVERY (to late 1998)

WHAT'S GOOD

High driving position good for sightseeing. Outstandingly competent and comfortable off road.

Diesels are surprisingly economical with 30mpg on the cards. Autobox goes well with the 4-cylinder diesel. Seven seat versatility (though the two back jump seats are not suitable for journeys). Revised, more expensive model from October 1998 with new 5-cylinder diesel engine, seven forward facing seats and much better road handling than the old model.

WHAT'S BAD

Very ponderous on the road due to high centre of gravity. Dangerous to carry anything on the roof. Generally poor build quality. Post-1973 '300 Series' gearbox has better change but suffers severe input shaft wear (can be alleviated by high tech gearbox lubricants). 300 TDi engines also prone to timing belt failure after 40,000 miles. Kits are available to extend timing belt life, but fitting them is a long job. V8s gobble fuel. Avoid the 2 litre 16v 'MPi' model. Lack of crumple zones mean it can be expensively damaged by hard impacts at speeds as low as 5mph.

WHAT TO WATCH OUT FOR

Signs of severe usage. Tow hooks (what's it been towing?) Underbody 'off roading' damage. Leaks from axles, transmission, transfer case. Worn suspension and steering bushes. Worn and noisy gearboxes (especially Post 1973 '300 Series'). Rust where steel chassis touches alloy body panels. 5-door models worth much more than 3-doors. If it's a TDi 300, has the timing belt modification been carried out? Check the trim carefully as dashboards of post '94 models can warp.

RECALLS

1995 (VIN LJ163104 to LJ172980 and LJ501920 to LJ504252): Check seat belts. 1997 (April '95–July '96: 22,723 vehicles): Possibility of failure of RHS front door latch. 1998: (build Jan '94–Mar '97): Airbag may go off involuntarily.

NEW DISCOVERY (from 1998)

WHAT'S GOOD

Revised, more expensive slightly longer model from October 1998 with new 5-cylinder diesel engine, seven forward facing seats and much better road handling than the old model. Same high driving position good for sightseeing. Outstandingly competent and comfortable off road.

WHAT'S BAD

Hard to distinguish visually from old model, so the neighbours may not realise you've got the new one.

WHAT TO WATCH OUT FOR

See old model, but most of the quality problems should be licked by now.

RECALLS

October 1999: all 9,296 new-model Discoverys sold to date recalled because of a problem with the ABS brakes. Ten minutes work required to rectify.

RANGE ROVER 'CLASSIC'

WHAT'S GOOD

'Classic' Range Rover, warts and all. Some people still love them. 4-cylinder diesels the most economical, and accepted in country circles. Unrivalled cross country performance until the new model arrived. Final metallic-blue 25 individually numbered '25th Anniversary' models the most valuable.

WHAT'S BAD

V8s gobble petrol. Misfires destroy 'cats'. Litany of quality problems which may or may not have been sorted by the previous owner. The three door CSK

(Cyril Spencer King) was an interesting aberration – not wanted at 2-3 years old, but might develop a cult classic following in years to come if kept clean. Air suspension fitted to LSE and Vogue SE can be troublesome.

WHAT TO WATCH OUT FOR

Signs of severe usage. Check suspension bushes for wear. Steering box may be worn. Look for oil leaks from gearbox, transfer case and axles. Make sure rear axle breather not blocked. Make sure diesel not suffering from cracked cylinder head (white smoke from exhaust; mayonnaise under oil cap). Sludge on dipstick is really bad news – a walk away fault because it means the oil has rarely been changed. Look for damage to leather seats and trim by dogs. Scuff marks and trim damage from shooting trips. Alloy parts of body won't rot, but steel parts and chassis do, particularly at the back, and electrolytically corrode where the steel and alloy meet. Check Boge rear suspension unit. Avoid cars with specialist, heavy duty tow bars (may have been pulling a 15 ton yacht or, worse still, a mobile hamburger stand). Try to buy town cars rather than country cars. May be reliable, but you can still expect niggling faults.

RECALLS

1998: (Jan '94–Mar '97 build): Airbag may go off involuntarily.

NEW RANGE ROVER

WHAT'S GOOD

Undeniable road presence. Far less vague on the road than the old model. 4.6HE is a powerful car. All are brilliant off the road, soak up the bumps and are the most comfortable way to travel cross-country.

WHAT'S BAD

BMW powered diesel version is exceptionally slow on the road – especially in automatic form. 4.6HE drinks petrol, may be hit by future 'guzzler' taxes. 4.0 V8 a bit less juicy. 4.6HE loses value fast.

WHAT TO WATCH OUT FOR

Signs of severe usage. Tow hooks (what's it been towing?). Listen for transmission noise on manual versions. Make sure all gearbox functions work (manual and automatic). Look for oil leaks from axles, gearbox and transfer case. Look for damage to leather seats and trim by dogs. Scuff marks and trim damage from shooting trips. Check all electrics. Make sure wheels will come off as the alloy wheels have a habit of corroding to the hubs. If paying dealer prices, make sure it comes with a full service history.

RECALLS

1995 (VIN LP311035 to LP312917): ABS braking hose may fail. 1998 V8: Cooling system hoses found to be failing.

LEXUS

IS200 (from May 1999)

WHAT'S GOOD

Toyota's answer to the BMW 3-Series and Audi A4. Fresh, 'clean sheet' styling. Promising 153bhp twin-cam 24v 2 litre straight six. 6-speed manual gearbox has rifle-bolt precision (4-speed auto optional). Rear wheel drive with proper rear drive handling. Interesting instruments. Big 17" alloy wheels. Much sharper steering than other Lexus models. Sport has traction control, which is a mixed blessing for keen drivers. Prices start at £20,500. Recommended.

WHAT'S BAD

Needs to be revved to perform, otherwise doesn't feel powerful enough. Auto can be sluggish at times.

WHAT TO WATCH OUT FOR

Too soon to say.

GS300 (to 1998)

WHAT'S GOOD

Beautifully built and quite good looking with plenty of road presence. Smooth, 209 bhp 6-cylinder engines. Warranty lasts three years and 100,000 miles.

WHAT'S BAD

Steering, handling, roadholding and ride quality not up to BMW standards. Not as much space inside as length suggests. Will not endow drivers with the status of a Mercedes E-Class.

Sport model best looking but doesn't drive as well as it looks.

WHAT TO WATCH OUT FOR

Full Lexus service history. Evidence of having been carelessly driven by people with business rather than driving on their minds. Suspension damage from kerbing.

RECALLS

June 1999: All GS300s built July '95–July '97 recalled to replace potentially faulty suspension links.

GS300 (from 1998)

WHAT'S GOOD

VVT engine gives more power (218bhp); 5-speed auto helps to use it. Longer wheelbase give more room inside. Double wishbone suspension improves handling and roadholding. Traction Control and Vehicle Stability Control help keep drivers out of trouble while they're on the phone. 3-year, 100,000 mile warranty.

WHAT'S BAD

In dubious taste. Chopping off the front and the back did not improve the looks of this car.

WHAT TO WATCH OUT FOR

Full Lexus service history.

LS400

WHAT'S GOOD

World's most refined V8. Effortless acceleration. Brilliant, fully controllable, utterly obedient 5-speed autobox from Oct '97 (4-speed before, and 3-speed before that). Unobtrusive traction and stability control system. As luxurious, reliable and trouble-free as you'd expect of an S-Class competitor built by Toyota. 3-year, 100,000 mile warranty. Quentin Willson reckons they're fantastic buys at over 100,000 miles.

He has no trouble with them. Trade generally approves of quality levels, particularly trim and switchgear. Lexus servicing seems to be top notch. Pre-August 1992 cars can legally be 'de-catted' for better performance and economy (talk to BBR on 01280 702389). 241bhp 3-speed auto Jan '90–Oct '94; 260bhp 4-speed auto Oct '94–Oct '97; 280bhp 5-speed auto from Oct '97.

WHAT'S BAD

Lack of steering 'feel' (Cadillac Seville STS is better in this respect). Pre-1995 model year cars could suffer from engine surging. Limo 'stretchers' not happy about the thickness of the body panels. Lacquer coating on early model alloy wheels peels off, allowing them to oxidise badly.

WHAT TO WATCH OUT FOR

Underservicing. Some busy company directors run these cars very hard as mobile offices, clock up 75,000 miles a year, don't always have time to get services done on time. Check 'cats' (£610 each) Buy young with high mileage rather than old with low mileage. Toyota GB says:- "make sure the car has a full Lexus service history, that the automatic transmission fluid and filter have been changed every year, that the shockers and suspension are okay, that the timing belts have been changed at 60,000 mile intervals and that there is no excess wear on the rear discs through misuse of the parking brake."

RECALLS

1998 (April '95–June '96 build): Risk of underbonnet fire due to faulty wiring.

LIGIER

AMBRA MICRO-CAR

WHAT'S GOOD

Tiny French two seater micro hatchback built at the rate of 300 a week imported by Reliant from 1999. Has 2-cylinder 15bhp 505cc Lombardini diesel engine giving 55–65 mph and 85 mpg. Simple, exposed belt Variomatic transmission. Electric windows & stereo. Alloy wheels and RHD standard in UK. Under the weight limit, so can be driven on a motorcycle licence. Euro Type Approved.

WHAT'S BAD

Slow acceleration will take a bit of getting used to. Quite expensive at from £6,495, but £500 cheaper than originally mooted.

WHAT TO WATCH OUT FOR

Too soon to say.

LOTUS

ELAN

WHAT'S GOOD

Fine handling front-drive sports car with excellent grip. An instant 'classic' despite possibility of 'Kia Roadster' lookalike with not quite the same dynamics. Non-turbo Isuzu engine has 130bhp. Turbos 165bhp pre-cat down to 155bhp with twin cats. Engines and gearboxes tough and reliable. Holds its value well.

WHAT'S BAD

Eats front tyres. Promotes heavy wear of front driveshaft joints, bushes and bearings. Fizzy electrics. Hoods leak. Hard driven, underserviced turbos will smoke. Red examples can develop a paint problem

WHAT TO WATCH OUT FOR

Repaired accident damage. Smoking turbos. Kerbed alloys. Front suspension, hubs and driveshaft wear. Need to see evidence of proper servicing, in particular frequent fully-synthetic oil changes.

ELISE

WHAT'S GOOD

Mouthwatering little road racer in the mould of the Porsche RSK and Elva BMW. Brilliant, ultra-lightweight chassis design and construction. Tremendous handling and grip best checked out under instruction at a race circuit 'track day'.

WHAT'S BAD

Not enough power in standard 118bhp form for the track, but BBR does an Interceptor 2000 for better mid-range grunt (01280 702389). 'Sport' version's 190bhp almost too much for the road. Minimal weather protection. Not a 'girlie townie' fashion accessory. Not for wimps. Expect roof to leak.

WHAT TO WATCH OUT FOR

Typical track day 'off' damage underneath, bent suspension, crunched ends. Cat damage from misfiring off rev-limiter. Won't pass advanced emissions test at first MOT if cat has been removed.

RECALLS

Lotus modified the rudimentary soft top in Spring 1998 because owners complained of leaks. Daft, really. You just don't buy an Elise as an everyday car.

EXCEL

WHAT'S GOOD

A Lotus with four seats. Decent handling, fast, reasonably economical and quite reliable in the right hands.

WHAT'S BAD

'Collector's car' jokes still apply (you have to collect the bits that drop off). Fiercely defended by club members. Screen surround comes adrift. Trim comes unstuck. Needs to be revved to perform (not a town car). If you don't know these cars you need to find someone local who does.

WHAT TO WATCH OUT FOR

Make sure no leaks from heater matrix and that air conditioning works. Needs frequent correct maintenance by experts, not the bloke under the arches (unless he is a Lotus genius). May have been 'owner serviced' so make sure it's been done properly by cross-examining the owner. Fully synthetic oil preferred.

ESPRIT SE/S4/S4S/ SPORT 300/V8

WHAT'S GOOD

'James Bond' submarine car

still being made. In the 'junior supercar' league, light in weight with 264bhp or 300bhp turbocharged engines. Excellent handling and roadholding. Sport 300 is a lightweight 300bhp car. 3,506cc V8 has 349bhp. At £49,950 the V8 GT is a supercar bargain with Porsche beating grunt and safe yet fantastic handling.

WHAT'S BAD

Four-cylinder Lotus engines stretched to the limit. Poor gearchange. 'Lie down' seats. Apt to go wrong quite a lot.

WHAT TO WATCH OUT FOR

This car really needs expert and frequent attention. If it hasn't been checked over at least every six months, leave it alone. You don't want to hear any rattles from the engine, especially the timing belt tensioner. Look for smoke from turbo, oil leaks, fizzy electrics, leaking heater matrix, inoperative aircon, hotspotted cats. If 1992K or

later, make sure it has passed a recent advanced emissions test.

RECALLS

1998 – 200 V8 models recalled for new timing belt, idler pulley bearings, new clutch and 5th gear locknut, cost to Lotus at least £1,500 per car. Also check rear alloy wheels for hairline cracks. Lotus Esprit: 200 V8 models recalled for new timing belt, idler pulley bearings, new clutch and 5th gear locknut, cost to Louts at least £1,500 per car. Also check rear alloy wheels for hairline cracks.

MARCOS

MANTIS AND MANTA RAY

WHAT'S GOOD

352bhp 4.6 litre Rover Buick V8 with hefty 330lbs ft torque gives 4.1 second 0-60 capability. Well developed, safe, precise handling. Jem & Chris Marsh are nice blokes. At £43,995 a very serious alternative to a TVR. New Manta Ray range with engines from 2 litres and prices from £32,500 launched at 1998 Motor Show.

WHAT'S BAD

Basic shape was launched in 1964. Has a lie down seating position, poor rearwards visibility, only the pedal carrier adjusts, heavy but very tight gearchange gate.

WHAT TO WATCH OUT FOR

Second-hand needs an expert check.

MAZDA

121 HATCH

WHAT'S GOOD

Lived on as the Kia Pride. Full length electric sunroof cheered it up. All were pre-cat.

WHAT'S BAD

Even though its a Mazda, it looks like a Kia Pride. Front suspension bushes wear. Carburettor engine can give trouble.

WHAT TO WATCH OUT FOR

Treat only as a cheap, fairly reliable buy. Almost all will already have been scrapped in Japan.

DEMIO

WHAT'S GOOD

Neat and versatile small boxy estate, with sliding, folding and reclining rear seats that can be turned into a bed. 72bhp 1,324 cc engine. 3-year warranty. A bit more substantial than the Move/Wagon R/Atoz/Matiz brigade. Five CO_2 absorbing trees planted for every car sold to achieve first-year "carbon neutrality". Not too dear at £10,500 either.

WHAT'S BAD

Criticised for lack of things like internally adjustable door mirrors. A bit slow and stodgy to drive. If you're looking for a car like this, the base version of the bigger Colt Space Star is more powerful and better value at £11,200.

WHAT TO WATCH OUT FOR

Second hand 'school run' damage, but won't be many second hand around for a while.

121 SALOON

WHAT'S GOOD

Amazing headroom, fun looks. Late model spec (from April 1993) of manual gearbox, power steering and full length sun roof by far the best. 1,324cc 74bhp engine identical to stronger-selling 323. May have scarcity value in years to come.

WHAT'S BAD

Derided by motoring press and simply failed to sell in the UK. Pre-April '93 models had daft specification of automatic, but no power steering and no sun roof. So few UK sales that body spares situation is not promising in years to come.

WHAT TO WATCH OUT FOR

You have to ask yourself what sort of person would buy one. Look for eccentric modifications and evidence of bad driving, such as kerbing. Make sure the electric sunroof works properly and has no tears.

121 FIESTA

WHAT'S GOOD

3-year warranty, otherwise see Fiesta.

WHAT'S BAD

See Fiesta

WHAT TO WATCH OUT FOR

See Fiesta

RECALLS

1996 (1996 model year): Check for faulty piston seal in hydraulic clutch master cylinder. Check for contamination of brake fluid and incorrect front brake hose routing. 1997 (5-door models built Dec '95–May '96): May have faulty rear door latches. 1998 (Dec '95–Jun '96 Build): Possibility of brake failure due to front brake pipe chafing on bracket. Modified pipe and bracket to be fitted to both front brakes.

323 (1989–91)

WHAT'S GOOD

Beautifully built and attractive. Low-roofed 5-door F-Type hatchback more of a 5-door coupe. Neat 4-door saloon tends to appeal more to the elderly. Sweet engines, all 16-valve. (1,324cc 75bhp carb; 1,598cc 87bhp carb; 1,840cc 140bhp twin-cam injection .) Sensationally reliable. Typically Japanese slick gearchanges. Automatic choke problems of pre-October 1989 323s was solved for this model. SE Exec models very well equipped. I actually owned one for 6 months and still saw a profit.

WHAT'S BAD

Immensely complicated model range of 3-door hatchbacks, 5-door hatchbacks, 4-door saloons and 5-door estates. Handling and roadholding not quite to UK tastes. Very light power steering. Not immune to snapped timing belts. Excellent factory paint finish can be very hard to match. Average ventilation on saloon is poor on F-Type hatchback, which is prone to misting up. Not much room in the back seat of F-Types.

WHAT TO WATCH OUT FOR

Make sure car has been regularly serviced, at least every 6,000 miles. Damaged trim is expensive to replace. Make sure all the electrics work. F-Types may have suffered parking damage due to poor rearward visibility.

323 (1991–94)

WHAT'S GOOD

All got fuel injection, as from May 1991, same bodies as before. general good points as above.

WHAT'S BAD

All got catalytic converters. Power outputs now 74 bhp from 1.3, 89bhp from 1.6, but just 129bhp from 1.8. General bad points, as above.

WHAT TO WATCH OUT FOR

Make sure car has been regularly serviced, at least every 6,000 miles. Damaged trim is expensive to replace. Make sure all the electrics work. F-Types may have suffered parking damage due to poor rearward visibility.

323 (1994–95)

WHAT'S GOOD

Re-styled range introduced in August 1994. 'F; type 5-door hatchback became even more coupe-like. Unusual, but attractive. New 1,489cc 89bhp engine replaces 1.6. 146bhp V6 from Xedos 6 introduced to top of the range 323F models. V6 very good looking on its bigger wheels. Service miles extended to 9,000, but still better to stick to 6,000.

WHAT'S BAD

An odd period for the 323 with only a handful of a new 3-door hatchback and very pretty 4-door saloon imported and no estates. Power output of 1.8 drops to 115 bhp.

WHAT TO WATCH OUT FOR

Make sure car has been regularly serviced. Damaged trim is expensive to replace. Make sure all the electrics work. Uneven tyre wear may be evidence of kerbing. Paint is hard to match and a giveaway of accident damage. Make sure the central locking works on all the doors. If you buy a 'glassback' 3 door or the pretty 4 door, be aware that body panels will probably have to come from Mazda's HQ in Brussels, and any RHD bits from Japan.

323 (1995–98)

WHAT'S GOOD

Range shrunk to just one

body, the 323F, until 1997, when a new 1.3 hatchback and a new 1.5 saloon both appeared. Some of 3-year warranty may remain.

WHAT'S BAD

3-door hatchback and pretty 4-door saloon disappeared from range from 1995–1997. New model range arrives late 1998/early 1999. 'F' model to be dropped.

WHAT TO WATCH OUT FOR

As above. Make sure car has been regularly serviced. Some 1995 cars suffered from a faulty batch of clutches.

RECALLS

1997: 'Mystique' special edition based on 323F 1.5LXi may have loose wheel nuts on spare wheel.

323 (from Oct 1998)

WHAT'S GOOD

Back to just one body, but a

new five-door hatchback. Initially a bit bland, but still has a low roofline. Looks improved enormously by dropped suspension and a range of smart alloy wheels. Flat cornering from 'Diagonal Roll Axis' suspension. Clever interior touches such as a front passenger seat that folds to become a table and split, fully folding back seats. Engines: 1,324cc, 75bhp; 1,498cc, 87bhp; 1,840cc, 114bhp + 118 lb ft torque. Range topping Sport introduced Spring 1999 at £16,320.

WHAT'S BAD

.Needs alloy wheels to look good.

WHAT TO WATCH OUT FOR

Too soon to say.

PREMACY

WHAT'S GOOD

323-based mini MPV from the same mould as the Colt Space Star. Good to drive, practical and versatile. Scenic like separately reclinable, foldable and removable rear seats. Front passenger seat folds to form a table or support for long loads. 99bhp and 113bhp 1.8 litre petrol or 89bhp 2 litre turbodiesel. A/c standard on all and "electronic brake force distribution", which can be much needed on a short boxy car braking heavily. Priced from under £15,000 with three-year warranty.

WHAT'S BAD

Too soon to say.

WHAT TO WATCH OUT FOR

Too soon to say.

MX5

WHAT'S GOOD

Sweet, neat, 'back to basics' sportscar. The best small, affordable sports car ever made. Twin-cam 16-valve engines, 5-speed gearboxes. Nice 'works' hard-top. Hood opens with one hand from driver's seat. Revised in Spring 1998 with heated glass back window. 1.8s recommended.

WHAT'S BAD

Cheaper to build than a 323 but sells for a lot more money. Lots of dodgy second-hand imports about. Catalysed 1.6i engine from April 1995 not powerful enough (just 88bhp, v/s 114 bhp for previous 1.6, 130bhp for 1.8 and 150bhp for 1.6 BBR Turbo). Even the new 1.6 doesn't really have enough power.

WHAT TO WATCH OUT FOR

Uncertificated Eunos Roadsters imported by traders after May 1998 cannot legally be registered, so any Eunos Roadster might be a 'clone'. MX5s are sports cars, so could have been thrashed. 'Fashion accessory' MX5s may not have been serviced properly. SVA 'kits' available to get imports through SVA, but

non-SVA Japanese parts may then be put back. Check speed ratings on tyres (Japan has a 55 mph limit.) Series 1 headlight motors go. Uneven tyre wear probably signifies accident damage. Ageing MX5s can rust in the sills.

MX3

WHAT'S GOOD

Very sweet 1,846cc 134 bhp 24v V6. Electric roof. Oddball but inoffensive styling.

WHAT'S BAD

1,598cc 88bhp automatic much less impressive. Back seat strictly for small children. Power of V6 dropped to 128 bhp in August 1994.

WHAT TO WATCH OUT FOR

Don't buy at the 80,000 mile mark unless it has had a timing belt change. Look for a proper Mazda history. Don't pay a 'coupe premium' price without it.

RECALLS

1994: MX3 1.6 & 1.8 (Build March '92–Aug '94: VIN JMZ EC13**
00100001–00113020): Front suspension coil may fail and puncture tyre.

626 (1992–97)

WHAT'S GOOD

Nicely styled 5-door, with amazing built-in rear boot spoiler. Briefly available as 'GT' (Feb '92–Dec '94) with full-on 165 bhp 2.5 litre V6 from MX6, but not many were imported.

WHAT'S BAD

4-door less inspiring, but still well liked. Comprex supercharged 2 litre diesel not a success – only lasted from May '94–Oct '95. Body damage extremely difficult to repair, particularly to rear of 5-door hatchback. Paint quality virtually impossible to match. No estate cars except carry overs with older body.

WHAT TO WATCH OUT FOR

Repaired accident damage. Uneven tyre wear from kerbed suspension.

RECALLS

1997: 'Mystique' special edition based on 626 1.8LXi may have loose wheel nuts on spare wheel.

626 (from 1997)

WHAT'S GOOD

Same Mazda qualities of good build, excellent reliability, superb paint finish. Useful engine range of 89bhp 1.8, 113 bhp 2 litre and 134 bhp 2 litre GSi. Aircon standard throughout. Three three-point rear seatbelts. Estate car back in range.

WHAT'S BAD

Very 'ordinary' looking 5-door hatchbacks and 4-door saloons.

WHAT TO WATCH OUT FOR

Make sure has full Mazda

service history or warranty could be void.

RECALLS

1998 (Nov '96–May '97 build): Possibility of timing belt failure leading to total loss of engine power and power assistance to steering and brakes; 626 diesel (to May '98 build): Faulty fuel injector may stall engine.

626 (from 2000)

WHAT'S GOOD

New-look 626 with corporate pentagonal grille. Engines: 100bhp 1.8 and 122bhp 2 litre petrol, plus 2 litre diesel. ABS standard. Likely to be very reliable. 3-year warranty.

WHAT'S BAD

Not likely to set the roads alight.

WHAT TO WATCH OUT FOR

Too soon to say.

MPV

WHAT'S GOOD

Mazda has sold a 7-seat MPV model in the USA for years, but the 2000 model is a much more attractive vehicle. 2 litre 122bhp petrol engine. Complements Demio and Premacy. Likely to be highly reliable.

WHAT'S BAD

Not cheap at £19,800 on the road. Testers have criticised the gearshift quality. Competing in a very crowded niche of the market.

WHAT TO WATCH OUT FOR

Too soon to say.

XEDOS 6

WHAT'S GOOD

Beautiful looking car. Really stunning. Could have been the prototype for a new small Jaguar – with Mazda reliability. Sensationally smooth, free-revving 2 litre

24-valve engine (which powered Ford's Mondeo Touring Cars). Mirror-like thick lacquer over paint has to be baked on while the car is rotating on a rotisserie. Suspension and handling much improved from 'N' reg on.

WHAT'S BAD

Early suspension not up to the engine or the sporty looks. Really just a 626 with strut braces. Difficult to feel what's going on through the steering. Very difficult to match the original paint quality, particularly metallics, so don't think a £300 bonnet respray will work. MX5 powered 1.6 is underpowered.

WHAT TO WATCH OUT FOR

Early UK SEs did not have air-con, just an aircon button with a sticker over it, so make sure aircon blows cold. (Aircon standard on SE from 'N' reg on.) Look for clean oil on the dipstick and evidence it has been changed regularly. Any mayonnaise under the oil cap, leave the car alone. First jobs: change coolant and brake fluid. Check for uneven tyre wear.

RECALLS

1994 (VIN JMZ CA1***01100001–01119137) : Engine may stop without warning. 1997 (built March '92 to Aug '94): Suspension coil may break and puncture tyre.

MPV

WHAT'S GOOD

Third of Mazda's family of MPVs, but this one has 7 seats and is 626-based. Separately controllable front and back aircon, twin sliding side doors, comfortable, well-equipped with good luggage space behind the third row. 1,991cc engine with 121bhp and 129 lb ft torque, plus 5-speed gearbox. Pedigree comes from ten years of Japanese/American Mazda

MPVs. UK launch at 1999 London Motor Show.

WHAT'S BAD

No auto option, no more powerful petrol engines, no torquey and economical turbodiesels.

WHAT TO WATCH OUT FOR

Too soon to say.

MX6

WHAT'S GOOD

Interesting looks. Lovely 2.5 litre 24v 165 bhp V6. Decent American build quality. Automatic and air-con optional. May still have balance of manufacturer's 3-year warranty.

WHAT'S BAD

Looks not universally liked. Chassis not nearly as good as engine and gearbox.

WHAT TO WATCH OUT FOR

All that glass means it gets hot in summer, so air-con highly desirable. Check tyres for uneven wear – may be misadjustment or may signify suspension damage.

XEDOS 9

WHAT'S GOOD

Bigger Xedos 6 with MX6/626GT 165bhp V6 engine. Loaded with kit. Aircon, sunroof, ABS, 4-speed autobox all standard. Leather and walnut trim standard from June 1996. Balance of 3-year warranty should apply. Tasty new alloy wheels and lowered suspension from 1997 transform the car and make it an eye-catcher. Brought huge handling and roadholding benefits. Supercharged Miller Cycle 2.3 litre V6 for 1999 makes it an even better car.

WHAT'S BAD

Not the same stunning looker as the Xedos 6 – until it got those new alloys in 1997.

WHAT TO WATCH OUT FOR

Make sure has full Mazda service history so warranty is still valid. 97 model onward the one to go for second-hand. Be very wary of uneven tyre wear.

RX7 2+2 (1989–92)

WHAT'S GOOD

Attractive Porsche 944 lookalike with 200bhp turbocharged rotary engine. Good looking cabriolet with well fitting power top.

WHAT'S BAD

Needs specialist maintenance.

WHAT TO WATCH OUT FOR

Engine must idle smoothly (rough idle sure sign of rotor tip wear). Make sure no smoke. Uneven tyre wear signifies accident damage. Must see a record of specialist maintenance even if not all done by Mazda agents.

RX7 TWIN-TURBO

WHAT'S GOOD

Sensational looking retro minimalist classic. Searing 'junior supercar' performance from 237 bhp engine. Quick steering. In the same league as a Porsche 911 C2 or a Porsche 968 of the same age. Better looking than either.

WHAT'S BAD

Power had to be restricted to get through EU emissions laws. Not enough 'feel' in the quick steering. Heavy fuel consumption. Strictly a two seater. Needs expert specialist maintenance.

WHAT TO WATCH OUT FOR

Evidence of proper, regular specialist maintenance, with regular changes of all fluids. Worth having an MOT cat test done even if not due to check for excess hydrocarbons which could mean that the rotor seals are wearing out. Don't buy without getting the car properly checked by an expert in the model, even if the inspection costs you £250. There are a few dodgy grey imports about that won't pass a proper UK MOT emissions test.

MCC

SMART

WHAT'S GOOD

Quite powerful 599cc 45bhp to 55bhp petrol engines coupled to 6-speed sequential autoboxes. Much faster than other microcars. And, of course, has city style which other micros lack. Euro Type Approved. New 799cc CDI diesel from autumn 1999 has 41bhp, 74lbs ft, does 85mph and 85mpg – and, at 90g/km, has ultra-low CO_2 output. Convertible version from mid-2000. Low chassis sports roadster on the way. Four seater planned. Prices from £5,999. Did well in German TUV/Auto Bild front offside crash test. Dealers include: Smart Car UK, tel: 0500 123456; KSB, tel: 020 8995 3837, website: http://www.ksb.co.uk; and Wheelbase, tel: 01932 252515.

WHAT'S BAD

Gearbox and accelerator can take some getting used to. LHD only. Two seats only. Definitely doesn't handle like a hot hatch.

WHAT TO WATCH OUT FOR

Take care on corners.

MERCEDES BENZ

A CLASS

WHAT'S GOOD

Brilliant packaging. Choice of 1.4 or 1.6 litre petrol engines 1.7 common-rail direct-injected diesel or 125bhp 1.9. Manual, clutchless manual or automatic gearchanges. Various trim options. Interesting full length sliding sunroof. Double-skin floor lifts passengers into safer position in side impacts. Four Star performance in 1999 NCAP secondary safety tests. Loaded with anti-skid, anti roll over technology. The most status you can buy of its length.

WHAT'S BAD

Not as well built as you expect from Mercedes. Convoluted 'right hand wheel' to 'left hand rack' steering column. Ride quality far from brilliant. Still suffers from top-heavy 'roll understeer' on tight, adversely cambered corners. Essential to pay full attention on the motorway or can swap lanes. Long step up or down from seats for elderly or infirm unless parked against a high kerb. Expensive.

WHAT TO WATCH OUT FOR

Too soon to say.

190/190E 1.8 /2.0

WHAT'S GOOD

Build quality, solidity, door latching system. Takes age and mileage very well indeed if properly maintained. 1989 model year facelift brought more legroom in back. Hard., flat seats like those of W123 are longest-lasting seats I know. Good autoboxes. 190 2.0 carb engine has 90bhp, 1.8

injection 113bhp, 2.0 injection 122bhp. Was a 136bhp 2.3 injection in Europe, LHD only.

WHAT'S BAD

Hard, flat seats not comfortable for everyone. 'Simplex' timing chains on pre-1989 model year cars prone to snap at around 60,000 miles. Some facelift cars (with lower body side-moulding) used up old stocks of 'Simplex' engines. Tinny boot lid. Clumsy manual transmissions.

WHAT TO WATCH OUT FOR

If buying an 'F' or 'G' 4-cylinder 190 or 190E, open the oil filler cap and look at timing chain underneath. Single link = 'Simplex'; Double link = 'Duplex'. If buying high mileage, make sure service records show 5,000 mile oil changes. 190s more than 10 years old may have started to rust. Clonking autoboxes. Noisy rear axles. Power steering leaks. Kerb damage to front suspension (look for uneven tyre wear). Clocking of these cars is rife so a full service history with receipts and old MOTs tells you a lot more than that the car has been properly serviced. (A 93K with 140,000 miles makes £5,000 at auction. Don't pay £10,000 for the same car with a haircut.)

190E 2.3/2.5 16v

WHAT'S GOOD

The 'hot' 190 2.3 has 187bhp; 2.5 has 197bhp, rising to 204bhp from September 1990. Autobox available with 2.5 16v.

WHAT'S BAD

Manual gearboxes not the best.

WHAT TO WATCH OUT FOR

Clocking. Uneven tyre wear a particularly bad sign on this one as could have been crashed. Otherwise, see 190/190E 1.8/2.0.

190E 2.6

WHAT'S GOOD

This simple, smooth and brawny 160bhp chain cam engine is the best of the bunch. 130mph performance, 28 mpg and no running out of breath when overtaking. Ideal when mated to autobox. Properly maintained, can run well over twelve years and 200,000 miles without serious engine or gearbox problems. Recommended (if you can find a good one).

WHAT'S BAD

See 190.

WHAT TO WATCH OUT FOR

Will need new valve stem seals at around 120,000 miles (a £120 job at a specialist, but much more at a Mercedes agent). See 190 1.8 & 2 litre for other checks.

190 DIESELS

WHAT'S GOOD

The most economical 190s, if driven with economy in mind.

WHAT'S BAD

Slow and dreadfully boring. None more so than 72 bhp 2 litre diesel automatic. 5-cylinder 90bhp 2.5 is better. UK did not get turbodiesel engines.

WHAT TO WATCH OUT FOR

Clocking especially, otherwise see 190.

C CLASS (to 2000)

WHAT'S GOOD

Galvanized body has 30-year warranty. Extensive range of engines offer something for everyone. Start with 122bhp C180, 136bhp C200, 150 bhp C220 four, 148bhp C230 four, 193bhp C230 Kompressor, 170bhp C240 V6, 193bhp C280 straight six, 280bhp C36AMG; 94bhp C220D,

113bhp C250D and 150bhp C250TD. C250TD is a very good diesel – now replaced by new 125bhp/221 lb ft C220 CDI common rail indirect injected diesel. Estates are smart and offer more status than saloons. 5-speed autos standard on latest models. Top model, 4.3 litre 40-valve 310 bhp V8 C43 lists at £47,640 and originally sold for over list, as did 218bhp 320 CLK coupe and convertible. Progressive spec upgrades over the years.

WHAT'S BAD

Early build quality not up to scratch and headlamps poor (much improved later). C180 Classic manuals without sunroofs or aircon don't hold their value in the way Mercedes owners expect. Average performance in NCAP crash tests. CLK coupes ridiculously overvalued by snob market. Huge queue formed for CLK convertibles with some prepared to pay £10,000 'overs'. C180, C200 and C220 seems to be unusually prone to premature failure of the catalytic converter, leading to an £800 repair bill.

WHAT TO WATCH OUT FOR

Chip lots of price off if the car is scruffy (a good way to get a cheap, long-lasting car you would have damaged yourself over the years). Glut of cancelled Far East export orders hit used values hard in 1998. C180 Classic manuals without sunroofs became very hard to sell. If you change your mind, don't expect a Mercedes agent to give you your money back. Make sure wiper mechanism works because its prone to failure and costs £800 to replace. Cat failure also likely to set you back £800.

RECALLS

1996: Check for sticking bonnet catch and safety catch which may lead bonnet to fly open.

C CLASS (from 2000/2001)

WHAT'S GOOD

Complete new range including 4-door saloon, 3-door hatchback, 5-door estate. Galvanized body with 30-year warranty. Engines to be 122bhp 1.8; 136bhp 2.0; 170bhp 2.4 V6; 190bhp supercharged 2.0; 197bhp 2.8 V6; 143bhp 2.2 CDI. Later on will introduce new direct-injected petrol engines from 125bhp to 200bhp, a 6-speed manual and a CVT auto as well as the existing 5-speed auto. (FRANKFURT SHOW)

WHAT'S BAD

UK launch could be delayed until 2001.

WHAT TO WATCH OUT FOR

Too soon to say.

SLK

WHAT'S GOOD

Beautifully engineered electrically folding hard-top. High build quality. Galvanized body has 30-year warranty.

WHAT'S BAD

Silly premiums paid for the first few years cars on UK roads. Offset driving position. 'Kiddy car' looks from side and rear. Official UK imports are automatic 2.3 'Kompressor' only, so more a two seat roadster than a 'sports car'. Likely to be challenged by boy racers in souped-up Novas – and likely to lose. Autobox changes gear on corners when you don't want it to. 'Overkill' anti-skid device.

WHAT TO WATCH OUT FOR

Sellers may try to base used prices on premium price paid rather than market value. LHD 2 litre manual 'personal imports' can be a better bet at £15,000 v/s £30,000 for RHD 2.3 auto 'P' reg.

W123 E CLASS (to 1985)

WHAT'S GOOD

The last beautifully built working-class Mercedes. Solid as a rock. I've seen them with 350,000 miles still looking almost like new. The seats don't sag. 230E the most popular. 240D slow, but goes on for ever. 5-cylinder 300D slightly faster, with similar longevity, less likely to have been a taxi. 280E fastest. Handsome, useful estates.

WHAT'S BAD

They do rust and diffs do go. Don't take well to unleaded. Must have 3,000 mile oil changes and a new timing chain every 60,000 miles or five years whichever comes first. 1984-85 230Es tried to go unleaded and suffered premature valve guide wear. Slow changing manuals best avoided. Don't buy without a sunroof. Avoid the 250 6-cylinder engine because its badly engineered. A new engine for a 280E is £6,000.

WHAT TO WATCH OUT FOR

Most of the good ones were bought up by 'private hire' and mini cab operations who will have serviced them pragmatically but run up a mega mileage and don't let them go until they're knackered. If the big bumpers are damaged it means a heavy impact which may have deformed the structure. Find out when the timing chain was last changed. Listen for rattles and look for oil smoke signifying valve guide wear. Listen for noisy, clonky rear axle. Bounce the rear suspension to make sure shocks still absorb. Look for oil leaks underneath.

W124 E SALOONS

WHAT'S GOOD

Strong, reliable, comfortable, well-built, safe. Bigger, more modern car than W123. Best compromise engine in older models is the 6-cylinder 12-valve 260E (not available in UK estates). Best in newer models is the 280E. 260E is rare in the UK because large numbers were exported second-hand to Malaysia and Thailand in the mid-1990s.

WHAT'S BAD

Lots of quality problems when the model was launched. Four-cylinder 200E and 230E had valve trouble running on unleaded and can still wear out their valve stems in the guides. 'Simplex' timing chains not replaced by 'Duplex' chains on 4-cylinder engines until 1988 (see 190). American style foot parking brake on automatics. Manual gearchange slow and not very pleasant.

WHAT TO WATCH OUT FOR

Built to cover high mileages and many did, but may not show it. Listen for noises from top of engine, look for oil smoke in exhaust. Simplex timing chains on older 200E and 230E last only 60,000 miles and require 3,000 mile engine oil changes. No such problems with later Duplex chains or with 260E, 300E, 300E 24v, 320E 24v. Check for uneven tyre wear (kerbed suspension, worn steering or merely adjustment needed). Brake hard and check for judder (front discs may be warped). Look for oil leaks underneath. Avoid 4-Matic unless you really need a large four wheel drive saloon car. Make sure auto box works in 'sport' (if fitted), feel for 'slip', check colour of ATF (should be dark red), listen for diff rumble. Make sure ABS light goes on and off when it should (brake fluid changes may have been missed). Want to see a proper service history, if not by a Mercedes agent, by a competent specialist.

RECALLS

1995: Passenger Footrest. 1996: Airbag may inflate on wrong side.

W124 TE ESTATES

WHAT'S GOOD

Estate cars come no better. Strong, reliable, comfortable, well-built, safe with more floor to window loadspace than any Volvo. 6-cylinder 300E and 5-cylinder 300D best older engines. 280 and 320 24v best newer engines. Recommended as best estate.

WHAT'S BAD

200s are underpowered, especially automatics. 230TE autos with aircon struggle with a full load. (See W124 saloons)

WHAT TO WATCH OUT FOR

Very important to check the rear suspension as replacement shocks are expensive. Has it been towing? 200TEs and 230TE autos aren't really powerful enough to tow a caravan, so will be well worn if they have been trying. Engine and auto may have overheated. The electric tailgate closer is vulnerable to failure and expensive to replace. Otherwise see W124 saloons.

RECALLS

1995: Passenger Footrest. 1996: Airbag may inflate on wrong side.

E Class (from Oct 1995)

WHAT'S GOOD

Galvanized body has 30-year warranty. New, very good looking cars with slightly better ride and handling than W124. Engines range from 2 litre 136 bhp four through straight sixes and V6s to 280bhp E430 V8. 177bhp 300 Turbodiesel goes well with reasonable economy, and replaced by 195bhp 320CDI with massive 350 lb ft torque, 125bhp 220CDI boosted to 143bhp and 232 lb ft. Estate cars particularly elegant. Top model 5.5 litre 40-valve 354bhp V8 E55 lists at £60,540 and competes head on against Jag XJR8. Three Star NCAP crash test rating (marked down for distortion of pedal box). 40mpg 220CDI 5-speed auto recommended, or 320CDI for towing caravans.

WHAT'S BAD

These are expensive cars. Old 5-cylinder 113 bhp E250D slow, but would be the taxi driver's choice. Standard 'Brake Assist' caused lots of problems which took Mercedes years to sort out.

WHAT TO WATCH OUT FOR

Cancelled Far East export orders found their way back to the UK at mammoth discounts. Make sure any car you buy from a non-Mercedes agent is properly certificated with either an EU Certificate of Conformity or UK SVA.

RECALLS

1995: Passenger Footrest. 1996: Airbag may inflate on wrong side.

S CLASS W126 (to 1991)

WHAT'S GOOD

Good looking, carved from solid Mercedes from the same box as the W123. Engines range from 185bhp twin cam 12-valve 280 six to 300bhp 560 V8.

WHAT'S BAD

280SE and 300SE not significantly more economical than the smaller V8s. All these cars like petrol.

WHAT TO WATCH OUT FOR

When checking a V8, take off the top of the air filter plenum chamber and look for oil. If there's oil in there, the car needs a £12,000 new engine. Listen for timing chain rattle, signifying infrequent oil changes. Don't want to hear any coarseness from the engine, transmission, diff or rumbles from the wheel bearings. Look for uneven tyre wear – could signify suspension wear. Small dinks and donks in the bodywork cost an arm and a leg to fix properly. Remember, these cars only go on forever if frequently and expensively maintained. Cut back on the maintenance and they will break, leaving you with bills for more than the value of the car. Could have been clocked – especially if on its 2nd or 3rd owner.

S CLASS W140 (from 1991)

WHAT'S GOOD

Sensible engine range from 190bhp S280 through 228bhp S300, 286bhp S420, 308bhp S500 and awesome 408bhp S600 (power on this cut back to 389bhp in October 1992).

WHAT'S BAD

All these cars are just a bit too big. European mid-90s slump left a lot of 'S' Class unsold – sitting outside in compounds which won't have done them much good. Used prices go up and down like a lift in a department store. The coupes are pointless and merely tell the world you're rich. All were slow sellers in the UK, particularly in 1997-98. Official sales hit by diverted Far East exports at up to £17,000 less. New slimmed-down, far better looking range of S Class launched at 1998 Motor Show, priced £44,000–£107,000.

WHAT TO WATCH OUT FOR

Can be a huge amount of car for the money if bought right. Tyres are enormous, wear heavily and are very expensive, so budget for this.

RECALLS

1997 (1995-96 build): May lose brake fluid from hose.

NEW S CLASS (from 1999)

WHAT'S GOOD

Galvanized body has 30-year warranty. Nice looking, beautifully build, unaggressively styled big cars. Sensible engine range from S280 through To S600. Smaller 280 and 320 are new V6s. Rack and pinion steering gives good road feel and makes the cars much better to drive then 140 Series without sacrificing ride comfort. Excellent 'Tipfunction' side-flick manual control over 5-speed automatic. 320 V6 is just about adequate. 430 V8 probably the best compromise. Nothing better as a quiet, refined 140mph Autobahn cruiser. Reasonably priced for what you get. Could be considered as 'The Best Car in the World'. Recommended.

WHAT'S BAD

As length and weight increases from S320 to S600L, handling qualities deteriorate. Not a lot of boot space for such a big car. Huge options list can increase new price considerably, and spec needs to be checked carefully when buying second hand. Vulgar £554 walnut/leather optional steering wheel not nice to hold.

WHAT TO WATCH OUT FOR

Too soon to say.

RECALLS

None known

SL (to Oct 1989)

WHAT'S GOOD

Roadsters for movie stars, nouveaux riche and pools winners had very long model life from 1972 to 1989. Six-cylinder engines more economical and cheaper to repair than V8s. A lady in Weybridge used to drive her pet parrot around in one. It just sat there in the passenger seat chattering away.

WHAT'S BAD

I call these 'ribside' roadsters from the Fiat Panda like ribbing along the sides. To some eyes, they are really ugly and look like oversized fairground dodgem cars. But other people like them and there is still some status attached to driving one around with the top down. Unlikely ever to be as 'classic' as previous model 230SL, 250SL, 280SL 'Pagoda Top' and light years behind the 50s to early 60s 300SL.

WHAT TO WATCH OUT FOR

Fell into the wrong hands in those middle years between being old cars and becoming 'classics'. Lots driven by rich women, some of whom bounce them off kerbs, so check for uneven tyre wear signifying suspension damage. Be very wary of 'customised' SLs with oversize alloys, vulgar body kits and white leather steering wheels. If it has aircon, make sure the aircon blows cold. Faulty ABS means a very expensive MOT failure. Make sure the power hood works properly and has no tears. Must have had 3,000 mile fully synthetic oil changes.

SL (from Oct 1989)

WHAT'S GOOD

Vastly better looking top people's sports roadsters. Six-cylinder cars probably the most sensible because once you get past 90mph you get flies in your teeth and your wig blows off whatever engine you've got in front. 300 12-valve: 190bhp; 280 12-valve 193bhp; 300 24v 231bhp, 320 24v also 231bhp, pre-cat 500 V8 326 bhp, catalysed 500 from Sept '90 down to 308bhp, then power up again to 315bhp from May '95; 600 V12 has 389bhp; AMG SL60 is a bored-out

5,956cc 381bhp V8 – handles better than 600SL. All these cars came with a standard, lift-off hardtop which is a two person job to remove. Just about the safest way to travel with the top down and tell everyone you've won the lottery.

WHAT'S BAD

Splodgy fat car handling. Autobox apt to change gear on corners when you don't want it to.

WHAT TO WATCH OUT FOR

Lots of iffy cars with doubtful pasts in the trade: LHD to RHD conversions. Clones. Cancelled Far East Export orders. Check carefully for repaired body damage. Look for rust near the edges of the hard top. Make sure the aircon blows cold. Don't buy with the hardtop fitted and no chance to check out the hood operation and the hood itself for mould or tears. Really need 3,000 mile fully synthetic oil changes.

V Class

WHAT'S GOOD

Based on the excellent Vito van. New 2.2 litre common rail direct-injected diesel is powerful and economical. Lap/diagonal seatblelts for everyone in 7-seater version.

WHAT'S BAD

'V' stands for Vito van with rear side windows, but can't really stand the move up-market and loses buckets of value over the first two years. Many only had 6 seats. Bits drop off. Sliding side door mechanism fails. Van-like to drive.

WHAT TO WATCH OUT FOR

Dings and dents. Check all trim carefully inside and out. Watch for signs of hard usage.

RECALLS

1999 V-Class and Vito van (1996–98 build): Tread may separate from tyres.

MG

MGF 1.8i and VVC

WHAT'S GOOD

The car MG enthusiasts had been clamouring for and, true to their word, they bought it in droves. BBR does a cheap tweak to improve mid-range performance of both engines (01280 702389). Works hard-top looks made for the car. Clever 'crush' boxes built into front bumpers protect the structure of the car in low-speed impacts. Excellent brakes.

WHAT'S BAD

More of a modern MGB than an MGA or Midget. Fine for the over-40s and for women, but not a young man's car. Early MGFs suffered a lot of quality problems, most serious of which was a leaking top, windscreen and bootlid, but fixes were quickly found. Suspension and suspension subframe misalignment is more serious. Park the wrong way on an incline, though and the softtop may still leak. Started to lose value quite heavily in 1999.

WHAT TO WATCH OUT FOR

The MGF bulletin board is a useful means by which owners can swap information about faults on: www.ipl.co.uk/cgi-bin/forum/MG/sub69/cmtlist.html First look for uneven tyre wear which signifies misalighned suspension/suspension subframes. Then silly things, like a bent cable from the exhaust manifold lambda probe can lose its insulation on the hot pipes, short out and stop the car. British Racing Green paint chips easily on flexible front. Have a good look under the carpets for rust caused by water from leaking hoods. Look under the car for damaged coolant pipes from front radiator to mid-engine. Full agent service history essential or 'in service' mods may not have been made. Flexible under-engine exhaust joint gives up (like Cavalier diesel) and rattles. It's in unit with rear silencer and the section costs £380. Gear linkages can be troublesome so check for clean changes on test drive. Hard tops are £1,450 – worth remembering if car has not got one. If buying an MGF with a hard top fitted, take it off and check the hood for damage. Immobiliser frequency can suffer interference. The clutch and brake pedals share the same mounting shaft and the clutch pedal can interfere with the brake light switch.

RECALLS

Boot and windscreen seals carried out as 'in-service' modifications. No official recalls known 1995–98. 1998: 20,000 MGFs recalled to check for snagging of drivers seat belt webbing.

MICROCAR

VIRGO

WHAT'S GOOD

French two seater micro hatchback. Has 2-cylinder 505cc Lombardini petrol or diesel engines giving up to 68 mph and up to 78 mpg. Simple, exposed belt Variomatic transmission. Electric windows & stereo. Fibre-glass rather than polycarbonate body. Under the weight limit, so can be driven on a motorcycle licence. Euro Type Approved. From £6,402 on the road. 3-year warranty on engine.

WHAT'S BAD

Slow acceleration of diesel.

WHAT TO WATCH OUT FOR

Too soon to say.

MINI

MINOR, COOPER, COOPER S

WHAT'S GOOD

To be re-launched as a brand in 2001. Car will be a four seater hatchback with modern styling echoing 1959–99 Mini. Engines to be 90bhp 8-valve 1.4 (for Mini Minor); 125bhp 16v 1.6 (for Mini Cooper) and 150bhp supercharged 1.6 (for Mini Cooper S). Coopers will have 15" wheels; Cooper S's huge 17" wheels. Prices from £12,000 to £17,000. Own website at: www.mini.com

WHAT'S BAD

Not how the original Mini was conceived, but should offer plenty of fun.

WHAT TO WATCH OUT FOR

Too soon to say.

MITSUBISHI

COLT (1989–92)

WHAT'S GOOD

Pleasingly styled along same lines as larger Galant and Lancer. Better looking than Lancer. Engines: 1,298cc 68bhp; 1,468cc, 74bhp; 1,596cc, 123bhp GTi 16v grew to 1,836cc and 134bhp in April 1990 putting it firmly in the Golf GTi 16v league. All models run on standard premium unleaded.

WHAT'S BAD

Service costs and parts prices, particularly body parts.

WHAT TO WATCH OUT FOR

Rust in the seams and floor pan. Skimped, independent servicing after 3-year warranty ran out.

RECALLS

1996 (1991–1994 build): Check for loss of brake fluid.

COLT (1992–96)

WHAT'S GOOD

Quite a pretty car which became the Proton Compact when Mitsubishi restyled the Colt in 1996. 1,298cc 74bhp; 1,597cc 111bhp; 1,834cc twin-cam 138 bhp. Very well built.

WHAT'S BAD

Only one small three door body-style, more supermini sized than Escort sized.

WHAT TO WATCH OUT FOR

Skimped, independent servicing after 3-year warranty ran out. Tappety engines. Badly shifting autobox. Uneven tyre wear signifies kerb damage, possibly strained PAS rack. Could need a cambelt change.

RECALLS

1996 (1991–1994 build): Check for loss of brake fluid.

COLT (from March 1996)

WHAT'S GOOD

Smooth 88bhp 1.6 engine feels more powerful (more like the 111bhp it used to have). Gives excellent combination of performance and up to 42 mpg. Other engine option: 74bhp 1,298cc. Decent steering, ride and handling. Beautifully built. The best 3-year unlimited mileage warranty available. Recommended.

WHAT'S BAD

Only one small three door body-style, more supermini sized than Escort sized. Not as neat looking as previous model. Mirage bodykit ugly and rear spoiler not car-wash proof. Not much back seat room. Shorter people find restricted rear visibility makes it difficult to reverse.

WHAT TO WATCH OUT FOR

Must have been agent serviced to retain warranty. Aircon was a very expensive dealer aftermarket extra.

RECALLS

1997 (June–August 1997 build): 213 cars found to have sticking brake booster valve.

LANCER (1988–92)

WHAT'S GOOD

Essentially, a slightly stretched Colt with either a four door saloon or five door hatchback body. Looks very much like a shrunken Galant. Engines: 1,298cc 68bhp; 1,468cc, 74bhp; 1,596cc, 123bhp GTi 16v grew to 1,836cc and 134bhp in April 1990. Also, just to complicate matters, a 1,755cc 95bhp engine for the GLXi with four wheel drive. All models run on standard premium unleaded.

WHAT'S BAD

Not much rear legroom for a four door saloon. Looks a bit truncated. GLXi had an (unnecessary) catalytic converter. Lancers dropped from official UK line-up from 1992. Next generation Japanese Lancer became Proton Persona. Current generation very successful in international rallying. Some personal imports in UK.

WHAT TO WATCH OUT FOR

Rust in the seams and floor pan. Skimped, independent servicing after 3-year warranty ran out. Uneven tyre wear may signify suspension damage or misalignment on four wheel drive model. Very hard to re-set and get right.

RECALLS

1996 (1991–1994 build): Check for loss of brake fluid.

CARISMA

WHAT'S GOOD

Decent engines, especially 1.8GDI which gives 40 mpg plus economy or strong acceleration from 125bhp – but not both at the same time. Painless to drive and own. Excellent three-year unlimited mileage warranty. Designed for low servicing costs. Facelifted Summer 1999 with new beak-like front.

WHAT'S BAD

Bland Nedcar Eurobox, more Orion than Mondeo sized. Not great to drive. Diesel version much slower and not much more economical than petrol GDI.

WHAT TO WATCH OUT FOR

No known problem areas, yet. Ex-fleet cars may have been abused by drivers. Steering could have suffered damage from kerbing.

SPACE STAR

WHAT'S GOOD

New Carisma-based, Netherlands built 5-door mini MPV to compete against Scenic. Has 85bhp 1.3 Colt engine or 125bhp 1.8 GDI. 3-year unlimited mileage warranty. Versatile rear seats can be double-folded, slid forwards or reclined. Three proper three-point rear seatbelts. Prices from just £11,000.

WHAT'S BAD

1.3 will tug a family of four along at a reasonable pace, but economy suffers. Not powerful enough for five adults and their luggage. For this you need the 1.8GDi. No automatic option at the time of writing.

WHAT TO WATCH OUT FOR

Too new to say.

SPACE RUNNER

WHAT'S GOOD

Strange looking, but very practical car. rear seat comes right out leaving large cube of space. Excellent 3-speed plus overdrive automatic gives 35 mpg. Neat handling. Good performance from 121bhp 16-valve 1.8 litre engine. Upright driving position. Optional aircon does not hurt fuel consumption unduly. Excellent vehicle for the disabled. 3-year unlimited mileage warranty.

WHAT'S BAD

Rear seat in one piece and heavy. Needs optional £35 rear bumper protector to avoid scuff marks. Only one (left hand side) sliding rear door. Comparatively high used prices due to usefulness and scarcity. Replaced at end of 1998 by new Carisma based model. Regular timing belt changes essential.

WHAT TO WATCH OUT FOR

Check sliding door mechanism. Timing belts need changing regularly or engines destroy themselves. Have a good sniff for lingering doggy smells. Check for damage form clumsy wheelchair ramp modifications. Servicing may have been skimped after 3-year warranty period.

SPACE WAGON

WHAT'S GOOD

Car sized seven seater. Not as high as other MPVs. More car-like to drive. 121 bhp 1.8 litre engine replaced by 131bhp 2 litre in August 1992 ('K' reg onwards). Unlimited mileage 3-year warranty. Bigger, better new model with 2.4 litre GDI engine launched at 1998 Motor Show.

WHAT'S BAD

Rearmost seat slopes forwards, not very comfortable for adults. Heavier, so doesn't handle as well and not as much fun to drive as Space Runner. New model only a three star performer in NCAP crash tests (4 points front impact; 15 points side impact).

WHAT TO WATCH OUT FOR

Timing belts need changing regularly or engines destroy themselves. May have been mini-cabbed and run up huge mileage under 3-year warranty. Servicing may have been skimped after first three years. Check for uneven tyre wear. Cable gearchange of manual can become sloppy. Also quite a few grey imports knocking around, so satisfy yourself is to proper UK spec unless offered extremely cheaply.

GALANT (1988–93)

WHAT'S GOOD

Quite good looking and well equipped. GLSI an early beneficiary of ABS. Much improved by Diamond Option Pack. Wood trim packs also help. Normal models very reliable.

WHAT'S BAD

4WD/4WS model too complicated to make a sound second hand buy. Diesel engine only available briefly in 1989. Parts for major repairs are expensive.

WHAT TO WATCH OUT FOR

If fitted with ABS, make sure warning light goes out and that it works. Check for air con and if fitted make sure it delivers cold air. Independent servicing once warranty ran out may have been skimped. Water pumps go (check expansion tank level and check under oil cap for mayonnaise indicating a cooked engine and cylinder head trouble). Power steering pump or rack may leak fluid. Engines wrecked by timing belt failure, so best changed every 36,000 miles or every three years. Uneven tyre wear on 4WD/4WS could signify suspension problems which cost a fortune to put right.

GALANT (1993–97)

WHAT'S GOOD

Better looking, slightly bigger Galant, still in Mondeo/Vectra class.

WHAT'S BAD

2.5 V6 four wheel drive with four wheel steer a bit too complex to be a sensible second-hand buy.

WHAT TO WATCH OUT FOR

See 1989–93.

GALANT (from 1997)

WHAT'S GOOD

Grew from being Mercedes C Class size to Mercedes E Class size. (Made Sigma redundant.) Very Japanese, but very striking styling. By UK standards, quite good value. 2.5 litre V6 automatic estate is a big, heavy, luxurious car. Usual excellent three-year unlimited mileage warranty. Three three-point rear seatbelts from 1998 model year.

WHAT'S BAD

Quite hard to judge the front when parking. More suspension 'clonks' than a BMW. Don't hold their value as well as a Mercedes or BMW.

WHAT TO WATCH OUT FOR

Minor body damage could mean a major repair bill.

SIGMA (1991–96)

WHAT'S GOOD

Two cars: Japanese-built high-tech 202 bhp 24-valve 3 litre V6 'executive' saloon. Australian-built 168 bhp 12-

valve 3 litre V6 estate came later in Feb '93. Both front-wheel drive, both capable of over 130 mph and saloon capable of over 140. Engines sound wonderful. Steering a bit too light. Manual option on estate, but not saloon. Aircon standard on saloon, optional on estate. 3-year unlimited mileage warranty.

WHAT'S BAD

202 bhp Sigma saloon too complicated for long term reliability at more than three years old. Lots of geegaws to go wrong. Body parts can be hard to get. No serious problem areas known.

WHAT TO WATCH OUT FOR

Make sure estate has aircon. Check for damage in load area from loads and dogs. If it's had a towbar, what has it been towing? Look for skimped independent servicing once warranty ran out.

RECALLS

1996: (1991–1994 build):

Check for loss of brake fluid.

SHOGUN (1991–99)

WHAT'S GOOD

Big, but not 'aggressive' looking. Better on the road than a Discovery or Range Rover. 3-year unlimited mileage warranty from new. Very good 3 litre 24v V6. Auto available. 5-door is a full seven seater, but driver's rear vision badly restricted. Facelifted as from Autumn 1997 Motor Show.

WHAT'S BAD

Don't buy for economy. Even the 2.8 litre diesel in the 5-door body is pushed to better than 22 mpg. 3 litre V6s even more thirsty. Diesels are also a bit slow. Gearboxes are the first bits to break. (New Shogun due mid-Y2K.)

WHAT TO WATCH OUT FOR

Eventually, they do rust and its important to check all the

points where the body meets the chassis. Listen for transmission whine (used replacement gear and transfer boxes are available from API, tel: 0500 830530.) Make all usual 4x4 checks: underbody damage; grumbling wheel bearings; suspension alignment; if it's been towing, what has it been towing? Steering arm balljoints go, but are fairly cheap to replace and easy to get at. Quite a few 'exported' to BFPO squaddies and re-imported tax-free. Make sure it's a real UK market Shogun and not a 'Pajero' or 'Montero' badged as one. Pay less for Pajeros and Monteros.

RECALLS

1996: (1991–1994 build): Check for loss of brake fluid.

SHOGUN (from 1999)

WHAT'S GOOD

Still obviously a Shogun, but now more rounded looking. New '4M41' 3.2 litre 16-valve direct injected diesel replaces underpowered old 2.8, offering 173bhp and 282lb ft torque. 217bhp/257 lbs ft 3.5 litre GDI V6 replaces thirsty old 24v V6. Suspension now independent both front and rear which improves on road ride comfort and handling enormously.

WHAT'S BAD

Too soon to say.

WHAT TO WATCH OUT FOR

Too soon to say.
SHOGUN PININ

WHAT'S GOOD

Cute 'Shrunken Shogun' designed to compete with 3-door RAV 4 and Freelander. 120bhp 1.8 litre BDI engine helps economy. 5-speed manual or 4-speed auto options. Short overhangs and high/low-range gears should make it very capable off road.

WHAT'S BAD

Not as quick nor as fun to drive as RAV 4. Limited interior space, and not much room for luggage

behind rear seats.

WHAT TO WATCH OUT FOR

Evidence of heavy off road use or heavy towing.

NISSAN

MICRA (1983–92)

WHAT'S GOOD

Amazingly reliable until they get old. Can be run on a shoestring. Cambelt replacement is a cheap £60 job, but best to replace camshaft end seal and water pump at the same time. API can supply good quality second-hand replacement engines for £455 + VAT (0500 830530).

WHAT'S BAD

Bodies start to rattle after four years. Very light build makes occupants vulnerable in a crash. Scratches rust quickly. Cambelts need to be replaced regularly and camshaft end seals at the

same time. Waterpumps eventually go and either snap the cambelt or lead to severe overheating which can wreck the engine. Fuel pump diaphragms fail, leaking neat petrol into the oil sump leading to severe engine wear and possibly even an explosion.

WHAT TO WATCH OUT FOR

Far too many suffer from neglected servicing and 'short run syndrome'. Elderly owners simply forget to service them. Mayonnaise under oil filler cap may be condensation, but mayonnaise under the radiator cap is a sign of a head problem. If the engine overheats on the test drive, its cylinder head is warped. Requires coolant replacement with special Nissan coolant (or Trigard) every two years or engine will corrode internally. After high mileage, will start to burn oil and need either new valve stem seals or a replacement engine. If engine has been replaced or reconditoned it may be dodgy. Any 'rumbling' from the bottom of the engine is likely to be the water pump about to fail (allow £150–£200 for new water pump, timing belt, camshaft end seal). A smell of petrol under the bonnet usually signifies fuel pump failure (allow £100 for new fuel pump plus oil and filter change).

RECALLS

Early Micras from 1985-87 recalled for gearbox oil loss fault. Oil fed its way up the speedo cable and dripped onto the pedals. Many Micras did not come back for the modification.

MICRA (from 1992)

WHAT'S GOOD

Jewel-like 16-valve chain-cam engines. Broadened the market for the Micra, making it a young person's car as well as an old person's. Well built, in Sunderland. Sensible parts prices (cats are £200). Special pre-facelift 1998 run out 1 litre model had CVT and power steering.

WHAT'S BAD

Cute 'blobby' styling works for some, not for others. Most did not have power steering. Average performance in NCAP crash tests. Must have 6 monthly oil changes to avoid timing chain trouble.

WHAT TO WATCH OUT FOR

Clocking. Dirty oil. If the timing chain rattles and the car is out of warranty, leave it alone. You could be in for a £400–£500 tensioner replacement job. May have suspension damage from kerbing – most likely and most damaging on power steered cars. Clutches of early cars don't last, but most will by now have been replaced. Previously reliable CVT has started to develop the same electromechanical clutch problems as Puntos. If it thumps when you move the lever to drive, or if the lever is hard to move, leave the car alone.

RECALLS

1994 (Sep 92–June 94 VIN 000001–237783): Floor may crack next to handbrake.

SUNNY (1987–91)

WHAT'S GOOD

Easy to drive. Strong engines. Can be cheap to run and home maintenance is possible.

WHAT'S BAD

Hideous styling. Uninvolving to drive. Thin sheet metal

will rust quickly if paint is broken. Not built to last.

WHAT TO WATCH OUT FOR

Skimped or incompetent home maintenance. Rust (especially structural rust underneath). Oil smoke denoting either bore wear or worn valve stem seals. Suspension damage from kerbing by elderly owners (most likely with 1.6 litre power-steered cars). Need regular timing belt changes.

SUNNY (1991–95)

WHAT'S GOOD

Better looking than previous model. Reliable, easy to drive, reasonable build and decent equipment levels. 143bhp 2.0e GTi is quick

WHAT'S BAD

Nondescript 'Golf clone' styling, with excessive rear overhang for a car of this type. Apart from GTi, uninvolving to drive. 'K' reg 'carb and cat' combination is troublesome.

WHAT TO WATCH OUT FOR

Carry out reverse turn test fort driveshaft clonks. Look for oil leaks. Check for uneven front tyre wear signifying suspension misalignment or damage from kerbing by elderly owners. Never pay extra for ultra-low mileage. Look for front end damage on GTi from falling off the road. Best cars will have a full service history with oil changes every six months and coolant and brake fluid changes every two years, but most will have been serviced once a year if the owner remembered. Vital to see a recent MOT emissions check on K reg 'carb and cat' cars as they are very difficult to get through this test.

ALMERA (to 2000)

WHAT'S GOOD

Tough. Strong, chain-driven twin-cam engines. Decent handling, good to drive, good ride quality, good roadholding. 143 bhp GTi (launched 1996) is a good 'hot hatch'. Four door saloon version by far the best looking and has three three-point rear belts.

WHAT'S BAD

Hopeless styling of original hatchbacks. Some 1.4 litre models have very mean equipment levels. Diesels are slow. We pay about twice as much for them as they do in Japan. Comparatively poor performance of hatchback in 1999 NCAP secondary safety crash tests.

WHAT TO WATCH OUT FOR

Make sure engine has clean oil and that coolant has been changed every two years (a messy, but necessary service job, often neglected). Engines have two timing chains so any rattles in this department, don't buy. Expect noises

from multi-link suspension –
often cured by spraying with
WD40.

RECALLS

1998 (Dec '97–May '98
build): Inertia reel seatbelts
may not lock on impact.

ALMERA (from 2000)

WHAT'S GOOD

New Almera due Y2K. Has
more exaggerated 'beaked
front' look than new
Primera. 5 door hatch does
away with 'D' pillar side
windows and looks much
better for it. 1.5–1.8 litre
petrol engines. New 2.2 litre
direct injected diesel. British
built at Sunderland
alongside Micra and
Primera. Interesting Tina
MPV version seen at
European motor shows in
1999.

WHAT'S BAD

The UK taxpayer had to fork
out for it to be built in
Sunderland.

WHAT TO WATCH OUT FOR

Too soon to say.

PRIMERA (1990–96)

WHAT'S GOOD

Unbreakable chain-cam
engines on 2 litre petrol but
not diesel. 2 litre twin cam
petrol engine very punchy.
Decent ride/handling
combination. Very good
(Sunderland) build quality.
Big boot. 2 litre petrol
models are the best buy
among 1990–96 upper
medium size cars.
Recommended.

WHAT'S BAD

Not a great 'looker'. Steering
a bit light on Mk I models.
Gearbox a bit weak and
won't stand abuse. Complex
rear suspension develops
squeaks and rattles (easily
cured with a spray of WD
40). Non-turbo diesels are
slow and have timing belts

rather than chains. Very difficult to drain the block to change the coolant (needs to be changed every two years to prevent internal engine corrosion). Two timing chains in 1.6 engine are one too many, but still no record of problems from them.

WHAT TO WATCH OUT FOR

Clocking. Evidence of lack of oil changes (black sludge on the dipstick) and lack of coolant changes (highly likely due to difficulty of job). Uneven tyre wear will mean front suspension damage from kerbing or wear in suspension bushes. Rear silencer boxes rust out rapidly even on 25,000-mile-a-year cars.

RECALLS

1995 (VIN 000001 to 472213): Front brake hoses may chafe. 1997 (June '96–Feb '97 build): Fuel vapour may leak from tank.

PRIMERA (1996–99)

WHAT'S GOOD

Unbreakable chain-cam engines on 2 litre petrol but not diesel. Drivetrain feels exactly the same as previous model. But steering slightly better and roadholding from new rear suspension is astonishing. Very good build quality. Big boot. Comparatively good performance in NCAP crash tests.

WHAT'S BAD

Not a great 'looker' compared to the rest of the class. Gearbox still bit weak and won't stand abuse. Still difficult to drain the block to change the coolant (needs to be changed every two years to prevent internal engine corrosion). Still two timing chains in 1.6 engine.

WHAT TO WATCH OUT FOR

Clocking. Evidence of lack of oil changes (black sludge on the dipstick). Uneven tyre wear and front suspension damage from kerbing.

RECALLS

1997 (June '96–Feb '97 build): Fuel vapour may leak from tank.

NEW PRIMERA (from Sept 1999)

WHAT'S GOOD

New sheetmetal from September 1999 turned the Primera from an excellent car let down by nondescript looks into a real polariser of tastes. New flexible 1,769cc 114bhp engine develops 111 lb ft torque from 2,400–4,800 rpm. New 'Hypertronic' CVT transmission is the first CVT with a 2 litre engine. CVT also offered with six ratio electronic manual hold.

WHAT'S BAD

Do you like the way it looks? Do your neighbours like the way it looks?

WHAT TO WATCH OUT FOR

Too soon to say.

PRAIRIE (1989–92)

WHAT'S GOOD

Replaced box-like 1983–89 Prairie, Still Sunny based, but now with up to seven seats. Much liked by mobility converters because the design allows a drop floor and slightly raised rear roof so electric wheelchairs can drive straight in. 2 litre Bluebird engine.

WHAT'S BAD

No nicer to drive than old Prairie due to vague steering and body roll.

WHAT TO WATCH OUT FOR

Rust, sticking sliding side doors, suspension wear from overloading, dog-eaten upholstery, gears difficult to select, uneven tyre wear. Engine needs regular timing belt changes.

SERENA
(from 1993)

WHAT'S GOOD

Tall, narrow MPV, fits a normal car-size parking space. Rear wheel drive (though specials were made with front or four wheel drive). 2 litre 126bhp Primera engined SGX models with independent rear suspension and aircon by far the best. SLX and 'Excursion' models have standard aircon from May '97. The cheapest 7–8 seater. Reliable. Timing chains on petrol models. Three star performer in NCAP crash tests (5 points front impact; 16 points side impact).

WHAT'S BAD

A Step back from the 89–92 Prairie. Crude, commercial van-based design, built in Spain. Unpleasant to drive. 67bhp 2 litre and 75bhp 2.3 litre diesels plain awful, with horrible droning jerky drive-train like a pre-war double decker bus.

WHAT TO WATCH OUT FOR

Likely to have been airport taxis and to have covered more miles than on the clock. Some had two side doors; some had only one. Check for excessive smoke from diesels (dirty injectors or air filter). With its two timing chains, 1.6 petrol needs to have had regular oil changes. Electric windows stick.

200SX
(from 1994)

WHAT'S GOOD

Transformed by new body from October 1994. Squat, well-proportioned almost Italian looks. Very good looking. 1996 facelift made it even better. 197bhp 2 litre turbo four not bad either. Manual or automatic. Usually with leather and air. Rear drive handling. Better ride than previous version. More room inside, especially back seats.

WHAT'S BAD

Not as sharp to drive as previous model. (But still inclined to swap ends in the wet.)

WHAT TO WATCH OUT FOR

Oddball grey imports not to proper spec with 55mph limited Japanese tyres and wipers that lift off the screen at 70 mph. Must have been serviced zealously, with extra oil changes to protect the turbo bearings. Shift to synthetic oil at 10,000 to 15,000 miles a wise move.

300SX (1990–94)

WHAT'S GOOD

Very serious twin-turbo 280bhp junior supercar, killed off by European emissions legislation. 'Full on' manuals or 'Mr Softy' autos, usually with leather and air. Very comfortable. Goes like stink and handles surprisingly well.

WHAT'S BAD

Rear three quarters vision not good. Handbrake a long way back. To drive, the manual is best, but buy an auto.

WHAT TO WATCH OUT FOR

Grey imports without the twin turbos and other important items of kit. Noisy engines. Exhaust smoke (turbo oil seals), dirty oil, lack of maintenance. Look for uneven tyre wear – may be simple misalignment, may have been 'sausaged'. Manual boxes and clutches lead a hard life and boxes are mega expensive to replace. Cars which have been sitting require a full recommission or you'll be in for all sorts of problems. Tyres may have 'flat-spotted', discs rusted, exhaust rotted (especially rear silencer boxes). Targa rood panels may leak – not easy to get new seals for them. Power steering may have spring a leak.

SKYLINE GT-R

WHAT'S GOOD

Phenomenal four wheel drive junior supercar that looks like a tricked-up coupe. Astonishing performance and handling. Three different generations of GT-R among unofficial imports: R32 (1989–1994); R33 (1995–1998); and R34 (1999 on). Also V-Spec models. Have been chipped in Japan to more than 1,000bhp, but standard conservatively estimated 280bhp (more like a true 320bhp) is plenty.

WHAT'S BAD

Very limited official UK imports (and performance limited to get through SVA).

WHAT TO WATCH OUT FOR

Lots of grey imports about dating back to the early 1990s, so make sure you know what you're getting. New grey imports now restricted by quota so don't buy a car which isn't registered. Check for uneven tyre wear and for pulling to either side an a flat road. Extremely complex suspension and drivetrain difficult to get parts for, to repair and to set up. Make sure the car is a GT-R and not either an R33 GT-S or, worse still, an ordinary Skyline which could be eleven years old.

TERRANO II

WHAT'S GOOD

Unbreakable, simple, old fashioned 4x4. Vastly improved in July 1996, especially 2.7 litre diesel which gained intercooler and 25 more bhp. (This is the same engine as most London taxis.) 5-door LWB versions can have 7 seats. Carried on when Ford pulled the plug on the Maverick.

WHAT'S BAD

Tall and narrow, so you have to be careful on corners and better not pile stuff on the roof. Jerky on-road ride – partly suspension, partly due to driveline. Spanish build quality not 100% up to the mark, especially trim items.

WHAT TO WATCH OUT FOR

Quite likely to have been off-roaded, especially if registered in a country area. Farmers cars will have seen some work, though remember farmers drive to preserve their vehicles – it's the off road enthusiasts who break them. Look for weeping seals, noisy hubs, clonky driveshafts, driveshaft 'lash', noisy gearbox or transfer case, oil leaks from engine and drive-train. Smoke from diesel may indicate that turbo oil seals have failed.

RECALLS

1995 (with Michelin 215/80 R15 tyres: VIN 200000 to 242699): Tyres may lose pressure.

PERODUA

NIPPA

WHAT'S GOOD

Strong Sterling exchange rates against the Malaysian Ringit enabled importers to offer their EX model as low as £4,800, including a two-year 24,000 mile warranty. For the UK, that's cheap. Has same responsive 42bhp 850cc 3-cylinder engine as Daihatsu Mira, Cuore and Move. Sells well in North East England, but brilliant for cities, shopping, suburbia and the school run.

WHAT'S BAD

Very small. Very basic. Mediocre cornering abilities. For £4,800 you don't get a radio (can't have everything).

WHAT TO WATCH OUT FOR

If previously owned by an
elderly person, may have
suffered heavy clutch wear
and over-revving when cold.

Younger owners may have
revved the nuts off them
trying to find some
performance.

PEUGEOT

106

WHAT'S GOOD

All handle well. Stronger
(and actually heavier) than
bigger 205. Revised range
from June 1996 includes hot
GTi 16v generally reckoned
to handle better than
equivalent Saxo.

WHAT'S BAD

Twisted-spine offset driving
position. Tall people just
don't fit.

WHAT TO WATCH OUT FOR

Check spare wheel is in its
underboot cradle and not
nicked. Front suspension
wear. Oil leaks. Needs
frequent timing belt
changes. 1.5 diesels need

regular servicing and regular
coolant replacement – are
especially heavy on front
tyres. Check for falling off
the road damage to GTi 16v.
16vs tend to blow their cats
when run against rev limiter.

RECALLS

1997 (March–Nov '96 build:
15,821 cars): Ignition switch
harness may foul on steering
column.

205

WHAT'S GOOD

The definitive 1980s
hatchback. Brilliant 'wheel in
each corner' design, no
space wasted anywhere and
great looking. Excellent ride

and handling combination, very throttle sensitive with lift-off oversteer available on demand on GTis. Sold 5.3 million. Later post 88 'TU' sub 1.4 engines better than early small engines which still had their gearboxes in the sump. Diesels capable of 50mpg and late versions came with power steering. Clever cantilever folding front seats of three door bodies give good access to rear seat. I've done 950 miles in a day in a 1.6 GTi without even a twinge of backache.

WHAT'S BAD

Very light build, so vulnerable in accidents – especially at the back. Small front discs of early diesels lead to heavy pad wear. Single front reservoir of pre-86 cars could lead to problems with rear wash/wipe. Valve stem seals of GTis give out at around 60,000 miles. Cambelts and camshaft end seals of all XUs must be changed every three years and 36,000

miles. Coolant of diesels must be changed every two years to avoid cylinder head gasket problems. No underbody rust traps, but superficial rust a problem on early cars.

WHAT TO WATCH OUT FOR

Check spare wheel is in its underboot cradle and not nicked. Front suspension wear (205s and 306s tend to 'lean' on the front suspension and are particularly vulnerable to kerb damage). Oil burning petrol engines needing new valve stem seals (allow £120). Crash damage and rust in doors, window surrounds and brake pipes. Rusty rear discs on 1.9 GTis.

206

WHAT'S GOOD

Interesting new 3 or 5 door supermini sized between 106 and 306. 60bhp 1.1, 75bhp 1.4 and 90bhp 1.6 petrol engines from 106, but new 70bhp 1,868cc DW8 diesel based on XUD. PAS and height adjustable steering column standard. Same excellent 306 suspension. 136bhp 2 litre 16v GTi, 90bhp HDI diesel and 1.4 litre automatic all came later. More roomy inside than new Clio. 500 a day built in Coventry. Image promoted by 300bhp WRC rally version. Well thought out inside with options such as a folding passenger seat that turns into a desk.

WHAT'S BAD

Not a style classic like the 205 and 306 (styled in house by computer; not by Pininfarina). Mixed reactions from journalists to handling qualities, but Quentin Willson liked it, so the chances are it will be very successful.

WHAT TO WATCH OUT FOR

Too soon to say.

306

WHAT'S GOOD

Excellent ride and handling combination, best in class until Focus came along. 1.6 TU best petrol engine for family car – very nicely balanced. 167 bhp 2 litre GTi-6 is track-car quick with roadholding and handling to match, plus a 6-speed gearbox. All capable of 150,000 miles plus if properly looked after. Non-turbo XUD capable of 50mpg. D-Turbo surprisingly quick. Three Star 'above average' performance in NCAP crash tests.

WHAT'S BAD

High used values due to prettiness of body. 1.8 8-valve XU petrol is the worst engine and many were fitted with a wrong engine management chip leading to failed emissions tests. Autobox not recommended. Cambelts and camshaft end seals must be changed every three years and 36,000 miles. Coolant of diesels must be changed every two years to avoid cylinder head gasket problems. Like Citroen ZX, can have cat converter test problems. Build quality a bit 'light'. Easy to fluff 3rd to 4th gearchange on GTi-6.

WHAT TO WATCH OUT FOR

See above. Front suspension wear (205s and 306s tend to 'lean' on the front suspension and are vulnerable to kerb damage). Oil burning petrol engines needing new valve stem seals (allow £120). Not all diesels has PAS and all need it. Check spare wheel is in its underboot cradle and not nicked. If fitted with low profile tyres, check for tyre and rim damage. If fitted with aircon. make sure it works properly.

RECALLS

1995: Check accelerator cable. 1996 (July 1993–February 1996 bulld – 150,000 cars): Underbonnet wiring may chafe leading to short circuit and fire. 1997: possible starter motor fault on 1996 model cars. Free replacement. 1997 (Feb–May '97 build: 2,060 cars): incorrect brake compensator fitted. 1998: (Sep '97–Oct '97 build): Steering wheel hub may crack; (Nov '97–Apr '98 build): Front suspension may collapse.

307

WHAT'S GOOD

(Replaces 306 in Y2K.)

WHAT'S BAD

May not be as good looking as 306.

WHAT TO WATCH OUT FOR

Too soon to say.

309

WHAT'S GOOD

Not as bad as it looks. Stretched 205 floorpan gives good combination of ride and handling, plus decent sized square-shaped boot. Old 'suitcase engines' (they need to be unpacked before you can work on them) good for 170,000 miles. Later TU and larger XU engines good. Diesels were the best of their day. The 309GTi 1.9 outhandled the Golf GTi Mk II and many thought it a better (though flimsier) car. High back seats of 3-door GTi gives back seat passengers a good view. Clever levers next to handbrake to open rear windows.

WHAT'S BAD

Its looks. Truly dreadful British styling (Peugeot's only departure from Pininfarina between 1959 and 1998). Was supposed to be a successor to the awful American Chrysler Horizon. To see what good looks could do for basically the same car, read Peugeot 306.

WHAT TO WATCH OUT FOR

TU and XU cambelts and cambelt end seals need changing every 35,000–40,000 miles whatever the handbook tells you, especially now these cars are getting older. Mk I (high boot sill) rear hatchbacks are leak prone and this may have led to rusting of boot floor. GTis tend to start smoking at around 60,000 miles, but all they usually need are new valve stem seals.

405

WHAT'S GOOD

Fine Pininfarina styling. All handle and ride well. Practical estate cars. Narrow enough to fit most garages.

WHAT'S BAD

Light build. Rust. Not all had power steering and all need it. Aircon system on GTX models prone to problems.

WHAT TO WATCH OUT FOR

Check spare wheel is in its underboot cradle and not

nicked. Look for front suspension wear. Rusted brake pipes are an MOT failure point (later models had coated brake pipes). Many diesels were taxis so look for the signs. Clocking of diesels is rife. Run diesels with dipstick out to check for excessive fumes from worn engine. Check for mayonnaise under oil cap signifying had gasket problems. All 405s, petrol or diesel, need a cambelt and camshaft end seal change every three years and 36,000 miles. Early carburettor petrol cars suffered from fuel vaporisation. All XU engines can suffer premature bore and big end wear if the oil has not been changed regularly. Trim does not take a hammering. Look for fluid leaks from power steering rack and pump, clonky driveshafts, worn bushes in external gearshift mechanism.

RECALLS

1995 (1995 model year to VIN 71339513): Airbag may fail to inflate in an accident. 1996 (Sept '93–May '95 build): Check for seepage of fuel from feed pipe.

406

WHAT'S GOOD

Bigger 'classier' car than the 405. Spare wheel now inside boot. Excellent ride and handling compromise. Powerful and economical 2.1TD. New class-leading HDI diesel engine from October 1998. Three lap and diagonal rear belts. 7-seater estate. Spare wheel now in boot floor well.

WHAT'S BAD

Build still feels a bit light. 2.1TD is a nightmare for mechanics to work on. Average performance in NCAP crash tests. Have received a well above average number of complaints from owners.

WHAT TO WATCH OUT FOR

Small dings in sheetmetal. ECU problems not sorted out in 96N/96P reg cars. 'Clonking' (likely to be wear in anti-roll bar bushes). Clocking on diesels. Oil consumption of 1.8i and 2.0i 16v petrol engines. Wrong chips fitted to ECUs on first year's production may or may not have been replaced (an MOT emissions test will tell you). Aircon system prone to problems.

RECALLS

1996 (1.8i and 2.0i petrol): Free upgrade of engine management chip if owner complains of 'rough' running, flat spots and lack of power on hills. 1997 (Nov '95–Apr '96 build: 13,412 cars): Ignition switch harness may foul on steering column. 1997 (Feb '97 build: 333 cars) Incorrect front subframe mountings.

406 COUPE

WHAT'S GOOD

Impeccable Pininfarina styling. One of the best looking cars in the world – better looking than more expensive Volvo C70 and Mercedes CLK. A truly beautiful car. Plenty of room for four passengers. Big boot. Airconditioning a more sensible option than sun-roof. 2 litre versions go and handle like a sports car – much better than 406 saloon. 3 litre V6 has four pot Brembo front brake callipers. Hold their value reasonably well.

WHAT'S BAD

Steering and handling of 3 litre V6 not as sharp or as sporty as 2 litre 16v. Could suffer same aircon system problems as saloon and estate.

WHAT TO WATCH OUT FOR

The 2 litre engines are easily chipped and power can be anything from standard 135bhp up to 155bhp. They don't have the low back pressure tubular exhaust manifold of the 167bhp–180bhp GTi-6, though. Oil consumption may be quite high. 3.0 autos may suffer from warped discs due to owners holding them in gear on the brakes.

605

WHAT'S GOOD

Big car with the best rear legroom in its class. V6s handle well and can be thrown about like a 205GTi. 2.1TD is economical and a relaxed long distance cruiser. Build quality much improved after January 1995 facelift. 1990–94 SVE 24-valve had 200bhp and was a seriously fast car. 170bhp 12-valve V6 not a bad compromise. 150bhp 2.0 8v turbo not a bad engine.

WHAT'S BAD

Overlight power steering. Riddled with build quality and electrical problems. The UK market never took to it. 2.1TD very hard to work on. Manual gearboxes a bit weak for V6 engines. Plummeting residual values. 16-valve 2 litre engines had ECU problems. 2.1TD auto more suited to long distance than town work.

WHAT TO WATCH OUT FOR

Most 2.1TD covered mega mileages, so may have been clocked. Check all electrics. Make sure aircon blows cold. Make sure catalytic converters aren't hot spotted. (Put it through an advanced emissions test.) If manual, satisfy yourself that clutch and gearbox are in good health. ABS prone to failure and cost of repairing may be more than the car is worth.

RECALLS

(None known 1994–96 – but that's surprising.)

607

WHAT'S GOOD

Due mid-Y2K, Peugeot's new big car starting with new 2.2 litre 160bhp 'four' at around £23,000 and rising to around £27,000 for the 210bhp 3.0 V6. Also a new 2.2 litre HDI.

WHAT'S BAD

Likely to be doomed by the lack of success of the 605.

WHAT TO WATCH OUT FOR

Too soon to say.

806 MPV

WHAT'S GOOD

Same well-planned reasonably compact MPV as the Citroen Synergie, with the same PSA engines, including new HDI 110bhp. Three star performer in NCAP crash tests (7 point front impact; 15 points side impact).

WHAT'S BAD

See Citroen Synergie

WHAT TO WATCH OUT FOR

See Citroen Synergie.

RECALLS

1996 (Sept '95–Oct '95 build): Check airbag trigger.

PORSCHE

944

WHAT'S GOOD

A grown up 924 with a proper Porsche engine rather than the engine out of a VW LT van. 2.5 had 163bhp from Jan '86 to Sept '88; 2.7 had 165bhp from Sept '88 to June '89. 2.5S16v had 190bhp from Sept '86 to June '88; 2.5 Turbo had 220bhp from Jan '86 to

Sept '88, then 250bhp to May '92. 3.0 S2 had 221 bhp from Jan '89 to May '92.

WHAT'S BAD

Strong acceleration likely to have been used. Many were stolen. Likely to have seen time on 'track days' and could have come off the track. Confusing engine range, but 211bhp S2 the best overall. 165bhp 3-speed autos are comparatively slow.

WHAT TO WATCH OUT FOR

Getting old now and may have fallen into the hands of abusers unable or unwilling to afford proper maintenance. This doesn't have to be Porsche agent, but does have to be a respected Porsche specialist who knows what he's doing. (Visit the bloke who maintained it and see how many Porsches he's working on that day.) Has two timing belts (one for the balancer shaft) and periodic re-tensioning of these is critical.

968

WHAT'S GOOD

Very punchy 240bhp 3 litre 4-cylinder engine more powerful than 231bhp 1983-89 911. 6-speed manual gearbox. Near perfect balance. Brilliant rear wheel drive handling. Stripped out 'Club Sport' model for purists. Became a 'classic' as soon as it went out of production. Will do 160mph 'on the clock'. Recommended.

WHAT'S BAD

Will probably have seen a few track days on race tracks. (Club Sport models definitely will have – no point in the car otherwise). 4-speed Tiptronic cabriolet comparatively slow. Cabriolet hoods attract envy slashes.

WHAT TO WATCH OUT FOR

Check carefully, preferably by professionals, that it has not been thrashed and crashed. HPI or AA/Experian check will make sure it's not on VCAR, but if crashed on a circuit would not have been insured anyway. Make sure the clutch still has plenty of life left in it. Look out for damaged alloys (could be from kerbs, could have had an off.) Cat could be blown from running against rev limiter. Also as everything in this section under 944.

911 (1983–89)

WHAT'S GOOD

Some say the last 'classic' 911 (I don't agree, I prefer the '89–'93 C2). Galvanized body panels. Properly looked after, it will last for ever.

WHAT'S BAD

Can be a handful in the wrong hands, particularly the 300bhp 3.3 Turbo. Very likely to have seen a few 'track days'.

WHAT TO WATCH OUT FOR

Signs of accident damage (suspiciously new looking rear wing stays); clutch slip (a new clutch is a £2,000 engine out job); exhaust system (as expensive as a clutch); oil cooler (expensive). Feel the discs for ridges, wear and shouldering. Make sure callipers aren't sticking at the back. Find a good local independent Porsche specialist to inspect the car and give it a compression test before you buy it. Once you own the car, take it in for regular servicing at least every 6 months even if you hardly use the car.

911/964 model C2 AND C4 (1989–93)

WHAT'S GOOD

More power than previous 911 (250bhp v/s 231bhp). A great drive with far more controllable and exploitable oversteer than bar talk would have you believe.

Nothing to be scared of at all. C2 preferable to four wheel drive C4. 260bhp Carrerra RS Lightweight the pick of the bunch. Recommended.

WHAT'S BAD

Idiots still crash them on the road. 320bhp Turbos are for experienced racing drivers only. Very likely to have seen a few 'track days'.

WHAT TO WATCH OUT FOR

If they fall off the road, C2s still tend to do it arse-first. So check the back end very carefully. New rear wing stays inside the rear wings are a sure sign of damage repairs, as are rear reflectors full of condensation (once the car has been smacked, they're difficult to seal). C4s, on the other hand, go straight on, so you need to check the fronts of these. You need to see a full and consistent Porsche agent or respected Porsche specialist service history with no major gaps during which it might have been stolen or awaiting a rebuild. Proper histories also make clocking more difficult. A duff clutch is an engine out £2,000 job to replace. Town driven cars may wear out their oil stem seals – not easy to replace on a quad cam flat six (don't buy without a compression test). Exhaust systems and heat exchangers still expensive. Feel the brake discs for scoring and lipping through the wheels (when they're cool, of course). Make sure pop-up rear spoiler works.

RECALLS

1996 (1989–1993 build): 54,000 cars worldwide recalled (2,966 in UK) to check universal joint in steering column which may fail. Early signs are noises or free play in the system.

911/993 model (1993–97)

WHAT'S GOOD

The last incarnation of the flat six, air cooled 911 and also the cleanest looking. 272bhp from December '93 to October '95; 285bhp from then on.

WHAT'S BAD

Monster 408bhp four wheel drive Turbo not a very nice drive. All 911s still have floor-hinged pedals. Very likely to have seen a few 'track days'.

WHAT TO WATCH OUT FOR

See above, and then some. Pay an expert to inspect it for you.

RECALLS

1996 (1993 build): 54,000 cars worldwide recalled (2,966 in UK) to check universal joint in steering column which may fail. Early signs are noises or free play in the system.

911/996 model (from 1997)

WHAT'S GOOD

Top-hinged pedals at last.. Lighter, more powerful, adjustable suspension GT3 by far the best.

WHAT'S BAD

Watercooling may be a mixed blessing (it definitely was when the flat-four VWs went water-cooled). Surprising amount of understeer for a 911.

WHAT TO WATCH OUT FOR

Too early to say.

RECALLS

Porsche 911 Carrera (1998 MY 996 model: 540 UK cars): Wrong size pulley fitted driving ancillaries drive belt which may slip affecting PAS, brakes, water pump and alternator (announced 3/6/98).

BOXTER

WHAT'S GOOD

Of the MB SLK, BMW Z3 and Boxter, the Boxter is the best of the bunch. Some echoes of old RSK. £42,000 252bhp 3.2 litre Boxter S from autumn 1999 has made standard 911 cabrio more or less redundant.

WHAT'S BAD

Still selling for 'overs'. Engine is completely concealed behind difficult-to-remove panels (owner drivers aren't supposed to touch it). You check the oil and water and top them up from the boot. Standard model could do with a bit more power, which it got in the 'S' version.

WHAT TO WATCH OUT FOR

Must have fully stamped up Porsche agent service history, preferably itemised bills as well.

RECALLS

1998: 9574 cars recalled to replace steering lock assembly because of faulty ignition switches. 2692 Tiptronics recalled because "gear selector bearing sleeves could seize up over time."

928

WHAT'S GOOD

Sporty, reliable alternative to the Jaguar XJS V12 and to a Mercedes SL. Kids seats in the back will also take small adults for short distances. Manuals more satisfying to drive, but autobox less likely to give trouble.

WHAT'S BAD

A new engine will set you back £12,000. A clutch and gearbox rebuild could hit you for £6,000. Catalysed exhaust systems are also a fortune.

WHAT TO WATCH OUT FOR

Don't buy unless from a Porsche agent or after an inspection by an independent Porsche specialist. Automatics go through brake pads and discs. Feel the brake discs for scoring and lipping through the wheels (when they're cool, of course). Don't buy town driven cruisers.

PROTON

MPI

WHAT'S GOOD

Reliable with good first owner warranty package. Very cheap. Based on an old Mid- 80s Mitsubishi Lancer.

WHAT'S BAD

Hideously ugly and irredeemably naff. Has some of the most ridiculous wheeltrims ever seen on a car.

WHAT TO WATCH OUT FOR

Rear suspension can collapse. Highly likely to have been mini-cabbed at the bottom end of the market. Old ones mostly owner-serviced or simply neglected.

PERSONA

WHAT'S GOOD

Really a Mitsubishi Lancer model which never reached the UK, but which, when highly modified, was hugely successful in international rallying. Quite good to drive with perky 1,600cc engine. Light years ahead of ancient Lancer-based Proton MPI. Prices from £7,750 for 1.3LSi.

WHAT'S BAD

Slightly unfinished, undeveloped feel to gearchange and interior. Rattles.

WHAT TO WATCH OUT FOR

Trim doesn't wear well. Rattles become more pronounced. Cambelts need changing regularly. Could have been cabbed.

RECALLS

1997 (July–August '97 build: 1,797 cars): Mitsubishi sourced brake booster valve may stick. 1998 (13" wheels only Aug '97–Aug '98 build): Front tyres may lose pressure.

COMPACT

WHAT'S GOOD

The previous model Mitsubishi Colt hatchback with a Proton Persona front. Good engines. Decent handling. Autumn 1999 cuts brought prices down to from £6,750 with alloy wheeled 1.6 litre 'Spectrum' model at £9,999 and 133bhp 1.8 coupe at £12,499.

WHAT'S BAD

Just a bit cramped. See Mitsubishi Colt.

WHAT TO WATCH OUT FOR

As Persona.

RECALLS

1996 (from October 1995 build): Fuel pump can allow fuel to leak when tank is brimmed. 1997 (July–August '97 build – 1,797 cars): Mitsubishi sourced brake booster valve may stick. 1998 (13" wheels only Aug '97–Aug '98 build): Front tyres may lose pressure.

PERDANA

WHAT'S GOOD

Malaysia's economic recovery has allowed the UK launch of its larger car with looks a bit like those of the Toyota Camry. 2 litre V6 with auto, a/c, leather, etc.for around £16,000.

WHAT'S BAD

Criticised for "restless ride" and uninvolving handling at launch. Undercut in price by Kia Clarus 2.0 Executive at £14,295 and Chrysler Neon LX at £13,495.

WHAT TO WATCH OUT FOR

Likely to depreciate quickly from list, so should be a serious bargain second-hand.

RENAULT

5

WHAT'S GOOD

Simple, old car, quite rightly kept in production as 60 bhp 1.4 Campus until March 1996. Cheap.

WHAT'S BAD

Shows its age.

WHAT TO WATCH OUT FOR

May suffer cat converter problems.

RECALLS

1995 (Campus 1.4: VIN C4070510214892 to C4070511788781): Car may pull to left when braking.

TWINGO

WHAT'S GOOD

Great design, practical and fun. Looks like Kermit. Sliding rear seat aka Citroen ZX gives choice of bootspace or rear legroom. Lots of transmission options: 5-speed manual; 5-speed electric clutch 'Easy' or 3-speed 'Matic'. PAS also became available in 1996. Latest airbagged version did reasonably well in German TUV front offset crash tests.

WHAT'S BAD

LHD only. Never officially sold in the UK. Lots about with unconverted digital speedos and right-dipping headlamps which dazzle oncoming drivers and may fail the UK MOT.

WHAT TO WATCH OUT FOR

Second-generation multipoint injected 60 bhp 1,149cc engines much better than older single point injected 1,171cc engines.

CLIO (1991–98

WHAT'S GOOD

Amazingly quiet at town speeds. Decent ride quality from long wheel base. Hot and red hot Clio 1.8 16v and 2.0 Clio Williams. Engines start with old pushrod 49bhp 1,108cc ohv from Renault 8 in 1992 'Night & Day' special. Rise through 60 bhp 1,171 single point injected and 1,149cc multipoint injected OHCs, 75bhp 1,390cc OHCs, 110bhp 1.8s to 137bhp 1.8 16v and 150bhp 2.0 16v Clio Williams. Also a 65bhp 1,870cc diesel. PAS widely available from 1.4s up. 4-speed auto became 3-speed auto in 1.4s from Jan 1996. Facelift with new grille from March 1994. Second facelift with bigger headlights and high level brake light from May 1996.

WHAT'S BAD

'Nicole-Papa' Saga looks like it's written by committee of marketing people and researchers. To protect Clio sales, Renault UK wouldn't let us have the Twingo. Average performance in NCAP crash tests. Watch out for kerbing damage, especially on power-steered Clios.

WHAT TO WATCH OUT FOR

4-speed autobox cooling system (oil cooler within the water radiator) can cause problems. Kerbing damage to front suspension. 1998: (June '97–Nov '97 build): Possibility of "inadvertent deployment of airbags".

CLIO (from Spring 1998)

WHAT'S GOOD

Pleasingly 'different' with cute protruding bottom. Looks good on the streets. High spec includes power steering, sunroof and driver's airbag – from £8,850, undercutting equivalent Polo by £1,535. Vic and Bob 'Graduate' commercial showed its cracks repeated incessantly during 1998 World Cup.

WHAT'S BAD

Engine line-up nothing to get excited about.

WHAT TO WATCH OUT FOR

Too soon to say, but expect kerbing damage.

19

WHAT'S GOOD

1.4s surprisingly trouble-free. You can reckon on 8–9 years and 90,000–100,000 miles before they start to get expensive. Even the catalytic converters can last nine years and 90,000 miles. Diesels are rough but tough with good economy. 16-valve models are screamers and were one of the 'cars to have' in the mid-90s.

WHAT'S BAD

Dull looks before the beak-like facelift. Autos can give up at around 60,000 miles.

WHAT TO WATCH OUT FOR

If the paint has faded, it may come up with Mer polish. Torn seat trim difficult to do much about unless you call a local car upholsterer (Yellow Pages). Switches break. Non PAS have heavy helms. Autobox the first bit to break. Likely to be rust under plastic window sill trims.

RECALLS

1994 (Renault 19 Phase II – Apr 92–Mar 94): Faulty seat belt pretensioners and bonnet catch.

MEGANE

WHAT'S GOOD

Sweet, precise handling. Economical diesel. Even more economical TDI from May 1998. Joint top of the class for secondary safety in NCAP crash testing. Galvanized body has 12-year warranty. New 1.6 litre 16-valve engine from Summer 1999.

WHAT'S BAD

Silly things go wrong such as the flywheel sensor cable connector. 1.4s and 1.6s a bit underpowered by the standards of the day. Coupe pointless except as a basis for the smart cabrio. Engine has to come out to replace the clutch. Several *Telegraph* readers report needing a replacement engine around 8,000 miles.

WHAT TO WATCH OUT FOR

Kerbing damage, strange electrical faults.

RECALLS

1997 (Megane and Scenic July–Sept '97 build): 7,434 cars found to have potentially defective braking system.

MEGANE SCENIC

WHAT'S GOOD

By far the most popular Megane. Sensible, practical without being in the least dull. Brilliantly planned, versatile interior. Three three-point rear belts. Huge square-shaped boot. Economical diesel. Even more economical TDI from mid-1998. Galvanized body has 12-year warranty. Refreshed from October 1999 with a new front, new 95bhp 1.4, 110bhp 1.6 and 140bhp 2 litre engines and 35 different models. 1.6 16v reckoned to be the best of the bunch. 'Sporty' 2 litre criticised for harsh suspension and unsporty steering.

KANGOO COMBI

WHAT'S BAD

Non-electric sunroofs don't slide and serve as no more than pop-up vents. Clutch replacement is expensive. Don't try to carry things on the roof. Comparatively poor performance in TUV/Auto Bild offset crash test.

WHAT TO WATCH OUT FOR

Kerbing damage, electrical faults, stained seats, unspeakable smells left by incontinent babies.

RECALLS

1997 (Megane and Scenic July–Sept '97 build): 7,434 cars found to have potentially defective braking system. 1998: (June '97–Sep '97 build): Roof bars may fail under load. Replacements redesigned and sourced from a different manufacturer.

WHAT'S GOOD

Renault's answer to the Citroen Berlingo Multispace – with two more doors and a lower price. After years of protesting that they couldn't import the Kangoo Combi because its single sliding rear side door was on the wrong side, Renault have put an additional rear door on the other side. 75bhp 1.4 litre 8-valve petrol or 65bhp 1.9 litre non-turbo diesel. Prices from a very sensible £9,750 OTR which includes PAS and metallic paint. RXE versions (£750 extra) has passenger airbag and three three-point rear seatbelts. Extremely sensible.

WHAT'S BAD

Fairly basic and certainly not for the status conscious – unless, of course, the Kangoo Combi becomes trendy.

WHAT TO WATCH OUT FOR

Too new to say.

21

WHAT'S GOOD

Cheap. 175bhp Turbo and Turbo Quadra were flyers in their day. Comfortable enough, but the market's not really interested unless the cars are seriously cheap.

WHAT'S BAD

Cheap, flimsy build. Quite a few parts are hard to get, such as rear discs for turbos and TXis. 19 model tended to be much stronger, better built and more reliable.

WHAT TO WATCH OUT FOR

Have to be cheap to be worth buying. Check all electrics carefully. Look for uneven front tyre wear. Check coolant for mayonnaise (blown head gasket). If has ABS, make sure it works.

21 SAVANNA

WHAT'S GOOD

Estates have option of seven forward-facing seats with reasonable luggage space behind. Diesels are economical, but range was complicated: 67 bhp 2,068cc non turbo from Jan–Sept 1989; 65 bhp 1,870cc non-turbo from Sept '89 to Oct 95; 88bhp 2,068cc turbo from Jan '89 to Oct '90 – then again from Nov '93 to Oct '95.

WHAT'S BAD

Two completely different drivetrains – across the engine bay on petrol 1.7s and along the engine bay on anything bigger. Lousy ventilation – particularly bad for rearmost passengers on long hot summer journeys. Not cheap to repair.

WHAT TO WATCH OUT FOR

Repaired accident damage (high values made them worth repairing). Rust. Family and dog damage. Torn upholstery. Sagging suspension. Don't buy one that's been towing because seven occupied seats and a caravan is just too much.

LAGUNA

WHAT'S GOOD

Clever three lap & diagonal rear seatbelts fitted from Jan '95 (third belt retracts into offside 'D' pillar). New 110bhp 1.6 16v and 120bhp 1.8 16 v engines from Spring 1998. 2 litre twin cam 149bhp RTi 16v also good. Roomy inside, comfortable ride, big boot. Non turbo 2.2 12-valve diesels make good taxis – pleasant to drive in heavy traffic. But 115bhp TD better still. All much better built than old 21. New 194 bhp 2,946cc Peugeot powered V6 from October 1997 much better than previous Laguna V6. Estate cars have masses of loadspace, but 7 seater option is rear-facing and folds to the side rather than into the floor. Comparatively good performance in NCAP crash tests.

WHAT'S BAD

85bhp 2.2 diesels sluggish on the open road. Long backed drivers find themselves sitting too close to the top of the huge windscreen. Old 95bhp 1.8 and 115 bhp 2 litre 8-valve engines outclassed. Old 170 bhp 2,963 cc V6 not a very good package. Poor quality electrics lead to all manner of irritating failures. More than its fair share of recalls. Power steering failure common.

WHAT TO WATCH OUT FOR

Look for leaking power steering on all Lagunas. Check for 'clonking' from wear in front anti-roll bar bushes. 2.2 litre diesels highly likely to have been cabbed and clocked. Check tyres for uneven wear denoting crash damage, suspension damage or simple misalignment. Check automatic transmission fluid for signs of overheating (will be black instead of dark red). Need cambelt changes every 35,000–40,000 miles. Ex-fleet cars may be on borrowed time. Try to feel the brake discs as these may need replacing. If aircon fitted, make sure it blows cold. Make sure keyfob transmitter was replaced under free recall.

RECALLS

1996 (May '94–Aug '94 build): Automatic transmission may lock up. 1996 (Jul '94–Dec '94 build): Airbag warning light may be faulty. 1996 (April '96–Aug '96 build): Fuel injection system computer may be faulty. 1997 (April–August '96 build: 12,494 cars): Engine ECU may malfunction causing exhaust manifold to overheat and set fire to bulkhead insulation. 1998: 'Plip' key transmitters can go out of sequence due to static or fiddling with them in the pocket. Improved 'plip' key transmitters now available free of charge to Laguna owners. (Per BBC 'Watchdog' 12/2/98) 1998: 17,000 cars recalled due to possibility of "inadvertent deployment of airbags". Cambelt tensioner

on diesel engines may lead to premature cambelt failure. To be checked as a TSB item at services.

25

WHAT'S GOOD

Much loved by owners and many have clocked up 300,000 miles plus. Can be extremely cheap.

WHAT'S BAD

Automatic gearbox can give trouble. Heater matrix may fail. Huge labour cost in removing dashboard to replace heater matrix, or minor failures such as bulbs. V6 not a specially good engine and gobbles petrol. Turbos too old to remain reliable.

WHAT TO WATCH OUT FOR

May have covered more miles than indicated on odometer. Make sure ABS is okay (pump not as dear as some at £660, but ECU is another £460 + VAT). Check all electrics (even the dashboard bulbs give up). Check auto especially carefully (some 25s go through three of four in a lifetime). PAS pump or rack may leak (common old Renault problem). Try to feel discs for scoring, lipping or wear. You could easily buy a 25 for £750 than have to spend £2,000 on it immediately. Buy only from a careful, appreciative, enthusiastic owner who's had it for years. Definitely not a backstreet buy.

RECALLS

(None known 1994–98 but autobox a well known problem area.)

SAFRANE

WHAT'S GOOD

Very comfortable with cosseting ride and excellent rear legroom. Latest Volvo-engined 2.5 litre 5-cylinder automatic capable of covering immense distances at high average speeds.

Reasonable fuel consumption. Low used prices.

WHAT'S BAD

Electronic autobox problems on pre-1996 facelift versions expensive to fix. Lose value quickly. Jerky cruise control.

WHAT TO WATCH OUT FOR

Clonky autobox. Duff cats. Make sure aircon blows cold. Check all electrics.

RECALLS

1994 (Dec 91–Mar 94 build): Heat shield required to protect fuel tank from exhaust. 1996 (May '94–Aug '94 build): Automatic transmission may lock up. 1996 (Jul '94–Dec '94 build): Airbag warning light may be faulty.

ESPACE (to 1997)

WHAT'S GOOD

Immensely practical design. Individual seat removal

system only bettered by new Espace. Easy to see out of and to park. Early models up to the first (1991) facelift handled the best. Nevertheless, your best bet is the facelifted 2.1 litre turbodiesel. Clutches will last three years and 120,000 miles in mostly motorway use. Engines can run up to 200,000 miles with few problems.

WHAT'S BAD

Strange relationship between driver's seat and accelerator pedal leads to ankle pain. Low diesel air intake can scoop up floodwater wrecking the engine. There was a recall over a wiring loom problem. Trim is a bit flimsy, not up to hard family use. Automatic transmissions have a history of problems. Be very careful driving the diesel in standing water as apt to suck it up and blow its cylinder head off.

WHAT TO WATCH OUT FOR

Clocked ex-taxis. Dodgy electrics. Chipped or cracked windscreens (expensive to replace). Wear in front and rear suspension from carrying heavy loads. Clonking driveshafts. Wear in gearshift linkage. Clutch wear (can last up to 120,000 miles, but depends on usage). Leaking or groaning power steering. Duff cats in post 1991 facelift model. Automatics best avoided. Make sure 2.1TD has received regular oil changes. Pull the dipstick and look for clean oil in all petrol versions, especially the V6. Look for mayonnaise under the oil filler cap, signifying cylinder head problems. 'Family' damage from baby's bottles, food, sweets, felt-tip pens, dogs, etc. Check that seat locking mechanisms aren't damaged from misunderstandings. Make sure recall work has been carried out.

RECALLS

1995 (2.1TD built 3/93–6/94). Install fuse in preheater wiring circuit, reroute wiring away from main loom and install clip to keep it away from loom to prevent risk of insulation damage. 1996 (Espaces – on original tyres built March '91–Oct '92): Check for separation of tyre tread.

NEW ESPACE (from 1997)

WHAT'S GOOD

Revamp of the original design put it back at the top of the class again. No other MPV has such a versatile seating arrangement. Longer bodied Grande Espace overcomes lack of luggage space with seven aboard. Best buys are the diesels (air intakes now in mirror assemblies). Four Star performer and the best MPV in NCAP crash test (11 points front impact; 16 points side impact).

WHAT'S BAD

Have heard of one wiring fire, which was a recall problem on the previous model diesels.

WHAT TO WATCH OUT FOR

Chipped or cracked windscreens (it's a lot of glass). 'Family' damage from baby's bottles, food, sweets, felt tip pens, dogs, etc. Make sure the seat locking mechanisms aren't damaged.

ROLLS ROYCE

SILVER SPIRIT/ SPUR (1980–99)

WHAT'S GOOD

Plutocrat's car. Like driving along in a mobile gentleman's club. Poshest colour is a dark browny green. Gradually improved over the years with injection and ABS in October 1986, automatic ride control in

1987, four rather then 3-speed autobox in September 1991. Cats came in during June 1990, but were initially a no cost option. Company taken over by VW in Spring 1998.

WHAT'S BAD

Stink of cigar smoke clings to the headlining. 9 mpg in town. Likely be hit hard by engine-size or CO_2 based annual taxation. Resentful drivers don't let you out of side roads, particularly during recessions. Apt to get vandalised with rusty nails or keys while parked. White or cream tells the public it's a wedding hire car, or has been. Daft RR defensive habit of not giving power outputs. (1993 Silver Spur had 226bhp and 340 ft lb torque; 1994 Flying Spur turbo had 360bhp and 552 ft lb torque.)

WHAT TO WATCH OUT FOR

Must have a proper Rolls Royce agent or Rolls Royce specialist history. The Cosworth built engine is an old fashioned pushrod V8, so you don't want to hear ticking tappets or see any blue smoke from the exhaust pipe. Make sure the suspension is not unduly wallowy. Check expensive tyres for tread depth and uneven wear. Make sure aircon blows cold. Good Rolls Royces have a patina and aura about them. Bad ones make you feel uneasy. Best to have the car inspected by a different Rolls Royce specialist from the one who's selling it.

RECALLS

1997: 29 left hand drive cars found to have potentially defective braking system.

SILVER SERAPH

WHAT'S GOOD

The Rolls Royce version of the Bentley Arnage. Smoother BMW 5.3 litre V12 engine pumps out 322bhp through 5-speed auto in similar very British body

WHAT'S BAD

As Arnage.

WHAT TO WATCH OUT FOR

As Arnage.

RECALLS

1999: Possible wiring fault in heated seat circuit.

ROVER

METRO

WHAT'S GOOD

Decent new 'K' series 1.1 and 1.4 engines. End-on gearbox and up to 5-speeds at last. Front-end rust traps largely eliminated. Better built than Austin Metro and generally reliable. Simple CVT auto worked well – far less troublesome than Ford and Fiat CVTs. Comfortable. I've done 450 miles in a day in a Metro CVT. Decent fuel consumption. 1.4 TUD diesel engine comes from Citroen AX and Peugeot 106.

WHAT'S BAD

Cramped cabin due to bigger, more luxurious seats. Heavy, non power-assisted steering – the wider the tyres the heavier it is. Diesel very slow and not that economical if worked hard. Still rust prone in seams.

WHAT TO WATCH OUT FOR

Oil leaks from engine. Cracked cylinder heads (look for mayo under oil cap). Tappety noises. Abused 16-valve versions. Kerbed alloy wheels (suspect suspension damage). Many still went to driving schools. Some were built long before they were UK registered.

100 SERIES

WHAT'S GOOD

Restyled Rover Metro. CVT

auto one of the best and still has a small market. Killed off in early 1998.

WHAT'S BAD

Past its 'sell by' date. Poor performance in NCAP crash tests. Not much market for them.

WHAT TO WATCH OUT FOR

As Rover Metro.

OLD 200/400

WHAT'S GOOD

Product of Honda/Rover marriage and first to use 'K' series modular engines. English 'feelgood' factor from stainless steel kick plates, bits of wood fillet in the dash and doors. Honda 1.6 engine is the best engine, often wedded to smooth Honda autobox. 400 'Tourer' estate could be had with 143bhp 1.8 litre VVC 'K' Series engine.

WHAT'S BAD

Diesels are pretty terrible.

PSA XUD engines at their noisiest and least refined. Gearbox/clutch problems can occur relatively early. 220s seem to develop all sorts of problems. Turbos best avoided. Distributor ignition igniter of Honda 1.6 can fail at about 50,000 miles and might lead to catalytic converter damage. Rover 'K' Series modular engines not as reliable, particularly pre-'K' reg monopoint injected versions. Cylinder head problems not uncommon. Rover 2 litre M16 engine least reliable; later T16 from 'K' reg on (badged 'ROVER' on cam cover) more reliable, but even T16 apt to coke up its valves if run on cheap petrol with inadequate detergent content.

WHAT TO WATCH OUT FOR

Premature clutch wear. Noisy gearboxes. Clonking suspension. Cooling system leaks. Hidden rust around windscreen. Visible rust at top of hatch and around hinges. Coolant leaks from corroded coolant rail at back of engine (coolant should be changed every 2-3 years). Look under oil cap for mayonnaise – sure sign of distorted or cracked cylinder head. ECU faults causing misfires. Excessive oil consumption. Diesel turbo hose can rub on front bulkhead. No power steering (if PAS, look for leaks at the pump). Make sure cambelt has been changed. Allow £160 for new distributor igniter for Honda 1.6. Front anti roll bar drop links rattle, but cheap to replace. Clonks from rear could be trailing arm bushes which are £200 a side to replace, or one of the roof support bars come unstuck. Rear silencer box rots inside out quickly. If fitted with ABS, the pump may fail if the brake fluid had not been changed often enough. A smell of petrol may indicate a rusted and leaking petrol tank – especially on 'N' reg cars.

NEW 200

WHAT'S GOOD

Compact. Good looking. Low wind noise at speed. Stainless steel kickplate 'Rover' image. All good performers for their engine size apart from 1.1 and 1.4 8-valve. Vi, fitted with MGF VVC engine tremendously quick and also very economical. Perky 1.6 CVT automatic offers instant acceleration out of side roads. 1.1 replaces Rover 100 as a sub-£10,000 offering. All have three 3-point rear belts.

WHAT'S BAD

Slow, over-light steering spoils all models, including Vi. Not quite out of Rover build quality problems. T16 2 litre engine apt to coke up its valves if run on cheap petrol with inadequate detergent content. CVT could be too 'instant' for some elderly drivers not used to automatics.

WHAT TO WATCH OUT FOR

Variable gearshift quality. Different models have different linkage arrangements, but a hollow pin wears and may drop out. No big deal since a replacement costs just 6p. 'K' Series cylinder heads have been known to become porous (look for mayo under oil cap). Timing belt replacement essential every 35,000–40,000 miles or every 3–4 years.

25

WHAT'S GOOD

Successfully re-thought Rover 200, aimed at the younger market, now with faster steering, more sporty suspension, much more sensible pricing and, importantly, a 3-year warranty. Base model 1.1 comes without PAS but costs just £8,295. 84bhp 1.4s with PAS start at £9,395. New 'Steptronic' CVT autos with 1.6 and 1.8 litre engines. VI remains top of range.

WHAT'S BAD

Too soon to say if quality improvements are lasting.

WHAT TO WATCH OUT FOR

See 200.

NEW 400

WHAT'S GOOD

Honda 'Swindon Civic' in drag, but mostly with Rover's own 'K' Series engines and (Rover claims) better ride and handling. Automatic retains Honda's 1.6 engine and autobox with engine in front of passenger rather than driver. Available as 5-door hatch or good-looking 4-door saloon (not many good-looking saloons in this class). Falling sales led to cut prices in 1998 with a 1.4Si 16v with alloys selling for £12,000 OTR.

WHAT'S BAD

If it's been owned by an

elderly person, may be three years old and not yet run-in.

elderly person, may be three years old and not yet run-in.

WHAT TO WATCH OUT FOR

'K' Series cylinder heads have been known to crack. Timing belt replacement essential every 35,000–40,000 miles or every 3–4 years. Front suspension bushes tend to wear. T16 2 litre engine apt to coke up its valves if run on cheap petrol with inadequate detergent content. A smell of petrol may indicate a rusted and leaking petrol tank – especially on 'N' reg cars (applies to both 'old' and 'new' 'N' reg 400s).

RECALLS

1996: Driver's seat lock does not always click into place properly. May mean seat slides when car is being driven. Most likely on cars with several drivers where seat is moved to and fro.

45

WHAT'S GOOD

Not as well re-thought as 25, and aimed at the older market. Engine range includes a 2 litre KVS mated to the 'Steptronic' CVT automatic. New 3-year warranty. Prices from £11,995 to £18,995.

WHAT'S BAD

Testers thought the steering too light and the ride too soft, but this may suit the market. High-revving KV6 not very well matched with 'Steptronic' transmission.

WHAT TO WATCH OUT FOR

As new 400.

600

WHAT'S GOOD

The most reliable Rover. (Really a Honda Accord.) Nice looking car. Wood, leather and stainless steel kickplate image. 156 bhp 2.3 litre Honda engine by far the best. Chassis also greatly improved on 2.3s. All manuals have good gearchanges and 129bhp Honda 2 litre engines are smooth and economical. 113bhp 1.8 is an 1,850cc multipoint injected Honda engine, not a Rover 'K'. Automatics by Honda. Good metallic paint colours, such as 'Nightfire Red', 'Caribbean Blue'. Generally a very good second-hand buy.

WHAT'S BAD

Understeery handling, over-light steering on all but 2.3. Ride quality not up to luxurious image. Can rust prematurely. 620i Turbo with Rover 'T' Series engines apt to blow gaskets. Average performance in NCAP crash tests. Replaced by Rover 75.

WHAT TO WATCH OUT FOR

Check everything electrical (windows, roof, mirrors, seats, etc.). Look for rust on 'K's and 'L's. Will run to high mileages (150k plus) so might be clocked. A 50,000 miler should not have excessive paint and windscreen chips, front number plate should be original. Avoid the 'ti' petrol turbo model. Rover direct-injected 'T' Series diesels okay, but only gain about 7 mpg on the petrol 2 litre. Exhaust rear boxes blow on low mileage 'short run' cars.

RECALLS

1996 (built between 12/94 and 12/95): Check to ensure steering rack mounting bolts are secure – symptom of problem: stiff steering.

800

WHAT'S GOOD

Cheap big cars that don't look cheap. Wood, leather, etc. on Sterling models and decent trim levels generally. High revving 2 litre 16-valve engines. Smooth Honda 2.7 litre V6s. (Early Honda 2.5 and later 2.5 KV6 less highly regarded.) T16 2 litre engine better regarded than earlier

M16. Tough but gruff VM 2.5 litre diesel engines.

WHAT'S BAD

Clonky front suspension. Cambelts of 2 litre M16 engines (pre-1991 facelift) need replacing every three years or 36,000 miles and must be correctly tensioned. Water pumps fail, leading to distorted cylinder heads. Brake calipers seize. Power steering pumps of early cars pack up. Depreciate rapidly. Even T16 apt to coke up its valves if run on cheap petrol with inadequate detergent content. Jointly replaced by Rover 75.

WHAT TO WATCH OUT FOR

Front suspension can deteriorate alarmingly. Rust in seams, sills and particularly around all windows. Iffy electrics. Head gasket problems from failure to replace anti-freeze every 2-3 years. ECU problems. Duff cats in catted facelift model. Earlier M16 valves can burn out on unleaded petrol (a very quiet engine is a bad sign). Pay no more than £2,000 for a pre-facelift 820, however good it may look. Make sure aircon blows cold if fitted.

RECALLS

1994 (VIN RS 100001–117697 and RS 150000 to 187439): Front seat belt security.

75 (from Spring 1999)

WHAT'S GOOD

Replaces both 600 and 800. Good looking with styling cues from 1950s Rover P4. Looks a bit like a Rolls Seraph from the back, and sits in the market exactly where P4s did between 1955 and 1965. Nice retro-look cream oval dial instruments. I.8 litre 120bhp K Series four; 2 litre 150bhp KV6, 2.5 litre 175bhp KV6, or pleasant, very quiet and torquey 2 litre 115bhp BMW common rail direct-injected

diesel. All front-wheel drive.
JATCO 5-speed automatic or
Getrag 5-speed manual.
Softish, cosseting ride
quality. Not a sports saloon,
but still handles well. Prices
from around £18,000. Estate
car to arrive Y2K.

WHAT'S BAD

The badly-timed debacles
over the future of Rover
which marred its launch,
now, thankfully, forgotten.

WHAT TO WATCH OUT FOR

Too soon to say.

SAAB

OLD 900 TO 1993

WHAT'S GOOD

Eccentric, 'classic' Saab looks.
Much loved by the
entertainment industry and
often the car of the star.
Convertibles much loved,
despite scuttle shake.
185bhp Ruby Turbo (last of
the line) will be a classic is
years to come. Understeer
can be overcome by
judicious left-foot braking.
Heavy, solid and capable of
mega mileages if looked
after properly. Hatchback
has long, flat luggage area.
rear bumper makes a good
seat for events. Nice old cars.

WHAT'S BAD

Lots of understeer. Timing
chains and tensioners tend
to need replacing every
60,000 miles. Even non-
turbos are fairly thirsty.

WHAT TO WATCH OUT FOR

Rattling timing chains, dirty
oil, cracked cylinder heads
(check for mayonnaise
under the oil cap), cracked
turbo manifolding
(remember, it glows red
hot), can be gear-selector
problems, check suspension
bushes, front hubs and
Driveshafts carefully. Make
sure turbo not 'coked' as
Saab sourced replacements

are expensive. Make sure big bumpers have not been used as buffers. Make sure aircon blows cold.

RECALLS

1996 (900 convertible 1993–1995 = old shape): Check for loss of steering control.

NEW 900 (from 1993)

WHAT'S GOOD

Excellent safety features. Durable build quality. Hatchback, with big boot and proper passenger protection against load. Five 3-point safety belts. Good side protection. Interesting clutch-free 'Sensonic' 5-speed dropped for 9-3.

WHAT'S BAD

Cavalier based, so not a true 'Saab'. Disappointingly soggy steering, handling, roadholding and ride quality. Comes a bit more alive with turbo, but still not a car you'd ever choose for handling finesse.

WHAT TO WATCH OUT FOR

Timing chains of 4-cylinder Saab engines need clean oil or can give problems at around 60,000 miles. (GM V6s have belts, best replaced at 60,000 miles.) Clean oil also essential for turbo life. Turbos best run on fully synthetic. Put the car through a £70 check at a Saab agents, then buy a used Saab warranty. Average performance in NCAP crash tests. Make sure aircon blows cold if fitted.

RECALLS

1994 (VIN R2000001-R2028886): Delayed braking action. 1994 (5-door – VIN R2000001-R2022754): Cracking of driver's seat rails. 1995 (VIN R2027373 to S2009903 and S7000001 to S7013081): Welds missing from seat frames. 1997 (1996–97 build: 21,661 cars): Corrosion on the throttle housing can cause a sticking throttle. Relevant parts to be replaced with brass items which cannot corrode.

9-3 (from 1998)

WHAT'S GOOD

Steering, handling and roadholding all vastly improved over previous same-shape 900. Now a proper driver's car. Even better with 17" wheels and Michelin Pilot tyres. 2.2 litre direct injected diesel particularly good to drive – better than 2 litre petrol. Very impressive safety features include a full set of five 3-point belts, two airbags and excellent side-impact protection. Clever anti-whiplash head restraints. Rear boot sill has been lowered to make it more like the old 900 and you can used the rear bumper to sit on. 2 litre eco turbo engine replaced 2.3i for 1999 model year.

WHAT'S BAD

Scuttle-shake of popular convertible still sets your teeth rattling. Turbo a bit vicious. Diesel needs to be kept on the boil (above 1,900 rpm) so not too good for caravan towing.

WHAT TO WATCH OUT FOR

Timing chains of 4-cylinder Saab engines need clean oil or can give problems at around 60,000 miles. (No timing chain problems yet reported on GM 2.2 litre diesel.) Clean oil also essential for turbo life. Turbos best run on fully synthetic oil once run-in.

9000CS

WHAT'S GOOD

Great cars, none better than the 170bhp 2.3 eco turbo which covers the ground quickly and still returns 32 mpg. Capable of huge mileages if looked after properly. Decent 'big car' handling. Innocuous looks.

Wonderful seats. Good, old-fashioned 4-speed automatic does what you want and doesn't 'hunt'. Full-on 2.3 turbo Carlsson puts out 220bhp, which is very nearly too much.

WHAT'S BAD

Ride quality a bit firm, but made up for by the excellent seats. Direct ignition module can give trouble. ABS pump needs fresh brake fluid every year. Timing chains oil-sensitive (best run on fully synthetic – particularly turbos). 2.0 eco turbo not as well suited to autobox as 2.3i or 2.3 eco. V6 best avoided. Subject to quite a lot of recalls.

WHAT TO WATCH OUT FOR

Timing chain rattles. Smoky engines (especially turbos). Check for white smoke from blown head gasket or cracked head. Look under oil cap for mayonnaise. Huge discs are expensive to replace (feel them through the wheels). Look for wear in front suspension bushes, hubs and driveshafts. Best put though a £70 pre-check at a Saab agents, then purchase a comprehensive used Saab warranty. Make sure aircon blows cold.

RECALLS

1994 (VIN N1041085-N1049024 and P1000001-P1015289): Fuel leak. 1994 (9000/Turbo – VIN N1000001-N1049024, P1000001-P1042386, R1000001-R1027659): Oil leak and faulty brake light switch on some models. 1995: (*manual with TCS): VIN N1000001 to N1049024, *P1000001to P1042386, *R1000001 to R1026535: Loss of brake pressure and/or ABS. 1999: 1993/94 build (5,300 cars): Possibility of moisture corrupting computer chips which control passenger airbag trigger mechanism.

9000CD

WHAT'S GOOD

Booted, better looking 9000CS, so same general comments apply. Truly enormous boot.

WHAT'S BAD

As 9000CS.

WHAT TO WATCH OUT FOR

As 9000CS.

RECALLS

(See list under 9000CS)

9-5

WHAT'S GOOD

Saab's latest 'big' car loaded with safety features. Nothing quirky about this one. 170bhp 2.3 eco turbo and 150bhp 2.0 eco turbo. 2 litre much improved compared to 9000 series. Most people find the seats very comfortable. Should both be capable of over 30 mpg. Four Star NCAP crash test rating and best of all 'executive cars'. Super-safe estate version from early 1999 usurps Volvo as probably the safest estate car you can buy.

WHAT'S BAD

Vectra-based, so not a true Saab. No hatchback apart from estate. Early production did not share the latest thinking on front suspension with the 9-3. Had peculiar lurch understeer. Still understeers, but much more progressively now.

WHAT TO WATCH OUT FOR

No known problem areas yet.

SEAT

MARBELLA

WHAT'S GOOD

Cheap skate for cheapskates, especially in Spain where they sold for not much more than £3,000 new.

WHAT'S BAD

Hideous Panda re-style. Based on old Seat Panda, not post-1988 Fiat Panda, so has old 903cc pushrod engine and old unimproved suspension. Rust prone. Like Panda, clutch cables snap.

WHAT TO WATCH OUT FOR

Rust, front struts, wheel bearings, smoky and rattling engines. (The rattle is usually the timing chain tensioner.) Front suspension problems (check for uneven tyre wear). Don't touch one with a catalytic converter. Could you really live with a car this ugly that makes you look so much of a miser.

AROSA

WHAT'S GOOD

Cheap, well-equipped, very cheerful small cars, all with power assisted steering. Decent ride quality. Originally, numerous 'option packs' include comfort pack, safety pack and even air-conditioning. Now restricted to base and SE spec. 1.4 litre 4-speed auto one of the cheapest autos with PAS (1.4 manual introduced later at same price). Tall body good for entry and egress by the elderly. 1.7 litre SDI with unpainted bumpers the most practical city car, capable of 65mpg. Initially built at Wolfsburg, now Barcelona. 'SE' version replaces 'Comfort Pack'. Three-year unlimited mileage warranty. Did well in German TUV front offset crash test. New 118mph 100bhp 1.4 16v petrol engine and 106mph 75bhp,

66mpg 1.4 litre TDI from early Y2K. UK unlikely to get 1.2 litre '3L' super economy diesel because UK diesel tax is too high to justify the cost.

WHAT'S BAD

Handling not to standard set by Ford Ka, but it's okay. Clutch cables stick and may break. Door mirrors feel a bit cheap. Clutch replacement unusually expensive on 1.0 version (more tha £500).

WHAT TO WATCH OUT FOR

The 'Comfort Pack' of height-adjustable seats, parcel shelf, better trim etc. costs £245 new and is so good it's worth paying an extra £300 for second-hand. Make sure servicing up to date and warranty still in place. Have been known to misfire so make sure the cat isn't torched by having it MOT emissions checked.

RECALLS

SEAT has admitted a cold weather fault with the 1.4 automatic, manifesting itself in a loud noise when changing up from 1st to 2nd gear. Replacement parts are fitted free.

OLD IBIZA (to 1993)

WHAT'S GOOD

These did used to shift a bit on Spanish roads. Had 'Porsche design' engine, VW gearbox, good handling. Not bad looking in a chunky sort of way.

WHAT'S BAD

Not very well made. Rust-prone Fiat Ritmo underpinnings. The last of the pre-VW Seats. Neglect has nearly always taken its toll on the car's looks.

WHAT TO WATCH OUT FOR

Rust, fall-apart trim, rattly dashboards, groaning wheel bearings, total lack of maintenance by people who buy them for next to nothing and chop them is as a '£500 minimum part-exchange'.

RECALLS

1994 (1985–1991 VIN
09045074-D119002):
Fuel leak.

IBIZA (from 1993)

WHAT'S GOOD

The development car for the
current Polo, essentially the
same underneath but
slightly longer wheelbase.
Neat shape. Sporty image
from rally success. Fun
'Mediterranean' image. Ibiza
TDI 90 noisy, but goes well,
handles well, ideally geared
for city driving, does 55mpg
even at 80mph. Think of
Seats as 'fun' Volkswagens.
Now come with three-year
unlimited mileage
warranties. TDI
recommended.

WHAT'S BAD

No protection strip means
doors vulnerable to damage
in supermarket car parks.
Build not quite up to
Wolfsburg standards.

WHAT TO WATCH OUT FOR

Lots of model variations:
1.3s, then much better 1.4s,
etc. You need a Parker's
Guide or 'The Book' to find
out just how much of a
saving you're making. Make
sure servicing up to date
and warranty still in place.

NEW IBIZA (from Sept 1999)

WHAT'S GOOD

Reworking of the 1993
model, itself the first
manifestation of the Polo
platform, from the 'A' pillar
forwards. Better handling
and improved ride comfort
from new 'silentblock'
mounted front suspension.
Interior design and quality
much improved. Range
includes 156bhp 1.8 petrol
turbo. While TDI 110 with
switchable traction control
gives true GTi performance
plus 55 mpg economy.
Remember, Seats are 'fun'
Volkswagens – and Ibizas
are more fun to drive than

Polos. 68bhp SDI diesel available from October launch, at a reasonable £8,995 with PAS. New 'tax-break' 1 litre 16v 70bhp engine from early Y2K. Three-year unlimited mileage warranty. TDI 110 recommended.

WHAT'S BAD

Re-engineering the brake servo for RHD means no 1.8 Turbo or TDI 110bhp in the UK until Spring 2000. Steering wheel still only adjustable up and down and seats still only have old rocking adjustment of Golf Mk II GTi.

WHAT TO WATCH OUT FOR

Too soon to say.

CORDOBA

WHAT'S GOOD

Saloon version of Ibiza that also became the Polo saloon. Excellent 1.6 litre 100bhp engine. Cordoba Vario estate is the best looking of the range and comes with TDI 90 or TDI 110 engines. Same revisions as Ibiza from September 1999.

WHAT'S BAD

Cordoba coupe is ugly. Cordoba saloon has a bouncy ride. Vario estate not a true estate because it has a high load lip to give the body rigidity.

WHAT TO WATCH OUT FOR

VW's 'self adjusting' clutch cable that can lead to a slipping clutch. Make sure servicing up to date and warranty still in place.

INCA KOMBI

WHAT'S GOOD

Kombi version of Polo/Ibiza/Cordoba based Inca van. 75bhp 1.6i petrol and 60bhp 1.9 SDI. Very spacious in the back and surprisingly good fun to drive.

WHAT'S BAD

Doesn't ride as well as Citroen Berlingo Multispace. Not as practical as Renault Kangoo Combi.

WHAT TO WATCH OUT FOR

Second hand examples which have led an extremely hard double-life as weekday van and weekend transport for the family and its dogs.

LEON

WHAT'S GOOD

Great looking Golf IV based 5-door hatch, essentially a shortenend Toledo, pronounced 'Lay-on'. Not unlike a latter-day Alfasud. Shares Toledo's superior road feel and handling. Galvanized body with 12-year warranty; 3-year unlimited mileage mechanical warranty. UK engine range from 75bhp 1.4 16v to 143 mph 180bhp 1.8 20v turbo 6-speed with Haldex-clutched four wheel drive, and including the usual 90bhp and 110bhp TDIs. 4WD Haldex clutch allows use of different circumference wheels and for the car to be towed with two wheels off the ground. Four trim levels: Select, Stella, Signo and Sport (but not with every engine). Built in Brussels and Martorell. Proposed UK launch date: April 2000.

WHAT'S BAD

Too soon to say.

WHAT TO WATCH OUT FOR

Too soon to say.

TOLEDO (1991–99)

WHAT'S GOOD

Jetta based family hatchback with enormous boot. Had mid-life facelift in 1995. Most models very well equipped for their price bracket. TDI 90 is a good package with decent performance and economy at (for the UK anyway) a sensible price.

WHAT'S BAD

Not a great looking car. Seat built a special Taxi spec diesel Toledo.

WHAT TO WATCH OUT FOR

Toledos that began their lives as taxis. VW's 'self adjusting' clutch cable that can lead to a slipping clutch. Leaks from ill-fitting tailgate (it's big, so twists out of shape easily). Check all electrics, including lights. Make sure servicing up to date and warranty still in place.

RECALLS

1996: Cooling fan motor may seize, leading to overheating in traffic or on hills.

TOLEDO (from 1999)

WHAT'S GOOD

Golf IV based family saloon. Really good looking in the manner of the Alfa 156 now we're seeing more of them on UK roads. Much sportier than Skoda Octavia using lessons learned on the Skoda. Better steering and handling than Golf IV and Bora due to 15" alloys with 195/60 tyres, stiffer four-door body and softer suspension settings. Good ride quality, comfortable, rattle-free, galvanized body with 12-year warranty; otherwise 3-year unlimited mileage warranty. V5 has a perfect set of gear ratios and at £17,550 is a bargain for what you get. But 52mpg TDI S 110 with standard aircon is by far the best buy at £15,885. Highly recommended.

WHAT'S BAD

Deep boot, but you have to post your luggage through a narrow slit. V5 give nice, progressive power but lacks the grunt of the old VR6.

WHAT TO WATCH OUT FOR

Too soon to say.

ALHAMBRA

WHAT'S GOOD

Seat's version of Galaxy/Sharan all built on the same line in Portugal. All had air-conditioning, but otherwise fairly basic trim. VW 2 litre petrol and 1.9 litre TDI 90 110 or even chipped 130 engines. Also 125bhp 1.8 20v and 150bhp 1.8 20v Turbo. Three-year unlimited mileage warranty. More cheerful trim than Galaxy and Sharan. Similar VW Sharan was a three star performer in NCAP crash tests (6 points front impact; 15 points side impact).

WHAT'S BAD

Trim quality and damage from family use may let the vehicle down. Below average 'customer satisfaction'.

WHAT TO WATCH OUT FOR

Lowest list prices mean most likely of Galaxy TDI 90 family to have been used as a taxi, so look for signs of clocking. Make sure servicing up to date and warranty still in place. Make sure 7-seaters have rear compartment heater. Spec was progressively improved. Latest Alhambra TDI 110 has aircon and pop up picnic trays on backs of front seats. Make sure manual Ford gearbox isn't 'clonky'.

RECALLS

1997: Brake pads may overheat.

SKODA

ESTELLE

WHAT'S GOOD

Some people liken the oversteering handling to that of a Porsche. Engine in the back means you leave engine noise behind you.

Decent size front boot. Extremely cheap.

WHAT'S BAD

Skoda 'skip' image dating from the days when these cars were assembled by convicts. Fall apart trim. Becoming difficult to obtain spares (VW doesn't want to know about this model).

WHAT TO WATCH OUT FOR

Paying more than £100 for one. Screeching gearboxes, iffy electrics (check all lights and indicators – I've seen new Estelles where the indicator cables were cross-connected). Cheapskate home maintainers will have used the cheapest oil changed it grudgingly and never bothered to change the coolant. But buy a car from an obsessive DIY'er with a Haynes manual and the chances are he'll have sorted out all the faults.

FAVORIT

WHAT'S GOOD

Gave a massive boost to Skoda's image. Handles quite well. Decently engineered. A good, sound, practical blow budget car. Much better than a Lada.

WHAT'S BAD

Memories of Skoda image die hard. Build quality still 'pre-VW'. Fall apart trim, grotty plastic, iffy electrics (particularly lights). Soft brake pedal (like old Polos). Engines start to smoke if oil not changed regularly and decent oil not used. Starter motors fail and can chew up the starter ring.

WHAT TO WATCH OUT FOR

Penny-pinched home servicing using the cheapest oil. Duff cats on catalysed models. Does the owner impress you as someone who really knows how to look after a car?

RECALLS

1994 (VIN P0670305-R0916381 and P5019665-R5043486): Wheel bearing failure.

FELICIA

WHAT'S GOOD

Looks like a Favorit, but really a VW Polo in Skoda clothes. PAS now available with 1.6 petrol and 1.9 diesel engines. Sound practical cars. Well built. Excellent paint quality, good shut lines. Strangely, high quality trim and plastics seem as if they're deliberately made to look cheaper than those of Polo. 1.3 versions cheap, but the engines feel it. Haynes manual available from March 1999. 3-year warranty means dealer servicing for first three years.

WHAT'S BAD

Skoda image not good for the status conscious. Old-fashioned single-plane door and ignition key up to April 1998 grille facelift, when it was replaced by twin-plane key. Diesel version a bit front heavy for standard width tyres – can lose adhesion.

WHAT TO WATCH OUT FOR

Owners home -servicing using the Haynes manual from March 1999 may take short cuts and will miss any rectification work carried out by Skoda agents on TSBs.

RECALLS

1998: (models with airbags): Wiring for airbag may chafe.

FABIA

WHAT'S GOOD

First incarnation of the next VW Polo floorpan. Chunky good looks. Height and reach adjustable steering wheel and height adjustable drivers seat. Engines include a pushrod 68bhp 1.4 litre petrol based on the old Favorit/Felicia 1.3; a 101bhp 16v 1.4 from the Polo/Lupo and the 64bhp 1.9 litre SDI diesel. Will eventually get VAG's new 1 litre 16v 70bhp petrol engine, VAG's 75bhp 1.4 litre 16v; a 120bhp 2 litre ohc unit and a 98bhp 1.9 litre 'Pumpeduse-System TDI. 'Classic', 'Comfort' and 'Elegance' trim levels. Ten-year body warranty. Prices from £8,000.

WHAT'S BAD

More expensive than outgoing Felicia. Won't arrive in UK until late Y2K. High rear door sills contribute to strength, but make rear seat entry/egress difficult for the elderly. High boot sill. Centre rear belt only two-point.

WHAT TO WATCH OUT FOR

Too soon to say.

OCTAVIA

WHAT'S GOOD

Galvanized body has 10-year warranty. VW Golf Mk IV underpinnings. Excellent 1.6 litre 100bhp, 1.8 litre 125bhp petrol engines and 1.9TDI with 90 or 110bhp. Very well built. Estate car much better than hatchback. 2 litre VAG 120bhp engine replaces non turbo 1.8 from autumn 1999, as with VW Golf.

WHAT'S BAD

Still a Skoda in the eyes of the golf club secretary. Looks like a Passat with the back wheels in the wrong place. Early LHD examples understeered heavily, but later RHD production very well thought of by motoring press, especially TDI.

WHAT TO WATCH OUT FOR

Car did not arrive in the UK until mid-1998, so too early to say.

SUBARU

JUSTY (1989–96)

WHAT'S GOOD

Cheap, small, reliable four wheel drive hatchback. Multipoint injected, catalysed 73 bhp 1,189cc 3-cylinder engine from September 1992 (3-dr chassis 007401; 4-dr chassis 009601) the best, but previous 67bhp engine avoids the cat. Not great to drive, but excellent in the snow.

WHAT'S BAD

CVT automatic transmissions fail and a replacement is the wrong side of £2,000.

WHAT TO WATCH OUT FOR

Avoid automatics. Look for suspension, drivetrain, engine damage underneath from rocks. Be very suspicious of uneven tyre wear. Make sure drivetrain doesn't shriek or scream (expensive to fix). Have it emissions tested to make sure cat converter not smashed. Interior damage from children, dogs or farm animals should be obvious.

JUSTY (from 1996)

WHAT'S GOOD

Now Suzuki Swift based and built in Hungary, with four rather than three cylinders and no unreliable auto option.

WHAT'S BAD

Hungarian build quality not the world's best. Interior trim not particularly tough.

WHAT TO WATCH OUT FOR

1,298cc Suzuki Swift engine has been known to suffer from cracked cylinder head. Be suspicious of uneven tyre wear. Try to get it on a ramp for a good look underneath, or take a torch. Check for oil leaks, bent suspension, dents in underside.

GL SERIES

WHAT'S GOOD

A Texas bank got 600,000 miles out of one o these. Can represent a cheap, reliable car for those who need four wheel drive in the winter.

WHAT'S BAD

Starting to get really old now and onto their third or fourth owners. May be impossible to check history. Suspension bushes go. Remember, Japanese cars are designed to be very reliable for up to seven years. They aren't built to last longer than this.

WHAT TO WATCH OUT FOR

Avoid turbos (too old now to expect them to be reliable). Rust. Broken front subframes. Any signs of having been used by a farmer (bits of straw under the carpet, strange dents, farmyard smells). If it has seat covers, look underneath – especially the top of the back seat. If tyre wear is uneven, best to walk away unless car is sub-£500.

IMPREZA

WHAT'S GOOD

Came top of *Top Gear*/J.D. Power 'N' reg customer satisfaction survey. Excellent reports from owners. No complaints in the history of the column. Engines are 88bhp 16v 1.6 flat four, 101bhp 1.8 litre 16v flat four and 113 bhp 2 litre. Auto optional on 1.8 and 2.0. 2.0 obviously the best engine, but 1.6 much cheaper. Recommended.

WHAT'S BAD

There was a 1.6 litre two wheel drive version from 1994–96.

WHAT TO WATCH OUT FOR

Don't bother with two wheel

drive versions. All larger Subaru are prone to scoring of the rear discs. Try and feel them through the wheel when cold. Check underside with torch for rocky lane accidents. Check for uneven tyre wear.

IMPREZA TURBO

WHAT'S GOOD

Good anyway with standard 208bhp engine, but special import WRXs offer 240–280bhp and two door WRX has up to 300bhp. These cars are very fast indeed. UK 240bhp RSR offers a terrific drive. Recommended.

WHAT'S BAD

Not much. In short supply so WRXs command substantial 'overs'; ordinary Legacy Turbos hard to get.

WHAT TO WATCH OUT FOR

Check for underside damage from 'off road' rally stage excursions. Check for uneven tyre wear. Feel through the wheels for scored rear discs. Smoke from exhaust could mean burned out turbo oil seals. These cars really need 3,000 mile fully synthetic oil changes. All WRXs are non approved grey imports, so make sure they're legal with proper SVA certificates. To avoid the SVA 50 car quota, some may have been 'cloned' (more than one car on the same registration).

FORESTER

WHAT'S GOOD

Impreza-based four wheel drive estate with boxier body and more ground clearance than Impreza. 75bhp turbo very good.

WHAT'S BAD

Exhaust system hangs quite low and could be vulnerable on bumpy tracks. .

WHAT TO WATCH OUT FOR

Check for underside damage

from 'off road' use. Check for uneven tyre wear due to damaged suspension. Feel through the wheels for scored rear discs.

LEGACY

WHAT'S GOOD

The most sensible large country estate car you can buy. Spacious, strong and reasonably economical (25–28 mpg). Facelifted in April 1994 and October 1996. Clever 'hillholder' brake system. Low transmission range very useful for crawling along in a traffic jam. Avoid the 2.0DL or 2.0DLSE (Feb 92–April 94) which has only part time four wheel drive and lower rear roof line. New model has revised floorpan with less suspension intrusion into load area. Recommended.

WHAT'S BAD

Spartan interior. Frameless side windows. Propensity to score rear discs. Cheap old shape 'Classic' models dropped from line-up in autumn 1999 and new models £2,000 dearer.

WHAT TO WATCH OUT FOR

Have been known to sit around on dockside compounds for years before finding buyers. Always check the rear discs for scoring. If it has a tow-hook, check whether it's been pulling a single or a double horsebox. Use a torch to peer underneath just in case it's been up a rough track and suffered serious damage from a rock. Mk Is from 1989–94 are getting old now. Second or third owner may have skimped maintenance and used it for hauling animals. Have a good look under load area carpeting for dents. If the car has seat covers, take them off – a dog may have eaten the seats underneath.

LEGACY TURBO

WHAT'S GOOD

Described in the trade as the Subaru 'Lunacy', these are very quick yet full five seaters and the estate is a full-size estate car.

WHAT'S BAD

They do get crashed.

WHAT TO WATCH OUT FOR

Accident damage. Twisted shell. Suspension and or steering damage from 'falling off the road'. Smoke from exhaust could mean turbo oil seals have gone.

SUZUKI

OLD ALTO AUTO

WHAT'S GOOD

Cheap, tiny, basic car with 40bhp 796cc 3-cylinder engine and 2-speed autobox.

WHAT'S BAD

Very small indeed. Noisy. Too slow for the motorway. Very light build, so rusts easily.

WHAT TO WATCH OUT FOR

Rust will seriously weaken the structure. Suspension gets tired quickly. Uneven tyre wear a more than usually bad sign.

NEW ALTO (from 1997)

WHAT'S GOOD

No bad looking for a tiny car. 53bhp 993cc 4-cylinder engine. 3-speed auto option.

WHAT'S BAD

May be bought as a marginal retirement car. Perodua Nippa is better value.

WHAT TO WATCH OUT FOR

Dings in the very thin sheetmetal. Premature rusting.

WAGON R+

WHAT'S GOOD

Chain cam little screamer of a 64bhp 996cc engine revs to nearly 8,000 rpm. Light controls. Easy to drive. Holds its own on the motorway – just. Much more elbow room than Daihatsu Move. Not as small as you think it's going to be. Shopping basket, bucket hidden under passenger seat. Reasonable legroom in the back. 3-year warranty. More powerful 1.2 litre engine, front end restyle and automatic option from June 1998

WHAT'S BAD

Daft looking, but not as daft as the Daihatsu Move. Severe understeer. Little feel from power steering. overpriced on UK market. Should be £2,000 cheaper.

Wouldn't like to be hit by a Toyota LandCruiser while driving one.

WHAT TO WATCH OUT FOR

Make sure it's not coming apart at the joints.

SWIFT (to 1993)

WHAT'S GOOD

101bhp GTi 16v fast and furious. Odd 1,590cc 91bhp GLX four wheel drive saloon lasted from March 1990–January 1993

WHAT'S BAD

Cylinder heads of 8-valve 1.3s and 1.6s can crack.

WHAT TO WATCH OUT FOR

Cracked cylinder head on 8-valve 1.3. GTi 16v likely to have been thrashed – expect heavy tyre wear but look out for uneven wear. Country bought GLX four wheel drive saloons may be damaged underneath.

NEW SWIFT
(from 1993)

WHAT'S GOOD

Cheap, especially 1 litre GC 5-door version. GTi 16v by far the best.

WHAT'S BAD

Built in Hungary. Cylinder heads of 1.3 8vs can crack. Ex-rental 1.0GCs took forever to sell into the trade.

WHAT TO WATCH OUT FOR

Cracked cylinder head.

BALENO
(to Aug 1998)

WHAT'S GOOD

Range of 3-door hatch, 4-door saloon, 5-door estate, all with same 1.6 litre engine. Power steering. Decent equipment levels. Owners like them. Got the 'ladies prize' at the 1996 Birmingham Motor Show.

WHAT'S BAD

Comparatively poor NCAP crash test results, but not tested with standard UK spec. driver's airbag. Bland to drive with overlight steering. No image. New model arrived August 1998.

WHAT TO WATCH OUT FOR

No known problem areas.

SJ 410/413

WHAT'S GOOD

The smallest, cheapest off roader you can buy in the UK. Relatively light weight helps in snow and 'soft' conditions.

WHAT'S BAD

Santanas are Spanish built; SJs Japanese. Superseded by 'Jimmy' late 1998. Can suffer cracked cylinder heads after 50,000 miles (look for emulsified oil under oil filler). Not nice to drive on the road, but okay as a holiday villa runabout or as an off road working car where small size is important.

WHAT TO WATCH OUT FOR

Uneven front tyre wear means the tracking's out, so has the front suspension bee damaged? Has it been off-roaded (much more likely than Vitara because these are classed as a working vehicle). Check drivetrain for oil leaks. Make sure it slips easily into four wheel drive (transfer boxes have been known to take in water and corrode inside). Listen for gearbox rattles, especially with the clutch disengaged. Check everywhere for rust, especially the hood mechanism the joints of which can rust up and snap. Check under matting on cargo floor for rust in the seams. Take care on corners.

JIMNY

WHAT'S GOOD

Cute looking with decent off road ability. Reasonable performance (0-60 in 13.6 secs; top speed 100 mph) from 1,298cc 85bhp engine).

Separate chassis for strength. Part time four wheel drive on the road driving rear wheels only for economy. Soft-top launched at Barcelona Show in May 1999.

WHAT'S BAD

Noisy and unrefined. Poor 'on road' manners, especially with large wheels and tyres.

WHAT TO WATCH OUT FOR

Too new to say

VITARA SWB

WHAT'S GOOD

1.6 litre 8-valve engine range has four outputs: 74bhp, 79bhp and 80bhp. A bit of a hairdresser's favourite (especially convertible) and these cars don't go off road.

WHAT'S BAD

Spanish built. Cylinder heads can crack. Poor oil feed to rocker shaft may lead to premature wear. Superseded by Jimny late 1998.

WHAT TO WATCH OUT FOR

Cracked cylinder head. Avoid ludicrous fat wheeled, running boarded 'customs' because it's like wearing a chest wig and pedestrians will laugh at you helplessly. Make sure the four wheel drive works. Clean oil changed every 3,000 miles essential to avoid blocking oil feed. Brake callipers can stick (need servicing, not replacing). Avoid if drivetrain unduly noisy. Back seat and backs of front seats may have been crocodiled by dogs. Drive carefully, especially round corners.

RECALLS

1994 (Sep '93–Jul '94 build): Wheel bearing failure. 1997 (July–Dec '97 build): Steering shaft could detach. 1998: (Oct '91–Oct '93 build): Front seat belt stalk may break.

VITARA 5-DOOR (to Spring 1998)

WHAT'S GOOD

Tall body easy to get in and out of. Will carry 4/5 and their luggage. The only 4x4 of its size. Range includes a 95bhp 16valve 1.6 petrol, a 70bhp turbodiesel manual and automatic and a 134bhp 2 litre 24-valve V6. All have power steering.

WHAT'S BAD

Superseded by new model Spring 1998.

WHAT TO WATCH OUT FOR

Usual 4x4 checks: is it a town car or a country car? Has it been towing? (if so, what?) Check steering gear for play and damage from kerbing (even on town cars). Has it been rolled or turned on its side? Brake callipers can stick (need servicing, not replacing). Avoid if drivetrain unduly noisy. Back seat and backs of front seats may have been crocodiled by dogs. Drive carefully, especially round corners.

RECALLS

1994 (Sep 1993–Jul 1994 build): Wheel bearing failure.

1997 (July–Dec '97 build):
Steering shaft could detach.

VITARA 5-DOOR (from Spring 1998)

WHAT'S GOOD

By UK standards, quite well priced at just over £16,195

for the 2.5 litre V6 5-door. Turbodiesel option. Seats fold flat to make double bed. £800 Clip-on tent available.

WHAT'S BAD

Still not a great drive.

WHAT TO WATCH OUT FOR

Too soon to say.

TOYOTA

STARLET (1990–96)

WHAT'S GOOD

Toyota's smallest car (in the UK anyway). Good little 12-valve 1 litre 54bhp and 1.3 litre 74bhp engines. I litre dropped in January 1993. Totally reliable for the first five years. 3-year warranty.

WHAT'S BAD

No power steering. Not very well packaged. Limited rear seat and load area. Expensive new.

WHAT TO WATCH OUT FOR

Lots of 'specials' such as 'Kudos'. Tend to be owned by uninterested people who want no more than a very small, reliable car. Make sure it has been serviced regularly and that the owner hasn't 'forgotten'. Look for evidence of parking dings, behind bumper damage. May need a cambelt change.

STARLET (1996–99)

WHAT'S GOOD

Better styled, better value and better packaged. New 1,332cc 74bhp engine and 3-speed automatic option. PAS standard on 5-door manual and 3-dr and 5-dr auto. Totally reliable for the first five years. 3-year warranty. Wider range appeals to wider range of buyers than before.

WHAT'S BAD

'Sporty' SR version not exactly sporty.

WHAT TO WATCH OUT FOR

If a 3-door manual, check that optional PAS has been fitted. Must have Toyota service history for remaining warranty to apply.

YARIS (from 1999)

WHAT'S GOOD

New small Toyota 3 & 5 door hatch replaces Starlet, initially all with same 68bhp 1 litre 16v VVTi iron block engine, but 85bhp VVTi alloy 1.3 and 4-speed auto option from October 1999. Low parts prices, good repairability, low insurance groups, combined finance and servicing package, three-year 60,000 mile warranty, slide forward back seat, option of 'Free-Tronic' automatic clutch. High seats make it easy for the elderly to get in and out of. Praised by road testers for its excellent steering and the roominess of its interior. Unusual central digital speedometer set in a tunnel. Light years ahead of the badly packaged Starlet it replaces. Price competitive with alternatives on UK market. Even better Yaris Verseo mini-MPV on its way. Did reasonably well in German TUV front offset crash tests. Car of the Year.

WHAT'S BAD

Not quite as cheap as Toyota makes out, in the UK at least.

(Manual prices from
£7,495–£10,995 OTR.)

WHAT TO WATCH OUT FOR

Too soon to say.

PRIUS (from 2000)

WHAT'S GOOD

The first hybrid car on general sale. 1,496cc 58bhp VVT-i engine feels more. Combined dash mounted automatic transmission selector and parking brake. Excess power output charges a bank of nickel-metal hydride batteries, which are also charged by regenerative braking when descending hills. These feed a 40bhp electric motor. The engine switches itself off at rest and the car moves off on its electric motor, starting its internal combustion engine when needed. It works remarkably well and the car even has a lively feel to it.

WHAT'S BAD

Probably price.

WHAT TO WATCH OUT FOR

Too soon to say.

COROLLA (to 1997)

WHAT'S GOOD

The world's most popular car (even though Corolla can mean different cars in different markets). Blandly efficient and extremely reliable over first five years or so. Easy, but dull to drive. 87 bhp 1.3 quite powerful, but economical. 1.6 has 113 bhp. Autos on 1.3s are 3-speed; on 1.6s are 4-speed. Full range of hatchbacks, saloons and estates. Well regarded and hold their value well.

WHAT'S BAD

Too bland, too dull for enthusiasts (this is not a criticism – they are deliberately made this way).

WHAT TO WATCH OUT FOR

Early cars had 6,000 mile service intervals – all need an oil change every 6,000 miles or every 6 months (whichever comes first) if you want to them to last. Quite likely to have been mini-cabbed and clocked, so look for excessive back seat wear and tear, worn door mechanisms, etc. Look for signs of a tow hook as may have been towing something too heavy. Estates may have had a hard life visiting cash & carrys for small businesses. Look for signs of sagging rear springs, damage to trim inside load area.

COROLLA (from Spring 1997)

WHAT'S GOOD

The market seems to have taken to the somewhat jokey re-style. Looks by far the best as a 3-door in silver. Huge range of cars offered as 3-door or 5-door hatches, four door saloon, 5-door estate. 5- or 6-speed manual gearboxes or three or 4-speed automatic. GS models all have aircon. Limited range of engines – just an 85bhp 1.3 16v, a 109bhp 1.6, or a 71bhp 2 litre diesel. Best new buy is a 1.6 litre GS 3-door and you should have no trouble chipping at least £1,500 off the price. Manufacturer 3-year warranty. Five lap & diagonal seatbelts. Three Star above average performance in NCAP crash tests.

WHAT'S BAD

1.3G6 6-speeder with ABS is a bit of an oddity. 1.3 with 3-speed auto is fairly slow and can lead to worrying moments when overtaking. Very 'Corolla' like to drive, so expect bland efficiency rather than fun.

WHAT TO WATCH OUT FOR

Repaired accident damage (a surprisingly high proportion seem to be involved in minor 'dings').

Still a new car so to remain under warranty will have needed to be serviced on time by a Toyota agent.

CARINA II (1988–92)

WHAT'S GOOD

Fantastic reputation for 'high mileage, no trouble' motoring. Easy to drive, good engines, good automatic. Available as saloon, hatch or estate.

WHAT'S BAD

Bland to drive. 'Feel free' steering. I.6 engine sounds strained at speed. Ride quality not wonderful.

WHAT TO WATCH OUT FOR

Be very suspicious of any of these with a tow hook. Will probably have been pulling a large caravan. Starting to get a bit old for a Japanese car now, so look for rust, saggy suspension, shocked shock absorbers. Expect failures such as water

pumps, oil pumps, brake cylinders, etc. and parts are expensive because in Japan cars of this age are scrapped.

CARINA E (1992– late 1997)

WHAT'S GOOD

Derbyshire built upper medium size cars with quite powerful and particularly frugal 1.6 litre and 1.8 litre engines (40 mpg plus). Easy for anyone to drive. Useful estate cars. Decent build quality but not quite up to UK Honda and Nissan standards. Built to do a high mileage in a short time with no trouble.

WHAT'S BAD

Fairly ugly slab-sided body with high waistline. Reliability and 'customer satisfaction' factor not quite up to levels set by Corolla and previous Carina II. Unresolved damping causes handling problems. Lean-burn engines require unusual economy driving style of high revs with small throttle openings – not holding high gears. Front tyre wear can be heavy – 14,000 miles or so.

Check for missed services, clocked ex-fleet cars (could have had the haircut years ago). Once they're a few years old, must have six monthly oil changes. Had its fair share of immobiliser problems, cured by new keyfob transmitter. Rear shocks can spring a leak. Expect a few behind dash rattles. One report of timing belt failure at 39,000 miles, so change at 35,000 miles rather than the recommended 63,000 miles. 'Lean burn' lambda sensor failure quite common – costs £350 a pop.

RECALLS

1996: Anti roll bar linkages may fail (first sign us a rattling noise). Covered under 3-year warranty. Only affects 2% of cars. 1997 (Sept '93–Jan '96 build): Stop lights may fail.

AVENSIS (from late 1997)

WHAT'S GOOD

A much improved Toyota Carina E. Same range of lean-burn engines. 1.8 litre the most frugal (40–45 mpg) and fitted with Michelin Energy tyres as standard. Much better looking than Carina E; hides its slab sides and high waist. Three proper lap and diagonal rear seatbelts. Unless you tow a caravan, the diesel is made pointless by the 1.8 lean-burn. Good launch advertising campaign left impression of a high quality car. Range includes a useful estate. Has a 3-year manufacturer warranty. Nice unaggressive 'smiley face' cheers up other drivers.

WHAT'S BAD

Still Carina E based, so it's

not going to set your pants on fire with excitement. Lean-burn engines require same economy driving style of high revs with small throttle openings – not holding high gears and labouring the engine.

WHAT TO WATCH OUT FOR

Nearly-news likely to have been ex-rental. Look for minor damage from 'rental car carelessness'. May have been 'kerbed', so check for uneven tyre wear and damaged hubcaps. Some problems experienced with steering column, subject to TSB and replaced FOC if owners complain.

MR2 (1985–90)

WHAT'S GOOD

Better executed Fiat X19 successor, with revvy 1.6 litre twin cam sideways in the middle. Super handling, great fun to drive and just enough performance not to be dangerous. Good value new. Held its price extremely well.

WHAT'S BAD

So many were thrashed and crashed or rusted out that good ones are now regarded as classics and fetch top money (Parker's prices are usually about right.) No bootspace of any significance.

WHAT TO WATCH OUT FOR

They rust badly. Smart, fresh paint is likely to hide basinfuls of 'pudding'. Feel all round the edges for crumbly bits. Look inside the front boot for rust, fresh paint and signs it has been front ended. Brake balance is all-important on these cars – not enough bias to rear and fronts will lock up in the wet. DIY kerbside servicing can't do a proper job as they need to be up on a ramp. Driveshafts start to clonk, diffs whine, gearbox bearings get noisy, valve stem seals go, electric window and headlight motors fail. Check tyres for uneven wear – may signify crash, kerbing or simply misalighment. Check floorpan for leak damage from T-bar roof.

MR2 (from 1990)

WHAT'S GOOD

Bigger, much more powerful car than the original. Moved into a different league. Base model had just 119bhp, but 'GT' had 158 bhp. Improved from March 1992 with bigger 15" alloys, better suspension, Yokohama tyres. The real improvements came in March 1994 with better suspension, ABS and power boosted to 174bhp. March 94–August 96 is the model to have.

WHAT'S BAD

A much more 'lardy' car than the original. 1990–92 models had a reputation for swapping ends, especially in the wet. 92–94 variable rate power steering can be a liability on a mid-engined car and power catalysed down to 154 bhp. After 1994 boost, power cut back to 168bhp from August 1996. New, cheaper lightweight replacement scheduled for late 1998 or early 1999 in spirit of MX5 and original MR2.

WHAT TO WATCH OUT FOR

Grey Japanese second-hand imports may not pass UK emissions tests. Automatics are all grey imports. Check all wheels for uneven tyre wear which could be due to accident damage, falling off the road, kerbing or may simply be misadjusted alignment. Full service history essential – either Toyota or Japanese performance car specialist. Needs 6 month services with fully synthetic oil. Make sure front brakes aren't snatching (needs new front to rear compensator, but may need new discs as well). Feel the state of the discs through the wheels and budget accordingly.

MR-S (from 1999)

WHAT'S GOOD

MR2 goes back to its routes and becomes a sporty spyder once again. All new 1.8 litre 140bhp VVT-i engine. Sequential manual 5-speed sports shift works the right way round – lever back to change up; forwards to change down.

WHAT'S BAD

Too soon to say.

WHAT TO WATCH OUT FOR

Too soon to say.

CAMRY (1991–95)

WHAT'S GOOD

Large saloons and estates with extra rear facing bench on US built estate, making it a 7-seater. Good 134 bhp 2.2 litre four (manual or 4-speed auto) and smooth 185bhp 3 litre V6 (auto only). Spacious inside and comfortable. Very reliable for first 5–7 years.

Depreciates rapidly so makes an excellent value for money used buy.

WHAT'S BAD

Depreciation if you are the first owner. Estates discontinued and saloons only available to order from Sept 1995.

WHAT TO WATCH OUT FOR

Not much goes wrong, so look for signs of abuse, such as towing something heavy or carrying heavy loads. Make usual checks of front suspension geometry – look for signs of uneven tyre wear and reverse turn in both directions to check for driveshaft clonks.

CAMRY (from Nov 1996)

WHAT'S GOOD

Very good looking large four door saloon, high spec, badged as a Lexus in some markets. Three proper three point rear seatbelts. 2.2 litre down on power slightly to 128 bhp; V6 up slightly to 188 bhp. Available is standard or 'Sport' trim (lowered, with bodykit and 17" alloys). Far better than Scorpios or Omegas, but top models getting expensive. Four Star NCAP crash test rating among the best.

WHAT'S BAD

Over-light steering not quite in the BMW league. No 'image'. Likely to depreciate steeply over the first three years.

WHAT TO WATCH OUT FOR

No problem areas known, but wise to buy with full Toyota service history. (If not available, why not? No history disqualifies the car from its 3-year warranty.)

CELICA (1990–94)

WHAT'S GOOD

Weird looking coupe. 201bhp to 205bhp GT-Four has warts and growths over its bonnet area. 'Carlos Sainz' GT-Four was collectable. Very quick, with excellent rally pedigree – notorious for being banned for a year for ingenious flouting of air restrictor rule. Basic front wheel drive models have 158bhp, which is enough. Handle well. Good to drive.

WHAT'S BAD

It really is ugly in an organic way – like something designed for 'Alien' by Gigor. All models have a firm ride. The interior is black as a coal mine. Reliability of front drive models is typically Toyota, but GT-Four power train comes under strain.

WHAT TO WATCH OUT FOR

GT-Four is a gearbox breaker. Must have specialist service history, but even then gearbox may fail. All need six monthly oil changes, preferably using fully synthetic oil. Watch out for used RHD imports from Japan brought. May not be fully up to UK spec.

CELICA (1994–2000)

WHAT'S GOOD

Very good-looking car, especially convertible. GT-Four has 240 bhp. Front drive GT has 173 bhp. Cut-price 1.8 much slower with just 114 bhp, but this is enough for cruiser types. Good seating position and good steering. Typical Toyota reliability.

WHAT'S BAD

Strange set of gear ratios and generally a softer car than the previous Celica. Doesn't handle or hold the road as well.

WHAT TO WATCH OUT FOR

GT-Four may follow in footsteps of old model and break its gearbox. Must have specialist service history (Toyota or Japanese performance car specialists such as Intech or Protech) All need six monthly oil changes, preferably using fully synthetic oil. Watch out for used RHD imports from Japan brought in at half the UK price. May not be fully up to UK spec. Watch out for 1.8s disguised as 2.0s. Could have been a drug dealers car.

CELICA (from 2000)

WHAT'S GOOD

Entire car has been re-thought. Now 101mm shorter with much better steering and handling than previous car. 6-speed manual or sequential 4-speed auto. Standard 1.8 has 140bhp, but 1.8 litre GTS VVTi has 180bhp, and 133 lbs ft, giving 0–60 in 7 seconds and a top speed of 150 mph.

WHAT'S BAD

Styling won't appeal to everyone.

WHAT TO WATCH OUT FOR

Grey imports not to UK spec.

PICNIC
(from 1997)

WHAT'S GOOD

Scenic-sized six or seven seater. Seems to handle quite well. Powerful 2 litre 126bhp engine same as RAV 4. Same 5-speed manual or excellent 4-speed auto as well. 2.2 litre IDI Turbodiesel gives more mpg at expense of performance. GS is basic model with 7 seats. GLs and GXs have aircon and ABS. Four star performer in NCAP crash testes (10 points front impact; 15 point side impact).

WHAT'S BAD

No luggage space when all six or seven seats in use. Seats don't fold very cleverly, but rear pair can be removed.

WHAT TO WATCH OUT FOR

Unlikely to have been a taxi. Most likely to have been privately owned. Trim may have received 'deposits' from very young children, sticky sweets may be stuck in seams. Dogs may have crocodiled the upholstery.

PREVIA
(1990–98)

WHAT'S GOOD

One of the bigger MPVs with room for up to 8 and their luggage inside. 5-speed floor-change or 3-speed + overdrive column shift auto. Good build quality. Now eight years old so oldest are affordable and can be 'de-catted' if necessary to save expense.

WHAT'S BAD

Only one sliding side door on the nearside. No diesel, supercharged petrol or 4x4 in UK. Only one petrol engine (but ripe for an LPG conversion). Auto holds its gears for a long time, can be frenetically noisy and a bit juicy.

WHAT TO WATCH OUT FOR

One sliding rear door may

precludes use as a taxi under some local authority rules. Airport taxis do huge mileages they may not show. 8-seater versions best. 6 'captain's' chairs pointless. Cylinder head gaskets can go if coolant not changed every two years. Look for mayonnaise under oil filler cap and in coolant expansion tank (though, since these are remote from the engine, it may not have reached that far). White exhaust smoke also indicates head gasket problems. Rear diffs eventually whine. Interior may have been trashed by kids or 'crocodiled' by dogs. Catalytic converters go eventually.

RAV 4

WHAT'S GOOD

The first fashion 4x4 that really was car-like to drive. Strong performance from 126bhp twin cam 2 litre Celica engine. Manuals have a centre diff lock; autos don't. Autobox is typically excellent Toyota with good ratios and fully controllable (does 60 in second). 5 door versions more practical and handle better, 3 doors faster and more fun. Nice low rear load height for dogs, etc. reasonably economical (30 mpg). Typical Toyota reliability.

WHAT'S BAD

Not great in an 'elk avoidance test'. Rear seat of 5 door slopes forwards and situated over rear wheels, so not comfortable. Suspension wishbones hang too low for serious off-roading.

WHAT TO WATCH OUT FOR

Bent suspension wishbones. Uneven tyre wear. Don't buy one with silly, over-large wheels and ridiculous running boards or you'll lose a lot of money on resale.

LANDCRUISER VX

WHAT'S GOOD

Huge, big, brutal 4.2 litre diesel capable of towing a Jag on a trailer at 100mph. Has gear driven chamshaft rather than belt or chain. Recommended.

WHAT'S BAD

Almost certain to have been used as a towcar, probably pulling something heavy. A lot used by people of no fixed abode to tow chrome plated caravans. Clocking is rife. Too big to be safe for the school run.

WHAT TO WATCH OUT FOR

If history is not impeccable, highly likely to have been clocked. Avoid oilwell emptying petrol version.

TVR

ALL MODELS

WHAT'S GOOD

Hairy-chested all-British sports cars we can now feel proud of. Compact new AJP8 engine is utterly brilliant. New AJP6 'Speed Six' is promising, with 350 bhp 4,185cc six putting out 320 lbs ft torque and allied to 6-speed gearbox. Other models still used modified Rover/Buick pushrod V8s. S1s, S2s and S3s had Ford pushrod V6s, but still with 187bhp (S3C). Late cars reliable and well put together. Some owners do 25,000 miles a year in them. Buy one and you buy into a club. Tuscan racing series well worth a watch. You can meet the owner, Peter Wheeler, in person at The Motor Show.

WHAT'S BAD

Lack of problems is not 100% guaranteed. Many cars

have an extremely hard ride and are very noisy. Cerbrera coupe with AJP8 has very little flywheel effect and revs like a racing car which can catch out the unskilled.

WHAT TO WATCH OUT FOR

Only buy from true enthusiasts of from TVR specialists. Be prepared to spend a few grand to get a used car the way you want it. Use your judgement or get the car checked by a TVR expert. HPI or AA/Experian check also well advised as the car could have been bought on the drip, then the 'owner' hit hard times.

VAUXHALL

AGILA

WHAT'S GOOD

New four door minibox based on Suzuki Wagon R. 12-year anti-perforation warranty. Same 1 litre 58bhp and 1.2 litre 75bhp engines. On sale Summer 2000. 1.2 litre turbodiesel to come later.

WHAT'S BAD

See Suzuki Wagon R. Four, not five, seats

WHAT TO WATCH OUT FOR

As Suzuki Wagon R.

NOVA (1983–93)

WHAT'S GOOD

One of the better 'older' superminis. 3-door nicest and most valuable, but also available as 5 door and 2 and 4 door saloon. Most had decent ohc engines. Easy DIY. Lots of cheerful trim combinations on updated range from 1990. GTEs 'caught on' among young

'Max Power' and 'Revs' readers, who spend thousands of pounds doing them up

WHAT'S BAD

Stodgy handling and indifferent ride. 3-door not very space efficient.

WHAT TO WATCH OUT FOR

May have been couriers cars (especially diesels) and could have been clocked back at anything up to twelve years ago. DIY servicing may have been incompetent or skimped. Really needs an oil change every 3,000 miles or every 6 months, whichever comes first. Main problem is camshaft wear, which can, of course, be terminal for the engine. Listen for thrashing noises and look for signs of oil weeping from top of the engine. Early 80s fuel pump problems should have been rectified in service by now. Check for driveshaft clonks by reverse turning in both directions. Look for split driveshaft gaiters. Expect to have to replace some front suspension bushes. If it has an aftermarket 'pop-up' sunroof, expect water leaks and check carpets. Rust starts in area of hatchback and rear wheel arches. Always lift boot carpets (especially in saloons) to check for repaired accident damage, rust, or both. 'SR' gearboxes don't last long. Interiors weak on all but post 1990 facelift models. Dashboards fall off. If the brakes of the 1.5 litre Isuzu turbodiesel lack servo assistance, you're in for a £600 combined brake vacuum pump and alternator.

CORSA (1993–2000)

WHAT'S GOOD

Ageing design but still a good, 'different' and practical shape for a supermini. Plenty of room in the back of the 5-door version. Doesn't make demands on the driver. Good engines, especially the ultra-economical Suzuki 1 litre 3-cylinder 12-valve, often badged 'Breeze'. Generally reliable, last well and cheap to run.

WHAT'S BAD

Still based on the Nova floorpan, so stodgy and characterless to drive. I.4s have suffered cat problems. Average performance in NCAP crash tests. Short runs may lead to sticking valves on 16-valve models (usually cured by switching to a high detergent petrol).

WHAT TO WATCH OUT FOR

Could have been a courier's car or a driving school car ('Engineering Education Trust' on the V5 = BSM). Clutch cables can be troublesome (cheap to replace). Heavier diesel engines promote high front tyre and suspension wear. All Corsas prone to front suspension wear. Check driveshafts for clonks by reverse turns in both directions. Cracking around door hinges on 'A' pillars of 2-door models (also look for cracks in the paint on 'B' pillars – an MOT failure point). Feel front discs for grooves, 'shouldering' and wear. GTEs may have been thrashed by kids.

RECALLS

1995: Static sparking during refuelling. 1997 (1993–1996 1.4 & 1.6 16vs only – 27,000 cars): Possibility of plastic cambelt idler pulley breaking which can snap cambelt. 1998 (diesel K to N reg: 26,000 cars): Live cable may rub against bonnet hinge, lose insulation and cause a fire; (1.0 12v – P to R reg: 8,000 cars): Cable may touch engine inlet manifold. (Vauxhall Recall Helpline: 01582 427200) 1998: Vauxhall Corsa diesel (K to N reg: 26,000 cars): Live cable may rub against bonnet hinge, lose insulation and cause a fire. (3/6/98.)

Vauxhall Corsa 1.0 12v (P to R reg: 8,000 cars): Cable may touch engine inlet manifold. (3/6/98: Specific Helpline: 01189 458500.)

CORSA (from 2000)

WHAT'S GOOD

New model due Autumn 2000.

WHAT'S BAD

Too soon to say.

WHAT TO WATCH OUT FOR

Too soon to say.

TIGRA

WHAT'S GOOD

Cute, cleverly repackaged Corsa. 'Girly' car image. Decent pair of 1.4 litre and 1.6 litre 16v engines. Reasonably economical. Enough of a 'sports car' for less demanding drivers.

WHAT'S BAD

All it really is underneath is a Corsa. 'Girly' car image (if you're not a girl). Glass hatchbacks leak. Can suffer from sticking valves if used for short runs on petrol lacking an adequate detergent. Rear seats too small for adults.

WHAT TO WATCH OUT FOR

Must be serviced regularly (preferably every 6 months). Look for uneven tyre wear. Broken wheel trims or damaged alloys denote a kerb prone driver, so expect suspension and steering damage. Feel front discs for grooves, 'shouldering' and wear.

RECALLS

1997 (1993–1997): Possibility of plastic cambelt idler pulley breaking which can snap cambelt. (Vauxhall Recall Helpline: 01189 458500 or 01582 427200)

ASTRA (to 1991)

WHAT'S GOOD

Well-liked and still good enough to form the basis of the 1994 Daewoo Nexia. GTE 16v was quick in a straight line. Nicely judged end-of-the-line SX and SXE hatches and estates.

WHAT'S BAD

Solid blue and red paint oxidises. Lacquers on metallics peel off. Hard, jiggly ride not matched by good handling and road feel. Dodgy digital instruments on GTEs. ABS pumps very expensive to replace. Belmont saloon is hideous. Pretty convertibles suffer severe scuttle shake.

WHAT TO WATCH OUT FOR

Could have done 400,000 miles, particularly diesel estates, so look for all the signs. Clutches stick (may need a cheap new cable or may have damaged bulkhead). Suspension bushes wear. Main problem is camshaft wear, which can, of course, be terminal for the engine. Listen for thrashing noises and look for signs of oil weeping from top of the engine. Fuel evaporation problem with all late injected models. Check for driveshaft wear by doing reverse-turns in both directions. Split driveshaft boots are common and an MOT failure point. Regular 3,000 mile oil changes essential. If not engines will sludge up an d rattle. Cambelts must be changed every 35,000 miles; tensioners every 70,000 miles. Always lift the boot carpet and look for signs of accident damage repairs because bodyshells are very difficult to pull back into proper alignment. Check the floorpan of convertibles for rut caused by leaks.

ASTRA (1991–98)

WHAT'S GOOD

Not bad looking and, with

metallic paint, gives impression of reasonable quality. Estate car the most practical in the class. Useful improvements for 1995 model year ('vee grille') include power steering across the range and 'low pressure turbo' GM diesel. LPT diesel estate the best buy and deservedly the most popular. I.6 E-Drive petrol engine slow, but very economical (45 mpg) – a good choice if worried about diesel price increases. 'High torque' 60bhp 1.4 the most popular engine, but even more short of puff.

WHAT'S BAD

Better than the Escort when it came out in 1991, but not much better. 4-door versions are hideous. Over-light power steering and severely lacklustre handling, even on 'Sport' and 'GSi' versions. 16-valve versions criticised for sticking valves – usually the owner's fault for driving short distances from cold starts on the cheapest petrol

(switching to Texaco CleanSystem 3 might cure the problem in a few hundred miles).

WHAT TO WATCH OUT FOR

Sagging rear suspension on hard-used ex-fleet estates. Kerbing damage to front suspension (look for uneven tyre wear). Worn front suspension bushes and steering joints. Damaged suspension arms from jacking by them. Unpleasant clutch action (might be cured cheaply with a new cable). Electric front windows can stick. Valve gear gets noisy with mileage and ambitious 9,000–10,000 mile oil changes. Valves of 16vs may stick if run on cheap petrol. Petrol engine cambelts need changing every 35,000–40,000 miles. Ex Vauxhall Masterhire cars on full service contracts come with very comprehensive computerised service histories, itemised down to light bulb replacements. Watch out for dodgy histories in kerbside or auction sale cars. May be clocked.

RECALLS

1995: Fuel pipe, airbag. 1995 (TD: VIN S5000001 to S5241939; S2500001 to S2707652 and S8000001 to S8216827): Chafing of wiring harness and possible fire risk. 1995: Airbag may fail to inflate in an accident. 1995: Static sparking during refuelling. 1997 (1993–1996 1.4 & 1.6 16vs only): 1999: Possibility of failure of plastic cambelt idler pulley GF50 on 16v engines 1993–96, which can snap cambelt. Changed as an 'in service mod' when cambelts are changed at 35,000–40,000 mile intervals. (Vauxhall Recall Helpline: 01189 458500 or 01582 427200)

NEW ASTRA (from Spring 1998)

WHAT'S GOOD

Vastly better than previous Astra. Steering, handling, roadholding now class-competitive. Better steering 'feel' than 4-cylinder Golf Mk IVs. Three proper three-point rear seatbelts standard across the range. Ski-hatch to boot. Useful 'head up' information display. Four stars for secondary safety in 1999 NCAP tests. Direct-injected 16-valve small turbo 'DI' diesel works well in this car allied to excellent 4-speed autobox – gives 45mpg. Decent build quality. Aircon usually fitted. 160bhp 2 litre GSi from autumn 1999.

WHAT'S BAD

Nondescript , 'hamster'-like road-hugging styling. Ride quality may be too firm for some. Might, unfairly, be regarded as 'also ran' to Golf Mk IV and Ford Focus, so not as likely to hold its value. However, this is something for the second-hand buyer to take advantage of.

WHAT TO WATCH OUT FOR

Only 6–18 months old during the life of this book, so second-hand examples likely to be ex-rental. Look for minor carelessness damage and signs of kerbing. Check front tyres for uneven tread signifying suspension misalignment.

RECALLS

Depending on source of supply, some models developed noisy power steering pumps. Free-of-charge replacement programme Spring 1999.

ZAFIRA

WHAT'S GOOD

Seven seats in a body the same length as an Astra hatchback. Rearmost fold into floor. Centre seats fold forward, giving completely flat load bay. 1.6 litre and 1.8 litre 16v engines on launch, DI came later. Did quite well for driver and front passenger protection in TUV/Auto Bild offset crash tests.

WHAT'S BAD

Cramped driving position and you have to reach behind to change gear. Suffers usual MPV roll understeer on tight bends. Pricey at £14,500 to £18,500 for petrol models. No DI automatic due to weight problems.

WHAT TO WATCH OUT FOR

Too soon to say.

CAVALIER

WHAT'S GOOD

Popular, reliable, good build quality, comfortable, cheap spares, cheap servicing, cheap and easily replaced clutch. Good, smooth, economical Japanese (Isuzu) turbodiesel engine. Cheap to replace ABS from 1994.

WHAT'S BAD

Stodgy handling. Rust in seam on rear wheel-arch.

Brakes can develop judder. Combined alternator/brake vacuum pump of turbodiesels is very expensive. ABS pump of early SRis is eye-wateringly expensive (more than some cars are worth). 6-speed gearbox on 4x4 turbo fails and costs a fortune to replace. Timing belt tensioners can fail on 16-valve engines built August 1993–January 1996.

WHAT TO WATCH OUT FOR

ABS light on early SRis (make sure it hasn't been disconnected). Signs of clocking as lots of 200,000 milers have received haircuts. Damage from being jacked up by front suspension arms. Timing belts not changed at 36,000–40,000 mile intervals. Camshaft wear on 1.6 litre 8-valve engines. Serious engine oil leaks. Track rod end wear. Shot shock absorbers. Juddery braking due to warped front discs. Non-fused wiring can rub against base of battery holder and cause a short. Alternator may short out due to ingress of water through worn rubber steering rod sleeves.

RECALLS

1994: (1.7 TD Mar 1992–Mar 1994 VIN NV201488–R7560941): Loss of braking efficiency. 1995: Static sparking during refuelling. 1999: Possibility of failure of plastic cambelt idler pulley GF50 on 16v engines 1993–96, which can snap cambelt. Changed as an 'in service mod' when cambelts are changed at 35,000–40,000 mile intervals. (Vauxhall Recall Helpline: 01189 458500 or 01582 427200)

VECTRA

WHAT'S GOOD

Half a step forward from the Cavalier. Reasonable build quality, comfortable ride, cheap spares, smooth ride.

Especially good on motorways. Smooth, economical Japanese (Isuzu) turbodiesel engine in early diesels. Important improvements for 1997 model year include height-adjustable steering wheel, better seats and Trafficmaster. Standard aircon from Sept '97 in lieu of sunroof. Potentially long-lasting chain-cam direct-injected (DI) diesel engines in later diesels. Vastly improved SRi and GSi models from Spring 1998 with steering and front suspension modifications developed jointly with Saab. Comparatively good performance in NCAP crash tests. Major facelift in Spring 1999 made it a better, but not better looking car.

WHAT'S BAD

Until the 1998 improvements, a whole step backwards from the Cavalier. Clutch replacement remains a five to six hour job involving engine removal instead of the simple half hour job it was on the Cavalier. Earlier cars suffer stodgy handling with severe understeer, which is not entirely cured even in the latest 1999 model Vectras. Terrible drivers seat on early models with no steering wheel height adjustment (corrected from 1997 model year). Styled mirrors give limited view. Replacement due 2001.

WHAT TO WATCH OUT FOR

Ex-Vauxhall Masterhire cars come with trustworthy print-out of full service history, including cambelt changes every 35,000–40,000 miles. Vectras from other fleets might have been clocked, so be sure to check mileages properly. Older SRis on Firestones may suffer premature tyre wear. Best tyres for older non-sporty Vectras are Pirelli P6000s. Best for new SRis and GSis are Yokohamas. Front suspension can wear prematurely. Make sure ABS light comes on, then goes out when it should. If engine misses, may have faulty ECU and cat may be hot spotted. May suffer steering column rattle. May have been run on cheap petrol and suffering sticking valves as a result. Readers also report problems with air-conditioning systems and window regulators.

RECALLS

1996 (8/95 to 2/96 build – 40,000 cars): Check front seatbelt mounting bolts and tighten if necessary. 1997 (1995–1996 1.6 16vs only – 27,000 cars): Possibility of failure of plastic cambelt idler pulley GF50, which can snap cambelt. Changed as an 'in service mod' when cambelts are changed at 35,000–40,000 mile intervals. 1997 (Jan–May '96 build): Fuel pipe may come off at tank. 1998 (all 200,000 built before July 1998): Handbrake cable subject to premature wear. Modified cable free replacement service. 1998 (automatics only): In service modification to autobox ECU mapping. 1999: Possibility of failure of cambelt idler pulley on petrol engined 'P' to 'R' reg Vectras (Vauxhall Recall Helpline: 01189 458500 or 01582 427200)

CALIBRA

WHAT'S GOOD

Good-looking, practical four-seater coupe with a big, golf club sized boot. Some good engines in the line-up. Some very fast, very powerful cars such as 6-speed 4x4 turbo. Some nice trim combinations. 2.5 V6s with leather and white instruments on 'R' plates can represent a lot of coupe for the money.

WHAT'S BAD

Hard to see out of and very difficult to reverse. Based on the Cavalier and though it handles better it still suffers from the understeering limitations of the Cavalier. Front drive Calibras will always come off the road front-first. 6-speed gearbox on 4x4 turbo fails and costs a fortune to replace.

WHAT TO WATCH OUT FOR

Ex-Vauxhall Masterhire cars previously on service contracts come with trustworthy print-out of full service history, including cambelt changes every 36,000–40,000 miles.

RECALLS

1999: Possibility of failure of plastic cambelt idler pulley GF50 on 16v engines 1993–96, which can snap cambelt. Changed as an 'in service mod' when cambelts are changed at 35,000– 40,000 mile intervals. (Vauxhall Recall Helpline: 01189 458500 or 01582 427200)

CARLTON

WHAT'S GOOD

Solid, German-built saloons and estates capable of extreme mileages of 300,000 or more with little trouble. Big, comfortable, well-liked by many owners, particularly 'Strasbourg' box automatics. Strong loyalty factor. Good handling and ride. Pre-August 1992 may be pre-cat (check for fuel filler restrictor). Estate car has a huge capacity. 3.0GSi 24v is quick. Lotus Carlton is seriously quick.

WHAT'S BAD

Power steering a bit vague. Can suffer from electrical glitches. Diesels are lacklustre. Obstructive manual gearboxes. Starting to get a bit 'old' looking. ECU connector block prone to hairline cracks which allow moisture in and lead to intermittent faults which could hot spot a 'cat'.

WHAT TO WATCH OUT FOR

Clocking, obviously, because these cars take the miles so well. Some engines require timing belt replacement every 35,000–40,000 miles – others have chains. Vital to check special rear shock absorbers in estates as these are expensive. Want to see evidence of regular maintenance, including biannual autobox ATF and filter change. Beware of clonky or noisy manual boxes – they're expensive to rebuild. Oil breathers of 4-cylinder engines sometimes get blocked. Noisy valve gear often denotes missed oil changes. If it has a tow hook or signs of one having been fitted, be extra careful. Watch out for clocked ex-taxis.

SENATOR (1987–95)

WHAT'S GOOD

The policeman's favourite police car. Highly successful re-style looks longer and lower than Carlton and garish 'chip-cutter' grille is just right, especially pitched against bland looking Granada. High-spec 3.0 24v CD obviously the best (not all had leather). Glovebox of air-conditioned CD can be used as a fridge or drinks cooler. Later 2.6 12v CD is okay, 3.0 12v also okay. The police liked these cars so much, they stored them and some did not come into service until 'M' reg. May still be a chance to pick up some of the last ex-police 24vs at West-Oxfordshire Motor Auctions. The public will think you are driving a police car, so it's still the best car for flashing plodders out of the way.

WHAT'S BAD

Top spec 3.0 24v CDs with less than 75,000 miles now increasingly rare. Lots of electrical glitches on CDs, particularly autobox electrics. Early 2.5 12v lacked essentials such as proper engine cooling. Police spec had no sunroof or aircon, wind-up windows and manual 5-speed boxes. They're not that easy to drive because the engine lacks the expected low down torque.

WHAT TO WATCH OUT FOR

Re-trimmed ex-police cars. Repaired accident damage on ex-police Senators. Police cars are very well maintained, usually with new clutches and 'cats' at around the 80,000–90,000 mile mark. Check all electric windows and sunroof (if fitted). Make sure aircon blows cold (if fitted). Privately owned cars may have suffered skimped maintenance, leading to camshaft wear. Beware of Senators used for 'private hire' (i.e. taxis). Servotronic steering should have 'over centre' feel (more steering effect at extremes of lock). Check for evidence of having had a tow bar. Bounce each corner, especially the back two as springs may have sagged and left shocks in a state of shock. Try to feel the discs through the wheels and budget for replacement accordingly. Timing chain tensioners on privately-owned cars not serviced and driven to police standards tend to fail at around 90,000 miles and the timing chains themselves at 100,000–110,000 miles.

OMEGA

WHAT'S GOOD

Well equipped, comfortable, handles well with more road feel than Senator. both 2.5 litre and 3 litre V6's nice to drive. 150 mph 207 bhp 3.0 MV6 is almost good value by UK standards at £24,445. Manual boxes better suited to engines than Senator manuals. Get a white, grey or otherwise a dark-coloured one and the cars in front will still think you are a police car. Three Star NCAP crash test rating. Comprehensively facelifted and re-engineered in autumn 1999 with option of new 2.2 litre 146bhp 4-cylinder engine offering 151lb ft torque.

WHAT'S BAD

Poor paint quality on some early cars. Large number of quality problems and complaints, often over BMW powered 2.5 litre straight six diesel. The police had great difficulty getting their kit into the limited dashboard and front-of-engine space. Started looking at Volvo T5s instead.

WHAT TO WATCH OUT FOR

Electrical and electronic problems (check everything works, including computer and especially ABS warning light). BMW diesel must have had 4,500–5,000 mile oil changes (easy for busy company drivers to forget).

RECALLS

1995: Static sparking during refuelling. 1995 (16v: VIN R 1000001 to S1155206): Fuel feed pipe may chafe. Reposition and clamp into place. 1999: Possibility of failure of plastic cambelt idler pulley GF50 on 4-cylinder 16v engines

1994–98, which can snap cambelt. Changed as an 'in service mod' when cambelts are changed at 35,000–40,000 mile intervals. (Vauxhall Recall Helpline: 01189 458500 or 01582 427200)

FRONTERA

WHAT'S GOOD

Not bad looking, in a chunky sort of way. Right car at the right time when launched in 1991 to feed 4x4 fashion fad. Initially well-priced as alternative to a Cavalier. Held value well until the public started to wonder why they were driving crude old-fashioned 4x4 trucks instead of proper cars. Reasonably competent off-road. 1998 'round the world' endurance run helped improve public perception of reliability. 2.5 litre from 1996P the best engine. Range revamped for 1999 with 2.2 Direct injected diesel or 3.2 litre V6.

WHAT'S BAD

Really no more than a
dressed-up Isuzu pick up.
Legion of quality problems.
Short-lived direct injected
2.8 Isuzu diesel withdrawn
due to emissions problem.
2.3 and 2.2 petrol engines
gobble petrol. If you want a
chunky 4x4 to use as a day
to day car the Honda CRV
and Land Rover Freelander
are vastly superior.

WHAT TO WATCH OUT FOR

Is it a townie's car (never
gone off road) or is it a
farmer's car? Big difference in
likelihood of damage to
underside and drive train.
Has a towing hook been
fitted at some time? If so,
what has it been towing?
(Anything from a one horse
horsebox to a mobile
catering stand, so look for
saggy rear suspension,
groaning rear diff., nosy
wheel bearings) Look for oil
leaks from engine and drive
train. Check that it tracks
straight. Look for wear in
front suspension and

steering joints. Listen for big-
end rattles, noisy tappets
(signs of insufficiently
frequent oil changes). Check
dipstick for clean oil.

RECALLS

1995: VIN NV500400 to
RV628644: Faulty bonnet
safety catch. 1996 (Sport): Fit
heat shield between exhaust
system and petrol tank (fire
risk). Replace catches for
removable roof section.
Spring 1999: Warning issued
to all known owners to take
vehicles to Vauxhall agents
at four years or 40,000 miles
for a replacement timing
belt and timing belt idler
wheel. 1999: all 'new'
Fronteras built June
1998–September 1999
(6,557 vehicles)officially
recalled for 'a check on
steering components'.

MONTEREY

WHAT'S GOOD

Badge-engineered Isuzu
Trooper.

WHAT'S BAD

Slow seller and lots hung around unsold in compounds for more than a year. See Isuzu Trooper.

WHAT TO WATCH OUT FOR

See Isuzu Trooper.

RECALLS

See Isuzu Trooper.

SINTRA

WHAT'S GOOD

Vauxhall's large MPV. Previa-sized, with advantage of two sliding rear side doors. Powerful 201bhp 3 litre petrol V6, 141bhp 2.2 litre petrol four. 1998 introduced 2.2 litre direct Injected diesel the most sensible choice, but a bit short of low down grunt.

WHAT'S BAD

American built, so trim not up to European standards. Not especially different or particularly attractive. Blitzed in the market place by the Chrysler Voyager. Poor two and a half star performer in NCAP crash tests (3points front impact; 15 points side impact).

WHAT TO WATCH OUT FOR

Has it been an airport taxi? (Late introduction of diesel means this is unlikely.)

RECALLS

1998: Catches for removing rear seats may sever fingers. Covers to be fitted to seat release lever mechanism.

VOLKSWAGEN

LUPO

WHAT'S GOOD

High build quality. Same car as Seat Arosa, built at Wolfsburg, with cute front end styling, much nicer interior, twin airbags., height-adjustable driver's seat and steering wheel as standard. Formed basis of '3-litre car' capable of 100kms on three litres of petrol, equal to 94mpg. 1.4s have new twin-cam 16v engine. 1.7SDI charming, economical and not too slow – a far better bet than the 1 litre petrol version. 100bhp 1.4 16v Sport from September '99. 1.4 litre direct injected petrol engine with 105bhp and 56mpg capability unveiled at Frankfurt show. 75bhp 1.4 direct injected diesel on the way. Lupo FSi with direct injected petrol engine giving 105bhp and 50mpg shown at 1999 Frankfurt Show. Lupo did well in German TUV/Auto Bild front offset crash test.

WHAT'S BAD

Prices higher than Seat Arosa. Power steering a £450 option on 1 litre base model. 1 litre horribly, painfully slow.

WHAT TO WATCH OUT FOR

Too soon to say.

OLD POLO

WHAT'S GOOD

High build quality whether put together in Germany or Spain. Steel 'factory' sunroof a desirable extra adds £200 to price. Euro Car Parts (0541 506506) supplies cheap parts.

WHAT'S BAD

Weak front suspension. Not very roomy. Tiny boot. Surprisingly heavy steering. No brake servo prior to 1991 facelift. The most expensive second-hand supermini. If water pump seizes, will usually snap cambelt.

WHAT TO WATCH OUT FOR

Piston-slapping tiny mileage shopping cars, serviced 'every two years whether they needed it or not'. (They need an oil change every six months.) Pre-hydraulic cam cars (pre-'86) more expensive to service. Need cambelt changes every 36,000–40,000 miles or every four years, preferably tensioner too. Sump pan can rust, especially if engine has been 'steam cleaned'. A dirty engine with peeling paint on the cam cover is a good sign. Check spec carefully. Some 1.3 CLs were 4-speed, not 5-speed. Will eventually rust, so check round the edges. Normal for cam covers to lose their paint. Engines should look scruffy, not 'steam cleaned' because steam cleaning washes off rustproofing.

NEW POLO

Strong UK image. A bottle green two door Polo with a sunroof has been described as the "most middle-class car you can buy'". (Bottle green is the 'right' colour and two rather than four side doors says 'it's a second car'.) All have good, fairly upright driving position, second only to the Fiat Punto. Big car ride (much better than Punto). Now come with 3-year dealer warranty, necessitating VW franchise servicing. Best engine now a 125bhp 16v 1.6. Comparatively good performance in NCAP crash tests. Cordoba Vario based estate launched Spring '98. Facelifted inside and out in autumn 1999.

WHAT'S BAD

Gearchange quality varies. Despite VW's best efforts, Spanish build quality in general can vary. PAS not available even as an option on slow 1.0 versions. 1.4 automatic not really powerful enough. Surprisingly old-fashioned dashboard. Sky high used prices. 1.9 diesel not very economical when pushed. Ugly Cordoba-based saloon versions not as comfortable as hatchbacks, but have big, deep boots. 1.9SDi diesel frugal but noisy. Dashboard shows its age compared to much more cheerful Lupo.

WHAT TO WATCH OUT FOR

Paying too much for a two or three-year-old. Particularly paying too much for a used Polo saloon, which is really nothing more than a Seat Cordoba. Very variable gearshift quality. Faulty self-adjusting clutch cables may cause premature clutch failure. Electric windows can play up.

RECALLS

1996 (to June 1996 build): Faults in steel wheels may lead to loss of tyre pressure.

POLO CADDY KOMBI

WHAT'S GOOD

Kombi version of Polo/Ibiza/Cordoba based Caddy van. 75bhp 1.6i petrol and 60bhp 1.9 SDI. Very spacious in the back and surprisingly good fun to drive.

WHAT'S BAD

Doesn't ride as well as Citroen Berlingo Multispace. Not as practical as Renault Kangoo Combi.

WHAT TO WATCH OUT FOR

Second-hand examples which have led an extremely hard double-life as weekday van and weekend transport for the family and its dogs.

GOLF MK II

WHAT'S GOOD

Image. 16v the one to have. Unlikely to rust in the seams. Long life engines, exhausts, batteries, shock absorbers. Euro Car Parts (0541 506506) supplies cheap parts.

WHAT'S BAD

Rattles. Needs a cambelt change every four years or 40,000 miles and a tensioner change every 80,000 miles. Plastic door membranes go, leading to soggy carpets. Water pumps, clutches, front strut top bearings, etc. have only average life. Clutch cable self-adjusters go, leading to premature clutch wear. Hubs go in 8–12 years (80,000–120,000 miles). Underfloor fuel pump on fuel-injected cars springs a leak after 9–10 years. Water pumps last 5–10 years. Radiators last 5–10 years. Rear disc callipers on GTi can go and cost £300 each. Pneumatic central locking starts to fail on rear doors after eleven years. Steel wheels can fleck with rust after six years.

WHAT TO WATCH OUT FOR

Make sure heater matrix bypass has been installed (major recall 1995–97). Check oil filler cap for black sludge (oil not changed regularly enough) or mayonnaise (cylinder head gasket problems). Check driveshafts by reversing car on full lock in both directions. Easily clocked so look for signs of more miles than the odo shows. Rear discs rust first, become pitted and fail MOT. Clutches last 70,000–80,000 miles average, less with town driving. Driver's seat upholstery should last twelve years and 100,000 miles before starting to wear through. Bonnet slam panel should be matt black, not body colour. After twelve years, cam cover of all but 16v should have lost almost all its paint unless owned by someone particularly fastidious. Engines should look scruffy, not 'steam cleaned' because steam cleaning washes off rustproofing. Look for a square white sticker showing the vehicle identification number on the inside of the boot sill. No sticker is a sure sign that the car has been rear-ended. Went hydraulic tappets in 1986 – cheaper to service. Rusts first on top of scuttle between screen and bonnet.

RECALLS

1995 (Golf 1.6 & 1.8 1983A to 1989G): bypass valve to be

inserted into heater pipe; heater matrix to be replaced if degraded. 1996 (Golf 1.3 1983A to 1989G): bypass valve to be inserted into heater pipe; heater matrix to be replaced if degraded.

GOLF MK III

WHAT'S GOOD

Strong image. High residuals. Best engines: TDI, 2.0 16v and 2.8 VR6 engines. Also 100bhp 1.6 fitted to last Golf GLs. Euro Car Parts (0541 506506) supplies cheap parts.

WHAT'S BAD

Strong image not completely justified. Prices paid in late 1997, early 1998 were probably too high. Residuals likely to drop sharply once Mk IV arrives in quantity. Three-door models flex quite badly (five-door models are better). Handling and roadholding not brilliant by 90s standards. Though car may remains solid and rust-free, many replacement parts will be needed over 10-year life. More than its fair share of recalls.

WHAT TO WATCH OUT FOR

Premature clutch wear due to faulty self-adjusting cable. Oil-burning TDI engines. Clocking. See Mk II.

RECALLS

1995 (Golf GTi, 16v, VR6, Convertible: VIN 1HPW 439315 to 1HSW 418237 and 1ERK 000001 to 1ESK 025159): Headlamp failures. Headlight switch on RHD models can overheat, leading to headlight failure. 28,000 cars affected. 1996: (1993–95 build): Cooling fan motor may seize. 1997 (Single headlight models). January 1997 recall for headlight failure. Headlight switch on RHD models can overheat, leading to headlight failure. 9,700 cars affected. 1997 (1994–97 build): September 1997 recall for headlamp modification for all cars. Total 150,000 cars affected. 1997 (1991–94 models with electric front windows – 16,000 cars): Insulation on power cable may chafe and short circuit. Needs protective shield in cable opening of door. 1997 (Aug '93–Jan '97 build): Engine wiring loom may overhead.

GOLF MK IV

WHAT'S GOOD

Much better looking than Mk III. Excellent build quality. UK market cars have high equipment levels, including ABS. 3-year manufacturer + dealer warranty. More room, safer and better handling than Mk III. Super-efficient and quick 110bhp TDI available for first time in UK. New 115bhp TDI with 6-speed gearbox even quicker and 35mph/1,000 makes it even more economical at speed. 100bhp 1.6 petrol good 'cooking' engine. 150bhp VR5 makes a

wonderful noise, has a good set of gear ratios and the extra weight gives the steering more 'feel'. Joint top of the class for secondary safety in NCAP crash testing after side airbags fitted from August 1998. Excellent car-like estate not the biggest in its class but feels very classy. The qualities of these cars grow on you. Galvanized body has 12-year warranty.

WHAT'S BAD

Expensive in UK. Supply shortages ensure 'exclusivity' and lead UK buyers to pay high prices. Steering very light. Cable gearchange on all but 1.6 and 1.4. 1.8 20v and 1.8 20v Turbo work well but don't involve the driver. Modification to 'B' pillar delayed production. No VR6. Alarm sensitivity on early production corrected by unnecessary pillar mounted sensors (all drivers had to do was shut off the air supply to inside the car).

WHAT TO WATCH OUT FOR

RHD personal imports not to full UK spec – especially estate cars. Some TDI 110s suffered a low speed running problem which could only be cured by a modified flywheel and inlet manifold and in some cases a re-chipped ECU.

RECALLS

Announced *Daily Telegraph* 1/10/98: 9,500 Mk IV Golfs from SE spec upwards fitted with volumetric alarms recalled to fit less sensitive volumetric sensors. (Not actually necessary because problem can be solved by using ventilation control to shut off outside air.)

BEETLE (from 1998)

WHAT'S GOOD

Golf Mk IV based and an instant cult car in the USA and Europe. Standard engine is updated 8-valve 2 litre from Golf III, which is pleasantly torquey and suits town work. TDI 90 engine available.

WHAT'S BAD

No more than a Golf IV in a beetle shell, which is nothing like as practical as that of the Golf. Very little room in the back seats. Small luggage capacity. UK prices started at £15,775 for LHD with a/c, alloys and a full spec including a bud vase. Strictly a fashion accessory 'fun' car. Hard to park.

WHAT TO WATCH OUT FOR

Grey imports started arriving in the UK in 1998. Trade imports restricted to 50 by SVA, so don't buy a non-registered Beetle or you won't be able to register it. Look out for parking damage at the ends.

RECALLS

May 1998, first 12,000 recalled in USA because wiring could become trapped by battery, overheat and catch fire.

JETTA

WHAT'S GOOD

Underrated 'Golf with a rucksack'. Stiffer body so handles better than a Golf with fewer rattles. 16v seriously quick, does 60 in 2nd gear, and gets there in 7 seconds. 'Long life' bodies, exhausts, batteries, shock absorbers. Euro Car Parts (0541 506506) supplies cheap parts.

WHAT'S BAD

Dowdy image. See under Golf Mk II.

WHAT TO WATCH OUT FOR

See under Golf Mk II.

RECALLS

1995 (1.6 & 1.8 1983A to 1989G): bypass valve to be inserted into heater pipe; heater matrix to be replaced if degraded. 1996 (1.3 1983A to 1989G): bypass valve to be inserted into heater pipe; heater matrix to be replaced if degraded.

VENTO

WHAT'S GOOD

Like the Jetta, underrated and consequently cheap. Euro Car Parts (0541 506506) supplies cheap parts. TDI is roomy, sensible, economical and quite quick. VR6 (if you can find one) is a performance bargain. More rigid body shell and better protection from rear end impacts than Golf Mk III.

WHAT'S BAD

UK market treated them just like the Jetta. Otherwise as Golf Mk III

WHAT TO WATCH OUT FOR

As Golf Mk III.

RECALLS

(See Recalls for Golf Mk III)

BORA

WHAT'S GOOD

Good-looking saloon version of Mk IV Golf with stiffer suspension and V5 engine available from launch. Superb set of gear ratios in V5 giving nice, linear acceleration. Big boot. Higher specs than Toledos with similar power outputs. Galvanized body has 12-year warranty.

WHAT'S BAD

More expensive than Seat Toledo and Skoda Octavia siblings. Stiffer suspension might be an advantage on open roads in the dry, but lacks 'bite' and can make the overlight steering feel a bit frightening when turning in on a wet bend. Bora estate not available in the UK.

WHAT TO WATCH OUT FOR

Too soon to say.

OLD PASSAT

WHAT'S GOOD

Estates have excellent rear legroom, are comfortable and handle well. Was a 174bhp VR6, briefly, 1993–95. TDI 90 best

compromise engine. Estates hold value well. Saloons worth £2,000 less. Aircon available in lieu of sunroof.

WHAT'S BAD

Good, well-specified estates hard to find and sell for strong money. All diesel models may have been cabbed. Saloons have dowdy image.

WHAT TO WATCH OUT FOR

As Golf/Jetta/Vento. Make sure aircon blows cold. Make sure not cabbed. A lot of this model Passat began their lives on rental fleets.

RECALLS

1995 (VIN3ARE 0000001 to 3ASE 142536): Headlamp failures. 1996 (4-cylinder Passats 1988F–1989G): bypass valve to be inserted into heater pipe; heater matrix to be replaced if degraded. 1996 (1993–95 build): Cooling fan motor may seize. VW Passat (Dec '95–Mar '98): May be airbag activator fault.

NEW PASSAT (from 1997)

WHAT'S GOOD

The best car in its class; really a class above. TDI 90 and 110 engines better than 1.8 20v, but 20v turbo will do 140mph – and brake from 140mph safely. Very low levels of wind and road noise. Excellent economy from TDI 90 and 110 – most owners will better 50 mpg. Comparatively good performance in NCAP crash tests. Improved 115bhp 210 lb ft TDi for 2000 model year. Galvanized body has 11-year warranty.

WHAT'S BAD

High residuals make them expensive used buys. Steering a bit too light, especially on motorways. Not entirely without build quality faults and problems, such as leaks from screen area, under-dash rattles, whining 4-speed automatics when mated to 1.8 litre 20v engine (1.6 auto, diesel auto and 5-speed Tiptronic OK). Cats fail on TDIs built before August 1998.

WHAT TO WATCH OUT FOR

Check very carefully for signs of water leaks (feel footwell carpets for damp). Listen for rattles. Check front tyre wear. Blue exhaust smoke from diesel indicates faulty turbo oil seals.

RECALLS

1998: 11,450 cars built May–November 1997 recalled due to potential fault affecting front seat belts. Involves replacing complete belt units. 1998: Passat Synchro (Dec '97–Apr '98 build): Throttle and brake hose problems; 11,450 Passats built between May–November 1997 recalled due to potential fault affecting front seat belts. Involves replacing complete belt units.

CONCEPT D

WHAT'S GOOD

VW's rival to BMW 7 Series and Mercedes S Class. Shown at 1999 Frankfurt Show with 'green' 5-litre V10 diesel engine producing 313bhp, but also to be available with Audi V8 and a new V12 petrol engine. Built alongside Passat at Dresden. European launch in Y2k.

WHAT'S BAD

Not what you'd call a looker. Not endowed with MB status. Does the world need yet another big car?

WHAT TO WATCH OUT FOR

Too soon to say.

CORRADO

WHAT'S GOOD

The best application of VW's VR6, here in superb 2.9 litre 190bhp form. Excellent front drive handling. Best bought for sensible money left-hand drive in Germany. VR6

recommended.

WHAT'S BAD

They were part of the drug dealers 'uniform', so don't be surprised if low lifes edge up to the car and flash money at you. Can suffer more than their fair share of niggly faults. Demand exceeds supply, so these cars are expensive. Cheaper used German imports will, of course, have been driven at 150mph on the Autobahn and will suffer stone damage to the body and paint.

WHAT TO WATCH OUT FOR

Pre-digital odometers easy to clock. VR6s fashionable among drug dealers 1996–97–often evidenced by 'flash' modifications. If aircon fitted, make sure it blows cold. Superchargers of G60s wear out (can be reconditioned by Jabbasport from £320, tel: 01733 571769).

RECALLS

1996 (4-cylinder cars 1988F–1989G): bypass valve to be inserted into heater pipe; heater matrix to be replaced if degraded. 1996 (VR6 1993–95): Cooling fan motor may seize.

SHARAN

WHAT'S GOOD

VW badged Galaxy carries the most prestige and holds its value best. Got the 110bhp TDI engine before Galaxy or Alhambra. Also first to offer 110bhp TDI with 4-speed autobox. 1.8 20v from Spring '98. Falling used values led to price cuts and VW agents offering 'S' reg TDI 110 'S' specs with aircon for £16,450 at 4–6 months old. Three star performer in NCAP crash tests (6 points front impact; 15 points side impact).

WHAT'S BAD

VW 2 litre 8v petrol engines not as good as Ford's 2.0 and 2.3 litre twin-cams. Began to suffer from over-supply in 1998. Below average 'customer satisfaction'.

WHAT TO WATCH OUT FOR

RHD imports not to UK spec, missing important items such as air-conditioning, rear seat heating, etc.

RECALLS

1997: (built Jan '96–Apr '97): problems with optional child seats. 1997 (built Dec '95–July '96): Brake pads may overheat. 1998: (Aug '96–Feb '98 build): Loss of power due to wiring loom failure.

CARAVELLE

WHAT'S GOOD

Acres of space for 8 people and their luggage even in SWB versions. 2.5TDI engine by far the best engine, giving 80–90 mph cruising and 35 mpg. Good to drive. Multivan comes with curtains and seats fold flat into bed.

WHAT'S BAD

Earlier models were awful to drive. Only available from VW commercial vehicle agents. VR6 is a heavy drinker. TDI timing belt drives water pump and if water pump fails, so does belt.

WHAT TO WATCH OUT FOR

Van based, so paint quality of early models was not up to car standards. Much improved after 1996 facelift. Metallics the best.

VOLVO

440/460

WHAT'S GOOD

Plenty of attention to secondary safety. Crude but effective diesel. 1.8 CVT automatic probably the best combination. Many former 340/360 owners liked their 440s and 460s just as much and mourn the passing of this car.

WHAT'S BAD

Booted 460 an aesthetic compromise. Poor Dutch build quality of early production from factory in Born. Ride quality not brilliant, especially of 460

with a laden boot. May rust prematurely.

WHAT TO WATCH OUT FOR

Rust, especially in body seams. Oil-consuming 2 litre versions may have required 'mod 2371', carried out 'in-service' by Volvo agents. Look for at least four year's official Volvo agent servicing to make sure 'in-service' improvements were carried out. PAS not always fitted, but can be retro-fitted for about £600. Late, facelifted 440s and 460s the best.

RECALLS

1994: 440/460 2 litre (440

VIN 419000–602090; 460 VIN 419001–602089; 480 VIN 586300–590058): Airbag may deploy accidentally. 1996: 440/460 (1991–1995): Fire risk from faulty electrical connections.

480

WHAT'S GOOD

Coupe version of 440/460 on same floorpan from same factory in Born reached the market first. Owners seem to like them with a passion. The last of the line were the best with very comprehensive spec, including air-conditioning. Galvanized, so rust not a problem.

WHAT'S BAD

Poor Dutch build quality led one magazine to dub it 'the coupe from hell'. But the car was progressively improved and almost all problems will have been solved 'in service'.

WHAT TO WATCH OUT FOR

Oil-consuming 2 litre

versions may have required 'mod 2371', carried out in service by Volvo agents. Look for at least four year's official Volvo agent servicing to make sure 'in-service' improvements were carried out. Make sure aircon blows cold (if fitted).

RECALLS

1994: 480 2 litre (VIN 586300–590058): Airbag may deploy accidentally. 1996: 480 (1991–1995): Fire risk from faulty electrical connections.

S40/V40

WHAT'S GOOD

Top in class for secondary safety in NCAP crash tests. Turbo versions are vary fast. GDI versions economical.

WHAT'S BAD

Bright, quartz iodine daytime running lights can dazzle and infuriate other drivers. Ride, steering, handling and roadholding not up to expectations created by good-looking body and clever marketing. Lots of early production quality problems at Dutch factory, later rectified. Not the car the image leads you to expect.

WHAT TO WATCH OUT FOR

Minor accident damage buckles the inner-wing structure. Car may have been badly repaired to save cost.

240/260

WHAT'S GOOD

Built like a tank. Pioneered a lot of secondary safety features. Estate cars will take fairly large items of furniture if you don't mind blotting out your rear view. Capable of huge mileages.

WHAT'S BAD

Some drivers think that the safety features make them 'safe', but heaven help the rest of us. Hideous looks. Appalling steering. Horrible handling. Wallows like a

hippo in a mudbath. A dinosaur to drive. Load platform is high and rear overhang too long which make an overloaded 240 estate doubly dangerous.

WHAT TO WATCH OUT FOR

Kerbed front suspension (all too easy with no steering 'feel' at all). Saggy springs. Soggy shock absorbers. Rust does eventually attack these cars.

740/760

WHAT'S GOOD

Built like a tank. Better looking than antiquated 240 in a curious 1970s American way. 'Genteel', very middle-class, 'respectable' image (but see 'WHAT'S BAD').

WHAT'S BAD

Ugly looks. Horrible handling. Very mixed image: Genteel and middle-class, but, on the other hand, sometimes driven by very aggressive drivers. High intensity high level rear brake light on automatics must be fitted with low intensity bulb or will dazzle the driver behind in a traffic jam (technically an offence under the RVLR 1989). Duff old PSA V6 (don't buy a 760 with a 'V' engine). The market is for Volvo estates. Saloon versions are very hard to sell. Old estates that began with antique dealers end up with painters & decorators.

WHAT TO WATCH OUT FOR

Steering and front suspension damage from 'kerbing'. Baggy suspension from carrying ludicrously heavy loads. Drips near back wheels could be leaking rear shocks. Engine and exhaust system damage from 'short run syndrome'. With 3,000 mile oil changes engines will do 300,000 miles plus, but most of the other bits won't. Previous owners may have replaced alternators, water pumps and starter motors but may have offloaded the car because the gearbox or diff is about to give up. On autos check ATF – should be red, not grey-black. High risk of clocking or having run 100,000 miles 'unhooked'. Cats are £600, but can be ditched from pre-August '92 models.

RECALLS

1995: VIN 37400 to 39877 and 16300 to 38007: Battery short circuit leading to possible fire risk.

850 / S70 / V70

WHAT'S GOOD

The first sporty, modern Volvo. Changed Volvo's image completely, especially when estates were entered for 1994 Touring Car Championship. T5s are seriously quick. T5 saloons or estates replaced Senators on many police fleets. Ex-police two-year-olds available for around £8,000 (West Oxfordshire Motor Auctions, tel: 01993 774413). TDIs not far off T5 performance and give 35 mpg economy. Rock solid build quality. Good, predictable, safe handling.

More fun to drive than any previous Volvo. Changed the image of the company. S70 earned Three-Star NCAP crash test rating.

WHAT'S BAD

Daylime running lights can dazzle other drivers. Estates are only commodious if you load them to the roof. Hard ride and sharper steering came as a shock to old-school, traditional Volvo owners. Front tyre wear of TDi, T5 and T5R can be severe – manuals 6,000–8,000 miles; autos 12,000–14,000 miles. Ex police cars with over 100,000 miles still comparatively dear at auction. TDI timing belt drives water pump and if water pump fails, so does belt.

WHAT TO WATCH OUT FOR

Kerb-damaged front suspension and front driveshafts. Front tyre wear. Retrimmed, clocked ex-police cars.

RECALLS

1995: VIN 078000 to 120420 and 175000 to 220678: Fault with jack which could allow the car to fall. 1997 (1996 and 1997 model years): Check for sticking throttle.

940

WHAT'S GOOD

Lots of 'passive' safety features. One of the first cars with a built-in rear child seat. 'Genteel', very middle-class, 'respectable' image (but see 'WHAT'S BAD').

WHAT'S BAD

Boring to drive. Flabby handling. Very mixed image: middle-class, but, like 740, sometimes driven by very aggressive drivers. High intensity high level rear brake light on automatics must be fitted with low intensity bulb or will dazzle the driver behind in a traffic jam (technically an offence under the RVLR 1989). The market is for Volvo estates and saloon versions are very hard to sell.

WHAT TO WATCH OUT FOR

Steering and front suspension damage from 'kerbing'. Engine and exhaust system damage from 'short run syndrome'.

960 (from 1994)

WHAT'S GOOD

The ultimate 'Q' car. Stonking 204bhp twin-cam 3 litre straight six makes this old dowager really fly. Sports car drivers simply can't believe their eyes. Not over-dear once they've done a few miles.

WHAT'S BAD

Volvo image may or may not be what you want. Ridiculous damage-prone protruding alloy wheels fitted 1996 (though low-profile tyres did improve handling).

WHAT TO WATCH OUT FOR

Some 960 24vs have suffered from cracked cylinder heads Check very

carefully for water and oil leaks and for signs of water and oil mixing. Check for steering and front suspension damage from 'kerbing'. Engine and exhaust system damage from 'short run syndrome'.

S80

WHAT'S BAD

New, front-wheel drive, 960 replacement. Good looking, dignified, rounded body. Same 204 bhp 2.9 litre straight six; 140bhp 2.5 litre TDI, 144bhp 10v and 170bhp 20v 5-cylinder engines from S70. Flagship S80 T6 has 273 bhp 2.8 litre twin turbo and 4-speed Tiptronic auto. T6, 2.9 and TDI are all good to drive with lots of grip and nice steering. 2.4 litre is 'softer' and more vague, but still okay. All have excellent radios with knobs for volume, channel changing and function/waveband selecting. Integrated hands-

free car phone system. Lots
of bottle, cup and can
holders.

WHAT'S BAD

In the diesel, the 2.9 and the
T6 you feel every ridge and

draincover – not something
traditional Volvo owners are
used to.

WHAT TO WATCH OUT FOR

Too new to say

INDEX

NOTES

NOTES

NOTES